THE FLAG BOOK
OF THE
UNITED STATES

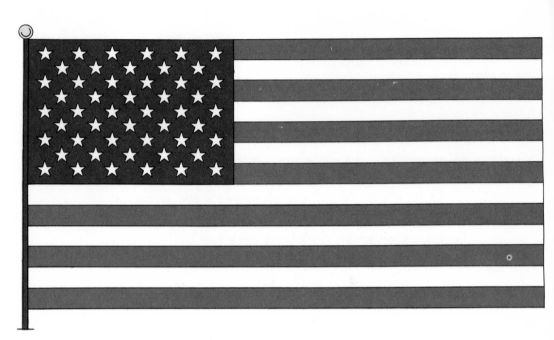

THE FLAG BOOK
OF THE
UNITED STATES

Whitney Smith

Director, Flag Research Center
Winchester, Massachusetts

Illustrations by Louis Loynes & Lucien Philippe

Revised Edition

WILLIAM MORROW & COMPANY, INC.

New York

for my parents

FRONTISPIECE:

UNITED STATES
State and national flag; ensign 4 July 1960—present
Basic design authorized 14 June 1777

UNITED STATES
Coat of arms 7 July 1884—present
Basic design authorized 20 June 1782

Revised Edition

Copyright © 1970, 1975 by Whitney Smith

Printed in the United States of America.

Library of Congress Catalog Card Number: 75-18701

ISBN 0-688-07977-6 (pbk.)

Designed by Robert Freese

PREFACE

Americans, more than most other people, are a flag-conscious nation. The flag of the United States is an everyday object, appearing not only on government buildings and ships and at military reviews, but on business blocks, private homes, and at schools; not only in history books, but in popular and patriotic art, folklore, literature, and even as an art motif in clothing. It would be hard to find an American who does not know the flag legends of Betsy Ross, Barbara Frietchie, and Iwo Jima. The flag has been further immortalized in their minds by famous paintings such as "The Spirit of '76" and "Washington Crossing the Delaware." "Old Glory," "The Star-Spangled Banner," "The Stars and Stripes," and "The Red, White, and Blue" are among the affectionate nicknames given to the national flag and repeated in countless songs, including the national anthem. The United States was the first country to have a Flag Day, a Pledge of Allegiance to the Flag, and a flag etiquette code. Lacking a royal family, Americans have turned the flag into the highest symbol of their nation and have willingly sacrificed their fortunes and their lives to protect and preserve it.

Yet despite their very real loyalty to the United States flag, Americans are surprisingly uninformed about its history, and much of what they believe to be true is erroneous. (How many, for example, can make a rough drawing of the United States flag which shows correctly the placement of both stars and stripes or a similar drawing of the flag of the State in which they live?) The myths surrounding America's flag heritage seem endless and an attempt to correct mistaken ideas is made difficult by the constant repetition which some of them have enjoyed in previous books and articles. A large number of people, for example, believe the field of the Bunker Hill Flag to have been blue (although it was in fact red) and they can point to a large number of books which "prove" this by illustrating such a flag. Nevertheless there has been a significant increase in serious scholarship on the part of individuals and institutions even in the five years since the appearance of the first edition of this book. Undoubtedly a large degree of this interest and concern, especially in historical flags, can be attributed to celebrations honoring the bicentennial of the American Revolution.

In very few other countries of the world is it possible for historical flags to be flown freely—not only on private homes and businesses, but even on government buildings. Americans do not always agree on the interpretation of these flags, either in historical or ideological terms, but they instinctively recognize that the freedom to express themselves by flying any flag and in any manner they choose is in fact one aspect of a liberty which Americans have always fought to preserve, namely the freedom to speak, write, and otherwise express opinions without fear or hindrance.

The Flag Book of the United States has been designed both for those seeking reliable factual information on all aspects of American flag history and for those who simply enjoy the color and drama surrounding such flags. The author, formerly a professor of political science, has sought to make clear that flags and other symbols from the very earliest days of man's history have been a vital and intimate part of the social structure of most countries. To deal with them, as many books have, as if they were no more than colorful decorations with no lasting significance, is a profound misunderstanding of the role of symbolism in human society. Vexillology, the analysis of flags and their usage in different countries, can give us a better understanding of national cultural characteristics—of the traditions and history of any society as it sees itself and of its aspirations for the future. For example, the diversity and proliferation of flags and flag customs in the United States mirror the strong pluralism that infuses the social organization of the country from the federal government down to the smallest neighborhood association.

Ultimately, American flags cannot be understood properly without the perspective which is gained from knowledge of flags used by other nations. Some attempt has been made in this book to discuss such contrasts, especially with regard to the role of heraldry, although space has not permitted extensive analysis. Fortunately, this book is only part of an ongoing series of publications and related programs, developed by the Flag Research Center to stimulate the growing interest of individuals and institutions in the fascinating world of vexillology.

At every stage in the preparation and revision of this book, the author has relied as far as possible on primary sources. While footnote citations have not been included, every historical fact and every illustration is solidly documented in the files which the author has collected in more than twenty years of research. He will be glad to correspond with interested readers concerning any aspect of the book or about flags in general and will be particularly pleased to receive further information on little-known types of flags (such as those of Indian tribes, cities and counties, religious and ethnic organizations) which have been presented here for the first time.

The author alone is responsible for the book, but he gratefully acknowledges the kind assistance he has received from countless librarians, government and military officials, and fellow vexillologists. Above all he is indebted to Louis Loynes and Lucien Philippe for their tireless efforts in producing superb artwork; to Narcisse Chamberlain for the professionalism of her editorial expertise and the warmth of her sympathetic aid to a young author; and to Ann for aid and assistance beyond the call of uxorial duty.

Whitney Smith, Ph.D.

Flag Research Center
Winchester, Massachusetts

CONTENTS

LIST OF
COLOR PLATES

Chapter I

AN INTRODUCTION
TO FLAGS

We do not know when man raised his first flag. Certainly it was thousands of years ago, for archeology has revealed pictures and sculptures of flaglike objects which date from the earliest days of organized society in the Near and Middle East. These "protovexilloids" generally consisted of animal skins or carved figures attached to poles so that they could be carried in battle, seen from a great distance, or mounted on a boat. Often—perhaps only for decoration—there were colored feathers or ribbons tied to such poles. Over the centuries more and more emphasis was put on the cloth attached to the pole and less and less to the figure at its top, although even today an important flag may be honored by the use of a special emblem, such as the eagle of the United States (see LVIII-a). Other changes also took place in the size, form, variety, and designs of flags and in the modes and extent of their uses. This book will illuminate many aspects of this development, but since its focus is on the flags of the United States certain interesting and important details will be left for discussion in the forthcoming books of this series.

In the past there were three principal areas where flags were commonly flown. The totemic standard and similar flags had a religious character and were placed in temples or carried in religious ceremonies. As the nature of religion changed, such flags became less and less frequent, and in the United States the influence of Puritanism (see pp. 36-38) very nearly has ended their use altogether. Closely allied to their religious use is the long service of flags in military units, both as holy symbols to inspire soldiers to sacrifice themselves for the glory and honor of their nation and as practical signals for rallying men in the field. The colors of a company or regiment came to be considered as a repository of the traditions of the unit; these colors are treated as living things not only in song and story but in practice on the battlefield and in ceremonies. At sea, flags became a necessity from the first time a ship ventured out of its home waters. Wherever men have sailed on the oceans their flags have indicated their nationality and allegiance and the ship without a flag has justly been recognized in international law as a pirate. Both military and naval flags appeared in America from the very beginning, when men still lived in tiny communities along the edge of a wilderness three thousand miles wide.

Today flags have many more uses and their display is more common than ever before. If the United States did not create the first truly national flag, a flag available to all its citizens for use on any and all occasions, at least it made major contributions to the development of this trend. We also have flags today for specialized use in advertising, distinguishing military and civilian ranks and offices, representing clubs and associations, and signaling all kinds of messages (including the weather). With the increase in the number and types of flags there has been a corresponding growth in the technical vocabulary of flags, and readers may wish to refer to the Glossary of this book before going on to subsequent chapters.

While flags have been an important part of men's lives for millennia, the study of flags (known as vexillology, from the Latin word for flag, *vexillum*) has developed very slowly. Until the seventeenth century flags were noted in books and charts only as decorative and incidental elements. The expansion of European navies in the 1600's made it necessary for identification purposes that tables of flags be made available for navigators and port authorities, and such information was gradually collected and published, especially in the Netherlands, England, and

France. It was not until 1912, however, that a substantial book* was published which dealt in a detailed and scholarly fashion with the origins, growth, and significance of flags. Since that time there has been more and more attention paid to vexillology as a serious area of study related not only to history but to political science and sociology.

The slow growth of vexillology no doubt reflects its long subordination to heraldry. Actually, both heraldry (the study and use of coats of arms) and vexillology are distinct parts of the general field of symbolism, along with sphragistics or sigillography (the study of seals), exonumia (the study of medals), and related studies. Although flags are incomparably older than coats of arms—which developed only about 800 years ago—and are found in all parts of the world and not just in Europe (to which heraldry is essentially restricted), it is true that flags were greatly influenced by the development of heraldry as a highly organized system of symbols. Traces of this influence can be seen in American flags, despite the fact that heraldry has never had any authentic roots in the United States. This subject is discussed at greater length in Chapter V.

In recent decades the study of flags has made rapid progress as an independent, organized discipline. The Flag Research Center (with its headquarters in Winchester, Massachusetts 01890) constitutes the international headquarters for vexillological activities. Its aim is to collect, preserve, organize, and disseminate information on all kinds of flags and other state symbols from all eras and countries. To accomplish this work the Center maintains a large library and extensive files; it compiles and publishes books, periodicals, charts, and other materials; it aids in promoting the coordination of vexillological studies throughout the world; and it serves as a consultant to governments, business firms, and others who need flag information. The Center welcomes correspondence from individuals interested in any aspect of flags. One of its publications, the bimonthly illustrated *Flag Bulletin,* has provided articles on all kinds of flags—especially flags of new nations—since 1961.

In 1965 the first International Congress of Vexillology was held in the Netherlands, and subsequent Congresses have met every two years in

* Rudolf Siegel, *Die Flagge* . . . Berlin: Reimer, 1912.

different countries. These Congresses, which give vexillologists a chance to meet one another and attend flag exhibits and lectures, are sponsored by the International Federation of Vexillological Associations. Member associations exist in North America (encompassing the United States and Canada), Britain, Switzerland, France, the Netherlands, and Japan, and groups are being organized in other parts of the world. Contact with these associations can be made through the Flag Research Center.

Almost all vexillologists are amateurs for whom the study of flags is an avocation or hobby. A vexillologist may be a great-grandparent, a school child, or anyone of any age in between. While vexillology is not yet as popular as philately or numismatics, it presents the same challenges and rewards. Many flag buffs have begun by collecting actual flags, usually of the small desk size. There are a few private flag collections in the United States which comprise over four hundred large flags, including one collection with more than seven hundred flags. There are also public exhibits, especially in museums and State capitols, which include flags of historic interest. Outdoor flag displays are becoming more common; probably the best-known ones are those in New York City at United Nations headquarters and Rockefeller Plaza and at the Flag Plaza in Pittsburgh. Large flag manufacturers such as Annin & Co. (Verona, New Jersey) and the Dettra Flag Co. (Oaks, Pennsylvania) can arrange for tours of their factories.

Vexillologists usually collect information about flags as well as actual flags. A few write books or articles for publication, but the greatest number pursue the subject simply for their own enjoyment. This is an inexpensive hobby and one which also has educational value because of its ties with geography, history, and many other subjects. The amateur frequently follows his interest not only by reading about it in the thousands of books on flags that exist,* but by making an album or card file with a record of flags he finds particularly interesting. Such an album contains a picture of each flag, the dates of its use, and other data collected from various sources. The most rewarding work may be in specialization on a particular era, or area, or type of flag, such as Civil War regimental colors, or Indian tribal flags, or yacht club pennants. So

* See the Bibliography on pp. 279-280 for a basic library.

much research remains to be done that even a beginner may discover a lost piece of information of considerable interest to others.

There are other areas of vexillology to be pursued. Some collectors sew their own full-scale flags; some paint small replicas to accompany military miniatures; some help organize flag activities for Scout groups or other associations; some promote correct display of the United States flag; some make a topical collection of flags shown on postage stamps. Many individuals design flags for themselves, friends, and associations. A few have the honor of designing a flag for a foreign country.

Readers of this book, whether or not they intend to take up vexillology, should be aware of the challenges of securing correct and complete information on flags. Very few countries have special agencies concerned with flag designs and use. In the United States the Army sponsors an Institute of Heraldry which provides flag-designing services for the military but does not conduct research or otherwise serve the general public. At the State level the Secretary of State is generally custodian of the State seal. Many Secretaries of State issue leaflets about State symbols, including the flag. Numerous inaccuracies exist in such publications, however; in one State, for example, the official booklet showed four versions of the same flag over the course of years. In another State the personal secretary to the Governor wrote the author that no personal Governor's flag existed, although such a flag had in fact been officially used for years.

Even books on flags frequently contain errors caused by inadequate research, faulty sources, or carelessness. Of course flags used a century or more ago are especially difficult to trace because data is usually fragmentary, confusing, or simply unavailable, and much of our information must be based on the process of historical reconstruction. Among the flags, old and new, which are habitually shown incorrectly in most books are those of Bunker Hill (VI-b), Rhode Island (VII-b), the Confederate Army (LXV-a), Colorado (XVII-b), and Illinois (XXIV-a). Every effort has been made in this book to avoid not only errors but misleading statements as well. For example, all flag illustrations based solely on a verbal description have been labeled "reconstructed"; indication has been made of variant patterns and of flags which are *de facto* but not *de jure,* i.e., ones in actual but unofficial usage. For the older flags, of course, no official specifications ever existed and variations in design were common. The correct width and length (e.g., 10 x 19) are given for every flag which has official proportions.

One problem of standardization which has not been resolved even today relates to flag colors. Although the human eye can distinguish among ten million different shades of color, those commonly used in flags are adequately represented by the twenty-plus colors used in printing this book. Most States and countries do not require specific shades and many manufacturers ignore official specifications for their own convenience. The problem is further complicated by the fact that the same dye will appear different if used on silk, wool, or paper, or under different lighting conditions. Readers who wish further information on the official colors or proportions of any flag in this book should write to the Flag Research Center which publishes existing specifications of all flags in standard format.

Chapter II

THE FIRST FLAGS
IN AMERICA

INDIANS AND VIKINGS

From the very earliest times man has sought to distinguish himself from other men by means of artificial marks or symbols of some kind. Even among primitive peoples who wear no clothes, a certain kind of painted or tattooed device on the body may set off the chief from the rest of the group and the tribe as a whole from its neighbors. In some societies particular forms of symbolism become very highly developed and are important in the religion, magic, government, art, and general economic and social life of the people. The forms of symbols which have been invented are almost infinite in variety, and the study of the different kinds—e.g., rings, feathers, staffs and maces, thrones, crowns, uniforms, coats of arms, medals, capes, umbrellas—is practically endless. Moreover, scholars have recently made studies which show that the role of such symbols is not only decorative, but plays an essential part in many of the institutions and processes of government. Just how significant symbols can be in the changing life of a people will become evident to the reader in the pages of this book.

It would be a mistake to think that any one form of symbol is always and everywhere the principal type. For example, the cluster of colored ribbons called a cockade and worn on a hat or coat used to be very common in Europe and America, but now is scarcely ever seen. Instead we have today the political campaign button which expresses our ideas in a slogan or picture. Many people consider heraldry, the use of coats of arms, as the chief form of symbolism. It is true that heraldry was a very important part of everyday life during the feudal periods of European and Japanese history, but it is much less important in the modern era and never existed at all in many societies. New forms of symbols are still being invented and new uses are being found for old types. The metal pennants planted on the Moon and planets by the Soviet Union and the flag which was hoisted by the American astronauts who visited the Moon are modern instances of the use of symbols.

Among the most long-lived forms of emblems is the flag. Basically only a piece of cloth attached to a stick, the flag has the power to arouse the intense emotions of loyalty, anger, love, or fear in millions of people. The flag can be used to assert independence, to provoke a war, to demand surrender, to demonstrate adherence to a political idea or program, to represent a group as small as a club or as big as an association of nations, to indicate the presence of a military force or of government authority, to honor a hero, to mark a victory, to lend dignity to a ceremony, to teach children the fundamental ideas of their society, to signal a movement of troops, or simply to provide attractive decoration. The first flaglike objects (protovexilloids) of which we have record date from the ancient civilizations of India and Egypt and are thousands of years old. Today there are thousands of kinds of flags, serving individuals, associations, businesses, churches, military forces, cities, provinces, nations, and world organizations. New flags are created almost every day. Untold millions of people have struggled, even given their lives, to protect and promote the ideas enshrined in flags.

I. FLAGS OF SPAIN

a. **SPAIN   State flag and ensign   c1230–c1516 (variant)**
b. **SPAIN   State flag and ensign   1580–1640 (variant)**
c. **SPAIN   Ensign   28 May 1785–27 April 1931   State flag on land 8 March 1793–27 April 1931**

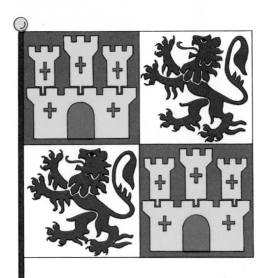

a.

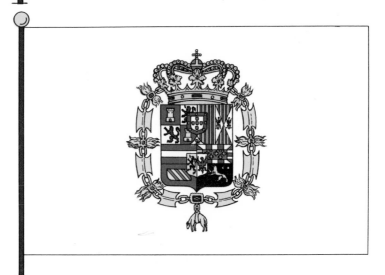

b.

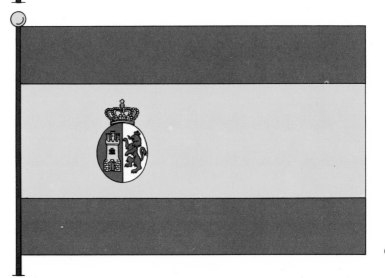

c.

As vital as the flag is, however, it cannot be found everywhere in all periods of history. In particular the use of flags seems to be closely associated with *urban* societies, those in which every person and group has a specialized task to perform. This is quite logical after all: in a traditional society where people all know one another, where there is little contact with outsiders, and where there are few formal groups into which people are divided, there is little need for distinctive flags or other symbols. It is for this reason that we discover few if any flags being used by the original inhabitants of what is now the United States. Unlike the Aztecs and Mayas to the south, most American Indians and Eskimos had only small settlements instead of cities and lived in groups of no more than a few thousand at most. The need for flags simply never arose. The emblems that did exist tended to be vexilloids, that is flaglike objects, rather than true flags. For instance Frobisher's second expedition to Newfoundland in 1577 records that the Eskimos there used as a signal a pole with animal bladders tied at the top. Plains Indians in the West used feathers tied to poles in their religious rituals.

One flag book from 1693 contains the following: "the Savages of America carry on different places of their Boats and their Canoes several little Streamers, split up the middle and cut into points, which are of diverse colors, but especially white." No source is given and the "Savages" are not identified. Perhaps research in the future will reveal other instances which will allow us to understand better the symbols of these peoples.

With the coming of white men, some of the Indian tribes adopted Western ways including the use of flags. In the early eighteenth century, for example, the Spanish marked with a red flag their border with the Apaches in south Texas. The Spanish word for flag, *bandera,* thus gave its name to the area which is known today as Bandera Pass. Later the Comanches made use of this red flag when they attacked the Spanish. Similarly, in the nineteenth century the Sioux and other Indians who warred against the United States Government sometimes carried flags and pennants that they had captured, such as Custer's cavalry guidon (X-c). The slow regrowth of self-respect and pride in Indian heritage in the 1960's has led to the adoption of tribal flags in a few cases. At the same time it should be noted that Indian emblems have been incorporated in two State flags, those of Oklahoma (XL-b) and New Mexico (XXXVI-b), and that the Alaska State flag was designed by an Indian. Indians are also pictured in the seals of Florida, Kansas, Massachusetts, Minnesota, North Dakota, and Oklahoma.

From the available evidence, it seems probable that the first true flags to fly in North America (and possibly in areas now part of the United States) were those which the Vikings are presumed to have brought with them in the tenth and eleventh centuries. Records dating from the era of the Danish rule in England indicate that the most common Norse flag was the one known as "Raven, Terror of the Land" or simply Raven. According to the legend, the original Raven was made in a single forenoon by the daughters of Ragmar Lothbroc, a ninth-century Danish warlord. The banner was in theory without any device on it, yet "in every battle where that flag went before them, if they were to gain a victory a live raven would appear flying in the middle of the flag, but if they were doomed to be defeated it would hang down motionless." In fact, of course, the story was probably inspired by the changing wind, which caused the flag first to flutter and then hang limp. That the flag actually bore a raven is evident from the illustrations on coins of the tenth century which have been found in England and Ireland. These coins also clearly show that the shape of the flag (see below) was an irregular triangle, not the rectangle which modern artists use in illustrating "the Viking flag." We do not know what colors were used for the raven and border of the flag, but the field was white.

RAVEN
Flag of the Danish Vikings
800's–1000's?
(reconstructed)

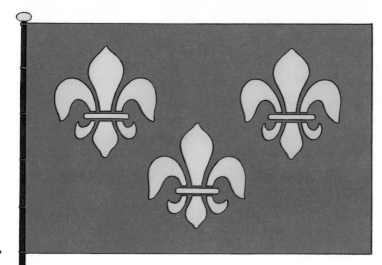

a.

b.

c.

Other claims have been made for early discovery and exploration of America: some even say that the Phoenicians or Irish visited the New World before the Vikings. More credible are the reports that English merchants from Bristol and various members of the Corte-Real family of Portugal visited the area between Labrador and Rhode Island a few years before Columbus reached the West Indies. There is not space here to examine these and other claims and consequently this is not the place to speculate about the kinds of flags such men might have carried. Instead the focus will be on those nations known to have sent explorers and settlers to the new lands—Great Britain, Spain, France, the Netherlands, Sweden, and Russia.* Since it was Britain which finally came to control most of the territory forming the nucleus of the United States and whose flags had the greatest influence on American flags, her story is the most extensive and will be saved for last.

SPAIN AND FRANCE

Columbus in his first voyage to the New World carried with him two copies of a special expeditionary flag (see p. 14) which is described in contemporary records as an "ensign with an F and a Y; above each letter its crown and one [letter is] on one side of the ✠ and the other on the other." The flags were white with gold crowns; the crosses and probably the letters were green. F and Y stood for the patrons of the trip, Their Catholic Majesties King Ferdinand and Queen Isabella of Spain. Although Columbus never reached the mainland of North America, on his second trip in 1493 he did discover Puerto Rico.

> * Although Columbus, Vespucci, Verrazano, Cabot, and several other early explorers were Italian by birth, all served under foreign flags because Italy was divided at that time into small states which could not afford to sponsor expeditions. However, Cabot in his voyage of 1497 to Newfoundland planted the lion flag of Venice as well as the flag of England.

II. FLAGS OF FRANCE

a.   **FRANCE**   **State flag and ensign**   **c1370–c1600 (variant)**

b.   **FRANCE**   **National flag at sea**   **9 October 1661–31 October 1790**

c.   **FRANCE**   **State flag and ensign**   **c1643–31 October 1790**   **Proportions 2 x 3**

CHRISTOPHER COLUMBUS Expeditionary flag 1492 (reconstructed)

The most important flag displayed by Columbus and other early Spanish explorers was the royal banner of Castile and Leon (I-a) which bore the arms of these kingdoms, namely a castle and a lion. From ancient coins we know that the lion was used as early as the reign of King Alfonso VII (1126-1157) and the castle as early as the reign of Alfonso VIII (1158-1214). The combined form appears in the era of Ferdinand III (1230-1252) and, with artistic variations, continues in use on flags until about 1516. After this date the changing arms of Spain, including not only Castile and Leon, but Aragon, Navarre, Sicily, Granada, and later on Austria, Burgundy, Flanders, Tyrol, Brabant, Portugal, Anjou, Parma, and Tuscany, are to be found on Spanish royal flags like the one in I-b. The other parts of these coats of arms—the Order of the Golden Fleece, the eagle of the Holy Roman Empire, the Pillars of Hercules, and the royal crown—often were painted or embroidered on such flags as well. Such variations of the royal flag were flown from 1516 until 1785 on most Spanish ships in the New World. The white field of the flag symbolized the Bourbon dynasty.

Many other Spanish flags were flown in the period 1492-1898 while Spain held a colonial empire in North America. The two most common flags, however, aside from the royal ensign already described, were the red saltire on white of Burgundy (see p. 15) and the red and gold flag (I-c) established on 28 May 1785 by King Charles III. The saltire in the former flag is a special kind, drawn to suggest crossed branches. Sup-

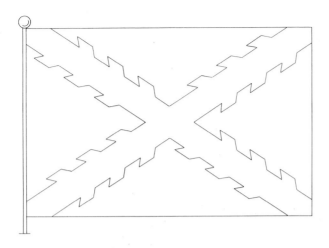

SPAIN State flag and ensign 1516–28 May 1785 (variant)

posedly its first use was by King Pelayo of Asturias in 718 A.D. It is most closely associated, however, with Burgundy and Spanish Flanders. The crossed branches were a favorite emblem of Philip I, Duke of Burgundy, who was Regent of Spain in 1506, and of his son, King Charles I (1516-1556), who was also the famous Holy Roman Emperor, Charles Quint. Thus from 1516 until 1785 a white flag with a red saltire was flown on the seas and in all the Spanish colonies in America. The red-and-gold-striped flag with the simple arms of Castile and Leon became the naval ensign of Spain in 1785, the flag of its forts and other military buildings on 8 March 1793, and the basic pattern for the Spanish regimental colors in 1843.

These flags flew over the few forts and settlements established by Spain in those areas now part of the United States which were then under their control. This included Florida; Texas, New Mexico, California, and other parts of the Southwest; Puerto Rico; certain Pacific islands; and (from 1763 to 1800) the Louisiana Territory. In Florida, these flags were replaced by the British flag (1763-1783) and by the flags of the West Florida Republic in 1810 and the United States in 1819. In 1821 Mexican flags substituted for those of Spain in the Southwest. In 1898 the Spanish-American War finally caused the Spanish symbols of authority to be lowered in Puerto Rico and the Pacific. Yet the era of Spain's dominion is not entirely forgotten, for their gold and red colors appear in the modern flags of Arizona and New Mexico. Castile and Leon are recalled in the castles and lions figuring in the seals or arms of such cities as Coral Gables, Los Angeles, New Orleans, and Santa Fe. The influence of Spanish heraldry and vexillology is especially strong in Puerto Rico.

France, like Spain, had a great number of flags up until the end of the eighteenth century. But here again the most important flag carried by explorers and settlers was probably the royal flag, since this was a symbol of the authority of the king in the new lands. (The royal flag was not the same as the king's personal standard, which would be flown only in his presence.) At the time of the expeditions of Verrazano and Cartier in the early sixteenth century the French royal flag was blue with three gold fleurs-de-lys (II-a), corresponding exactly to the shield in the royal French coat of arms.* Actually, we have no direct evidence that either explorer hoisted this flag on land. In claiming new territories the French, like the Portuguese, usually preferred a permanent marker indicating possession. Thus we have record that Cartier in August of 1535 set up a large cross bearing the arms of France to establish his claim to the St. Lawrence River region. In any event the use of the *bannière de France* was uncommon after the early 1600's.

Samuel de Champlain (?1567-1635), who contributed much to the growth of New France, left pictures in his memoirs indicating that he used the French merchant flag (II-b). This flag was the product of a long historical development. During the Crusades the major European nations identified their soldiers by crosses worn on the surcoat. The Burgundians used the red saltire already mentioned; the English bore the red cross of St. George; and the French were distinguished by a white cross. By the time of King Charles VII (1422-1461) the white cross had

---

* The first recorded use of the fleurs-de-lys in France dates to the twelfth century, when the field of the *bannière de France* (banner of France) was strewn with them. During the reign of Charles V (1364-1380), and afterwards, the number of fleurs-de-lys was usually reduced to three. The flag shown in II-a is attached to its pole in the manner current in the seventeenth century.

III. FLAGS OF THE NETHERLANDS, SWEDEN, AND RUSSIA

a. **(DUTCH) CHARTERED WEST INDIA COMPANY   c1650–1664 (in New Netherland)**

b. **SWEDEN   State flag and ensign   1638–1655 (in New Sweden)**

c. **RUSSIAN–AMERICAN COMPANY   28 September 1806–1861**

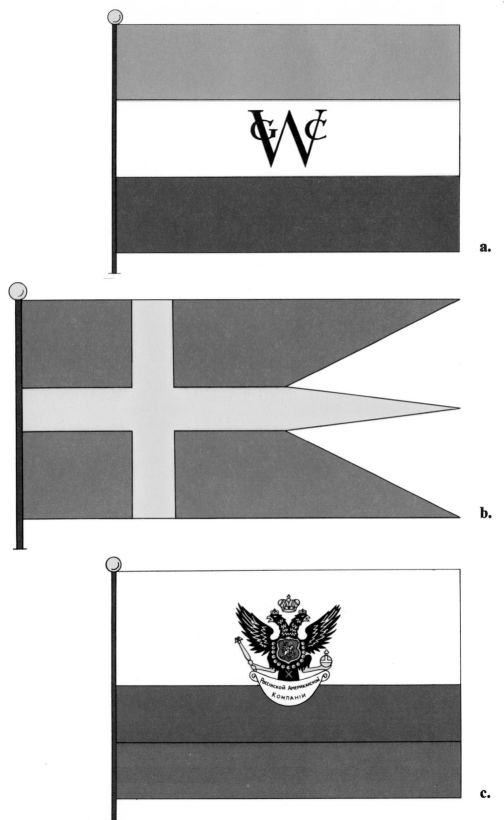

a.

b.

c.

become common as a mark on French military flags. At sea the usual form was a white cross on a blue field, with or without fleurs-de-lys on the blue field and the royal arms in the center. Although an official form (II-b) was decreed on 9 October 1661, private ships continued to fly other combinations of blue and white, including striped flags of these colors. The favorite flag of the merchant vessels, however, was the plain white flag specifically denied to them by the Order of 1661. Since it was the distinctive ensign of royal ships, the white flag tended to command greater respect at sea. So insistent were the captains of merchantmen in displaying this flag that it finally was recognized as a legal merchant flag on 25 March 1765.

The plain white flag was actually a simplified version of the proper royal ensign flown on ships and forts (II-c). This flag bore the entire arms of France and the field was strewn with fleurs-de-lys. Another simplified form showed the fleurs-de-lys but not the arms; we have record of such a flag being displayed in French territories in North America in the sevententh century. This was probably the flag carried by LaSalle, Marquette, Joliet, and Cadillac. It was the flag lowered in 1760 when the British conquered New France and effectively put to an end French aspirations for an empire in the New World.

Aside from the two royal flags and the merchant flag of the Ancien Régime so far described, one other French flag flew briefly in the Louisiana Territory. Following the rise to power of Napoleon, the Spanish were

FRANCE State and national flag; ensign 20 May 1794–13 April 1814

forced to cede this area to France, from whom they had originally acquired it in 1763. The involvement of Napoleon in European affairs and his need for money to finance his wars induced him to sell the Territory to the United States in 1803. During the brief three years in which it was under French rule, Louisiana flew the famous Tricolor (opposite). This flag of blue, white, and red stripes, which dates from 1794, has inspired the symbolism and design of many national flags in all parts of the world. In the United States its influence is to be noted in the flags of Iowa, New Orleans, and the 1861 flag of Louisiana. Parts of the older French flags have been incorporated into the flags of North Dakota, Detroit, New Orleans, and St. Louis.

THE NETHERLANDS, SWEDEN,
RUSSIA, AND MEXICO

As one of the great seafaring nations of the era, the Netherlands joined other European states in seeking to exploit the potential riches of the New World. In 1609 the Dutch ship *Halve Maen* (Half Moon) under the command of Henry Hudson explored the area of North America from South Carolina to New York, especially the river which now bears Hudson's name. Since the *Halve Maen* was sponsored by the United East India Company, it probably flew the Company's flag. The Company was divided into a number of Chambers, each with a flag of its own. It is quite possible, therefore, that the *Halve Maen* also flew the flag of Amsterdam Chamber which had sent Hudson out to find a passage to the East. Both these flags had the same basic pattern—a horizontal tricolor with an appropriate hallmark on the center stripe. The Chamber used the city flag of Amsterdam with its red (top), white, and black stripes, while the Company itself used the national stripes of orange (top), white, and blue.

The hallmarks (see p. 20) contained the three letters VOC for *Vereenigte Oost-Indische Compagnie*, the name of the Company in Dutch, and the same letters plus A for Amsterdam.* These flags were

---

* Occasionally, the VOC was shown upside down (see p. 20), which has misled some authors into supposing that the correct initials were AOC.

(DUTCH)
UNITED EAST INDIA COMPANY
Ciphers of the company and
of its Amsterdam chamber
Early 1600's

soon replaced by those of the United New Netherland Company and, after 1621, the Chartered West India Company. That latter used its initials (GWC for *Geoctroyeerde West-Indische Compagnie;* III-a) on the national flag. Company flags are an important part of vexillology in the seventeenth and eighteenth centuries because the companies, rather than the governments themselves, were in many cases responsible for the actual exploration, settlement, and administration of colonial territories in all parts of the world. Even today their role has not entirely been ended: in the Canal Zone, for example, the government is in the hands of the Panama Canal Company. Thus the Dutch settlements in New Netherland which began in 1624 and ended forty years later with the

IV. THE DEVELOPMENT OF THE UNION JACK

a. **ENGLAND (ST. GEORGE'S CROSS)** National flag c1277–6 March 1707   Merchant jack   5 May 1634–c1810

b. **SCOTLAND (ST. ANDREW'S CROSS)** National flag 1200's–6 March 1707

c. **GREAT BRITAIN (UNION FLAG)**   State flag at sea   12 April 1606–5 May 1634   Jack   5 May 1634–23 May 1649; 5 May 1660–1 January 1801   State flag on land   28 July 1707–1 January 1801

d. **IRELAND (ST. PATRICK'S CROSS)**   1600's–1700's (?)

e. **GREAT BRITAIN (UNION FLAG)**   State flag on land and jack 1 January 1801–present

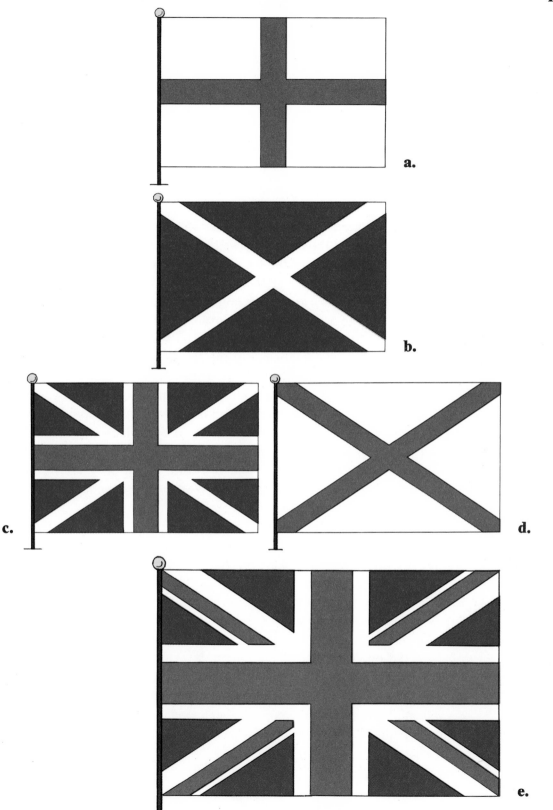

a.

b.

c.

d.

e.

British capture of New Amsterdam (renamed New York) probably flew both the Company flag and the plain national flag.

The history of the orange, white, and blue stripes—known as the Prince's Flag—goes back to April 1572 or perhaps even earlier. The Dutch at that time were fighting their 80 Years' War of independence against the Spanish, and Prince William of Orange became their leader. In honor of his name the various Dutch flags then in use, such as the saltire banner of Burgundy and the red-white-blue banners of the provinces, were replaced by the Prince's Flag. This flag, often with six or nine stripes instead of three, became well known on all the oceans of the world as the national flag of the United Netherlands. In the seventeenth century the orange stripe was gradually altered to the red which is still in use today, although this was not officially confirmed until 1795. The first reference we have to a red stripe is in November 1630 but the use of red apparently did not become common until 1650-1672 when the States-General refused to name a member of the House of Orange as the Head of State.

It seems likely that flags of both orange-white-blue and red-white-blue were used in New Netherland, which included parts of Connecticut, Delaware, New Jersey, and New York. The Dutch flags and coats of arms of the seventeenth century are recalled in the modern city flags of New York (see LXI-b), Albany, and Hartford, and in the flags of the Bronx, Kings, Queens, Richmond, and Westchester counties in New York.

To the south of New Netherland, in what is now Delaware, there existed the colony of New Sweden between the years 1638 and 1655. As a military undertaking the colony did not have a company flag but flew the Swedish state and naval flag (III-b). This followed the common Scandinavian swallow-tailed pattern, even though the Swedish national flag was (and is) rectangular. The blue field and gold cross form the basis for the city flag of Wilmington.

On the opposite side of the continent exploration and settlement were carried out by Russia during the late eighteenth and early nineteenth centuries. From Alaska down the Pacific coast as far as San Francisco came Russian fur traders and other merchants. Their flag was the white (top), blue, and red tricolor which Peter I had established first as a

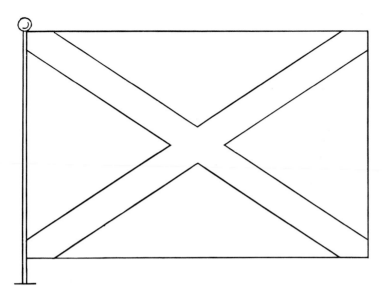

**RUSSIAN EMPIRE Ensign 1784–28 September 1806;
1861–18 October 1867 in Alaska**

naval ensign and then, after 1700, as a merchant flag. The colors had
long been used in Russian banners, but the horizontal stripes were apparently based on the flags Peter had seen in the Netherlands. The ensign
(see above), flown on state vessels, was white with the blue saltire of
Andrew, the patron Saint of Russia. These flags predominated in Alaska
until its sale to the United States in 1867. However, between 1806 and
1861 ships and buildings there also flew the special flag of the Russian-
American Company which administered Alaska from 1799 until 1861.
This flag (III-c) differed from the merchant flag in the width of its
stripes and the addition of the royal coat of arms (with the name of the
Company on a ribbon below).

Three other powers—Denmark, Germany, and Japan—also have
held territory in the area now controlled by the United States. However,
they did not significantly influence the flags in American colonial history
and so are dealt with under the separate sections on American Samoa,
Guam, the Ryukyus, the Trust Territory of the Pacific Islands, and the
Virgin Islands. On the other hand Mexico deserves notice here because it
once ruled vast areas now part of the United States. Until 1821 when its
independence was finally achieved, Mexico flew the flags of Spain.
Freedom was won by forces which flew a white, green, and red
tricolor, each stripe bearing a star. The stars and stripes represented the

V

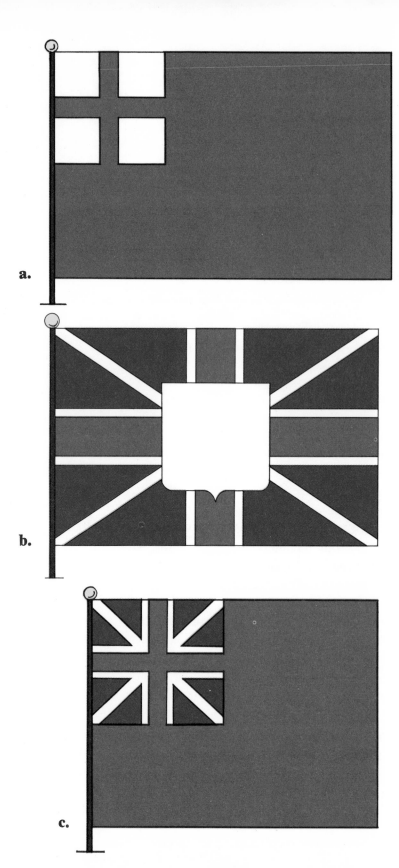

a.

b.

c.

MEXICO National flag adopted 14 April 1823; used until 1836 in Texas; until 1848 in the Southwest

"Three Guarantees" for which the Mexicans had been struggling—Religion, Independence, and Union. This flag lasted only a few months and was replaced on 2 November 1821 by one bearing the coat of arms of Mexico. Although there have been many reinterpretations of these arms since 1821 for political and artistic reasons, the flag has remained basically the same to this day. The model shown above was adopted on 14 April 1823 and remained the official Mexican flag until 1880.

Besides being a very ancient emblem in art and architecture, the eagle killing a snake which forms the central feature of the coat of arms has a special meaning for Mexicans. According to tradition, the Aztecs were to choose the site of their permanent settlement at the spot where they should see a snake being eaten by an eagle standing on a nopal cactus growing from a rock in the middle of water. After years of wan-

V. FLAGS OF GREAT BRITAIN
a.   **GREAT BRITAIN (RED ENSIGN)**   **Ensign and national flag at sea (unofficial) c1621–28 July 1707   Official as national flag after 18 September 1674**
b.   **BRITISH NORTH AMERICA**   **Merchant jack (in public service)   31 July 1701–?4 July 1776**
c.   **GREAT BRITAIN (RED ENSIGN)**   **Ensign and national flag at sea 28 July 1707–1 January 1801   (in America until 4 July 1776)**

dering the Aztecs did find this omen at Lake Tenochtitlán and there they created the town which has since become Mexico City. In honor of this event, which supposedly occurred in 1325, the eagle and snake became one of the chief Aztec emblems. Officially ignored under the Spanish regime (1521-1821), this ancient symbol was restored after independence. As a souvenir of Mexican rule, this coat of arms figures in the seals of New Mexico, Los Angeles, and Sante Fe.

GREAT BRITAIN

Mention has already been made of some of the crosses used on flags by European nations for rapid identification. From the standpoint of American flags the most important of these crosses were those borne by the English and the Scots, later combined to form the Union Jack of Great Britain, which flew in the colonies until independence was achieved. The custom of wearing a large cross on a surcoat or of carrying it in pennon form on a lance originated with the Crusaders ("cross-bearers"). Even at that time the chief characteristics of the cross as an emblem were evident. First, it provided a ready and sure means of identifying Christian soldiers from Muslims in the heat of battle. Indeed so important was this function that noblemen began to adopt their own distinctive personal emblems which could be seen from a distance to guide and reassure the troops of their leader's presence. One such example is the crescent and star badge employed by Richard I of England as a personal badge (see p. 63). Later many such emblems developed into the system of hereditary coats of arms known as heraldry. The common soldier never acquired such marks but continued for several centuries to wear the cross. Since each national group had a cross of a different color, the second function they fulfilled was to distinguish between the English, French, Flemings, and others. This usage tended to be perpetuated long after return from the Holy Land, as we can see in the Swiss use of a white cross on red military banners or the French display of a white cross on their blue merchant flags.

In war and in peace, on land and at sea, the third factor involved in the use of crosses was religious. Quite simply, the common soldier or sailor looked to a particular saint to aid him; in turn he offered that saint special devotion. At first there was no agreement in England as to which saint was primary. The banners of St. Edmund and St. John of Beverley frequently were hoisted in battle before St. George's flag (IV-a) became preeminent. And while the first recorded use of St. George's flag is in 1277, reference to the banners of other saints is still made as late as the end of Henry VIII's reign three hundred years later. In the seventeenth century the spirit of Puritanism forced the elimination of saints' emblems, but the cross of St. George was generally retained, being by this time considered as primarily a national symbol. It was thus the flag of St. George that most of the early English explorers flew when they traveled to the New World.*

When Queen Elizabeth I died in 1603, a new era in flags began for her realm. On her death the throne passed to King James VI of Scotland who became James I of England as well. As monarch of two kingdoms which remained separate in most respects, James issued a proclamation on 12 April 1606 to prescribe the correct usage of flags for all English and Scottish ships. On their mainmasts such vessels were to fly a new union flag. On their foremasts—ships in that era did not commonly fly either a jack at the bow or an ensign at the stern—the proper color was the national flag. In the case of England this was the banner of St. George; in the case of Scotland it was the banner of St. Andrew (IV-b). This flag had been borne by the Scots for centuries, although the white cross often was set on a background other than blue.** Early records are missing, but we know that the emblem dates from at least the thirteenth century and tradition carries it back to the ninth century. The saltire form of the cross refers to the supposed martyrdom on such a cross of Andrew, patron saint of Scotland.

The union flag (IV-c) combined the crosses of the two saints to show that England and Scotland had a common ruler. There have been some criticisms of this flag and its modern counterpart (IV-e), most of

---

* Two exceptions to this rule were the Cabots and Drake, who had special permission to fly the royal banner. This flag quartered the French royal arms of three gold fleurs-de-lys on blue (to symbolize the claims of the kings of England to be the rightful rulers of France) with the English royal arms, three gold "leopards" on red; these arms are shown in the first quarter of the Virginia arms (LV-c). Although the designs have changed, the distinction is still maintained in Britain today between the cross on the *national* flag and the heraldic patterns of the *royal* standard.
** In Russia, as noted earlier, St. Andrew's flag was blue on white.

them relating to the widths of the crosses. In particular the Scots protested from the very first until as recently as 1853 that the St. Andrew's cross should pass in front of St. George's cross instead of vice versa. But the real problem with the new Union Jack (as it came to be called) was the great popularity it enjoyed with ships of all kinds, whether or not they were entitled to display it. On 5 May 1634 James's successor, Charles I, had decided that merchant vessels should be distinguished from men-of-war and ordered the former to cease using the Union Jack. The owners and captains of English merchantmen were reluctant to return to the exclusive use of St. George's cross, however, for a number of reasons. The new flag was not only more striking in appearance and more visible at sea; its use entailed a number of benefits. In foreign ports certain customs duties could be avoided; in the Channel foreign ships were required to give a salute; and in general there was greater respect paid to a ship bearing the Union Jack than to one without it. Thus there began in the seventeenth century a contest between merchant ships which wished to fly the Union Jack or a flag very similar to it and the Board of Admiralty, which sought to restrict its use to warships. Only in the twentieth century has the Admiralty won its way.

Following the creation of the Union Jack in 1606, the most significant development in British flags was the unofficial growth in the use of ensigns.* In the sixteenth century merchant ships and especially war vessels sometimes flew a flag at the stern which included the red cross of St. George, across the whole flag or in the canton, plus stripes of various colors. There was no regularity of design until about 1625 when

---

* Flags on fore, main, or mizzen masts, ensigns, and jacks were all used on ships for purposes of identification. Changes favoring the usage of one or another have been principally influenced by changes in ship architecture.

VI. FLAGS OF NEW ENGLAND

a.   **MASSACHUSETTS BAY   General usage flag at sea; company color November 1634–c1686 (unofficial)**

b.   **NEW ENGLAND (ENSIGN)   (Pine tree flag; Bunker Hill flag)   General usage flag   c1686–c1707 (unofficial)**

c.   **NEW ENGLAND (JACK)   ?General usage flag on land   c1686–c1707 (unofficial)**

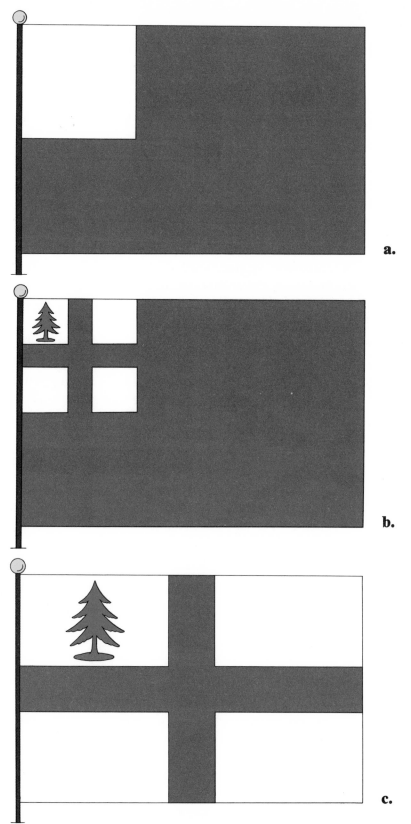

a.

b.

c.

the first "Red Ensign" (V-a) came into use. The hoisting of such a flag by merchant vessels was formally recognized in 1663 by Charles II and both private and public ships bore the Red Ensign until 1707. After that date merchant ships continued to display the Red Ensign, but ships of war frequently had ensigns in which the field was blue or white instead of red. These were based on the distinguishing flags of admirals and gradually developed into a regular system for identifying the red, white, and blue squadrons of the fleet during battles. The first instance recorded of this practical arrangement, which continued until 1864, was in 1617. The details of the development and the exact changes of flag are not of concern here, since the only ensign likely to be seen in American waters on either a merchantman or warship was the Red Ensign.

These two types of ships were most readily distinguishable in the period from 1634 until after 1800 not by their ensigns but by their jacks—except, of course, when merchantmen illegally flew the Union Flag which was supposed to be the exclusive naval jack. The proper merchant jack throughout the whole colonial period was the cross of St. George, even though England and Scotland formally ceased to exist after 1707 as separate kingdoms. Privateers sailing under letters of marque or reprisal, which in effect were privately owned ships recognized by international law as warships, were allowed after 1694 a special "budgee jack" consisting of the Union Jack bordered in red on the bottom and fly edges. Colonial merchant vessels in all parts of the New World normally wore exactly the same colors as those from the mother country. However, to distinguish such ships when acting on public service as commissioned by a colonial Governor, a special jack was created on 31 July 1701. It consisted of the regular Union Jack with a white shield in the center (V-b). There is no known instance of actual usage of this flag.

It is slightly misleading to refer simply to "the Union Jack of His Majesty's ships." Actually from 1606 to 1782, when Britain recognized American independence, four different jacks were employed on men-of-war to reflect the changing political structure of Great Britain. The personal bond between England and Scotland having been broken when Charles I was beheaded, the original Union Flag ceased to exist on 23 February 1649. At first the new Commonwealth government reestablished St. George's cross, but on the 5th of March of the same year a new Union Jack was created. It combined the cross with the traditional arms of Ireland, a yellow harp on blue.* Five years later Scotland was again united with England and the old Union Jack was revived, but with the arms of Ireland in the center. This was official from 18 May 1658 until 5 May 1660, although the previous jack appears to have been unofficially used after Cromwell's death in 1659. The Restoration under King Charles II brought back the original Union Jack (IV-c) in 1660.

Although this jack continued in use until 1801 an important change occurred in its meaning when, in 1707 under Queen Anne, the Kingdoms of England and Scotland and their separate navies, parliaments, and councils were dissolved and replaced by those of the United Kingdom. Thereafter the Union Jack was substituted for the cross of St. George and the cross of St. Andrew in the various ensigns. V-c shows the form of the Red Ensign used from 28 July 1707 until 1 January 1801. On the latter date a further change was instituted, following the formal recognition of Ireland as part of the United Kingdom, rather than a dependency of the Sovereign. This did not affect the United States directly, although it formed the canton of the national flag of the Kingdom of Hawaii, which is now used as a State flag.

The new Union Jack of 1801 (IV-e) included the red saltire of Patrick, the patron saint of Ireland. The new cross (IV-d) shared the space with the white saltire of St. Andrew and was fimbriated with white wherever it would otherwise touch the blue field or the red cross of St. George. Disunity prevented the development in Ireland of a true national emblem until the nineteenth century; moreover St. Patrick was not entitled to a cross since he was not a martyr. Hence the origin of this "flag of St. Patrick" is somewhat obscure; the cross probably derives from the coat of arms of the powerful Geraldine family. Its first appearance on an Irish flag dates from the sixteenth century. When the saltire was added to the Union Flag it also appeared in the various ensigns and continues as part of these British flags even today, despite the fact that southern Ireland is now an independent republic.

* Ireland had long been under English rule but had not previously been recognized in British national flags.

a.

b.

c.

BRITISH COLONIAL MILITARY COLORS

Although the 1701 jack of colonial public vessels (V-b) appears to have been the first officially recognized flag representive of the British colonies in the New World, it was not the first flag used in those colonies distinctive of the local peoples. From the very first settlements at Jamestown and Plymouth, the colonists in America had shown themselves to be strong-willed individuals. Facing a vast and largely hostile frontier, just as they readily adopted new solutions to meet problems unforeseen in the mother country, so they created their own symbols. At the same time the flags of the colonists, like the governments they set up, were generally based on British models and it is only over the course of a century or more that we can discern the emergence of purely American models. These trends are all made clear in the history of the New England pine tree flag; but in order to understand this story fully it is necessary to review general flag usage on land in the British colonies.

It must be remembered that the flying of flags on land has become more and more common in the United States with the spread of wealth and of democratic ideals. In the nineteenth century very few private citizens flew flags, except for ship owners, and in the eighteenth century even the concept of a national flag did not exist. In the 1600's the only flags to be found on land in America were of two kinds. On fortifications, government houses, and other public buildings—being Crown property—the Union Jack was usually flown, although this custom was not universal and was not confirmed by law until 1707. The other type of flag was the military color carried by local troops or, later, the regular army sent over from Britain. The separate colonies, so far as we know from present research, had no recognized flags of their own with the exception of Maryland.

VII. FLAGS OF THE AMERICAN REVOLUTION

a.   **UNITED STATES NAVY   Commander in Chief's flag   c1776–1778? (unofficial)**

b.   **RHODE ISLAND   Color of the 2nd Regiment   c1777–1781**

c.   **MASSACHUSETTS   Company color of the Bucks of America   c1780**

Until the reorganization of the English Army in 1661, following the Restoration, there was little regularity in the colors carried by British troops. This was especially true in the cavalry where each company was raised by its own commander and hence carried a flag of his devising. These "cornets" were about two feet square and generally bore allegorical pictures and mottoes. Two examples of such cornets are preserved in this country—the Moulton flag and the Bedford flag (see below). The latter is made of crimson damask with the arm, sword, clouds, etc., painted on in gold, silver, and black. There appears to be good reason for believing that this flag was made in the 1600's for the Three County Troop which operated in Essex, Middlesex, and Suffolk Counties in Massachusetts. Tradition asserts that one hundred years later Nathaniel Page, a minuteman, carried this cornet at the Battle of Concord on 19 April 1775. This battle, which with the engagement earlier that morning at Lexington signaled the beginning of the American Revolution, was commemorated in Emerson's now-famous poem:

> By the rude bridge that arched the flood,
>   Their flag to April's breeze unfurled,
> Here once the embattled farmers stood,
>   And fired the shot heard round the world.

Today this flag, the oldest still in existence in the United States and one of the oldest in the New World, is on display at the Bedford (Mass.) Public Library.

"BEDFORD FLAG" (obverse) Company color of the Three County Troop, late 1600's (used at the Battle of Concord, 19 April 1775) Proportions 1 x 1

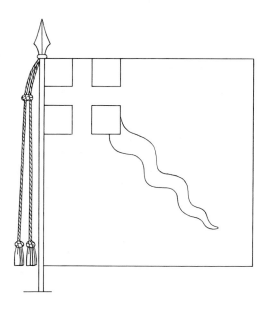

GREAT BRITAIN Major's company (infantry) color (example from Boston, 1679)

British infantry flags were larger than cornets (about four feet six inches by six feet nine inches) and more standardized in design. The companies within a regiment were commanded, in decreasing seniority, by a colonel, lieutenant-colonel, major, first captain, second captain, and so forth. Until 1661 in England and until about 1686 in America the system of ensigns, as the infantry colors were called, was generally as follows: the colonel's company had a plain flag of red, white, green, or blue; the lieutenant-colonel's company added a canton of St. George's cross; and the major's company added the canton with a ray (see above). The ensigns of the captains included the canton plus a circle in the fly of the flag for the first captain, two circles for the second captain, etc. References exist to a number of these infantry flags, although no American examples remain. The 1684 flag of Captain Thomas Noyes's company—green with a canton of St. George—has incorrectly been labeled by some authors as a town flag for Newbury (Mass.).

In 1661 St. George's cross was established as a background pattern for the infantry ensign. There is evidence that a flag of this type, the first captain's color of the King's Guards, was carried by troops in this country during the administration of Governor Sir Edmund Andros (1686-1689) in the Dominion of New England.* This was a square banner with a purple St. George's cross bearing James's royal cipher in gold. It had been mistakenly identified in some books as a flag for New England or for Andros himself.

In 1707 the Union Jack was introduced in regimental colors; as a canton it probably provided the inspiration for the general design of later regimental colors used in the colonies, such as the one shown in VII-b. In 1743 the number of colors per battalion was reduced to two regardless of the number of companies. One, called the King's Colour, usually had as its field the Union Jack; the other, or Regimental Colour, had the Union Jack only as a canton, the field of the flag being of the same color as the facings on the troops' uniforms. This system obviously inspired the American military colors adopted in 1780.

THE NEW ENGLAND FLAG

The 1600's were a time of religious turmoil for Englishmen, and one expression of this can be found in the symbols that they displayed. The Puritans who populated the Massachusetts Bay Colony were convinced that true Christianity required them to eliminate every trace of idolatry and paganism, which they understood to include all "badges of superstition." The extremists among them considered that the cross of St. George "was given to the King of England by the Pope, as an ensign of victory, and so [was . . .] a superstitious thing, and a relic of Antichrist." Spurred on by a sermon denouncing the cross, in November 1634 John

---

* The Dominion, established by King James II, combined the colonies of Connecticut, Massachusetts Bay, New Hampshire, New Jersey, New York, Plymouth, and Rhode Island. It was dissolved before it could effectively begin to operate.

VIII. THE FIRST UNITED STATES FLAG

a.   **UNITED STATES (CONTINENTAL COLORS)**   State and national flag; ensign   Fall 1775?–13 June 1777 (variant)

b.   **UNITED STATES**   National flag   ?1775–1800 (unofficial; variant)

c.   **UNITED STATES**   ?Ensign and jack   c1775–1776   (unofficial; variant)

a.

b.

c.

Endicott, a member of the local government, ordered the ensign bearer of Salem (Mass.) to cut out the red cross from the infantry colors then in use (V-a). Others, fearful that this act would be viewed in England as a sign of rebellion, brought the matter before the General Court (the local legislature) where Endicott was censured for "rashnes unchari-tablenes, indiscrecon, & exceeding the lymitts of his calling" and was "disinabled for beareing any office in the common wealth, for the space of a yeare nexte ensueing."

The question was far from settled, however. In March 1636 the much agitated General Court left it up to the military commissioners to determine the correct regimental colors and without exception they left out the cross. The Red Ensign flown on Castle Island at the entrance to Boston Harbor presented a special problem, however, since it was visible to all passing ships as well as the inhabitants of the town. After long and heated debate, it was decided to leave this flag undefaced since the Castle was the property of the king; yet Dutchmen who were in Boston in 1680 reported seeing the red flag with the plain white canton such as the militia used. Other references indicate that local ships also flew this form of the flag, so we may consider that between 1636 and about 1686 there existed, at least unofficially, a distinctive Massachusetts Red Ensign (VI-a). The leading student on the history of this flag suggests that it may have been flown elsewhere in New England, according to the religious ideas of the individuals involved. Agitation against defacement of the flag continued until the 1680's when the cross was again generally in-cluded. It is nevertheless clear that many people had serious misgivings about the restoration of the cross: Judge Samuel Sewall wrote that he was "afraid if I should have a hand in 't whether it may not hinder my Entrance into the Holy Land."

Just at the time that the cross of St. George reappears, another distinc-tive flag for New England came into use. This was the English Red Ensign with a tree in the uppermost corner (VI-b). There was also a jack form, consisting of the flag of St. George with the tree in the canton (VI-c). Although our sources are scanty, it seems clear from available evidence that the New England ensign and jack remained in use on both land and sea for almost a century, that is until the American Revolution.

The cross of St. George and the Red Ensign then ceased to be appropriate and the flag took on a somewhat modified form which has lasted to the present (XXX-a).

Certain problems exist concerning the exact design and display of the New England flag. First, the species of tree is unclear, or rather variable. In old drawings it is shown as either a pine,* willow, or oak. The same three trees occur on the early coins of Massachusetts which are known collectively as pine tree shillings. In a famous incident Governor Thomas Temple of Nova Scotia, who was discussing the affairs of the American colonies with Charles II, made a favorable impression on the King by suggesting that the "royal oak" on the Massachusetts coinage was in honor of the tree in which Charles had hidden when fleeing Cromwell. Nevertheless the examples of the flag from the eighteenth century suggest that the pine tree was the type most in favor, probably because of the contribution that the pine made to New England commerce. Certain books erroneously substitute a globe for the tree in this flag.

A more serious misconception about the New England flag regards the color of its field. It has already been pointed out that the Red Ensign became familiar through a century and a half of use on men-of-war, merchant ships, forts, and in military formations. As the universally recognized national colors of England, the Red Ensign was the logical basis for a flag representing its namesake in America. The Blue Ensign in contrast had only limited use as the least important of the squadronal identification colors, blue never having been an English color. Yet many books dating as far back as 1716 show a blue field for the New England flag. There are two significant points to note about the sources that show such a field. Comparison indicates that all of them copied heavily from a single source which pictured a blue field, but described it directly underneath as red. Moreover, the early sources were all published in France and the Netherlands, countries in which flag information from New England must have been second- or thirdhand. In contrast we have three contemporary English sources, each apparently compiled independently of the others, which show the red field. Unfortunately, historical evi-

---

* The first use of the pine tree seems to have been in the seal of Plymouth Colony made about 1624.

dence is all too frequently weighed by quantity instead of quality, and vexillology records a number of other imaginary designs that have achieved immortality through constant repetition.

With the New England flags we begin the transition which leads from the old era to the new in American flag history. In the six hundred years between the arrival of the Vikings and the settlements at St. Augustine and Plymouth, the flags carried to the New World were rarely planted on its shores. Yet once established the banners of the Old World quickly took root and provided the heritage of symbolism and design from which grew, a century and a half later, an authentic and vital flag tradition fed by native American aspirations and activities.

IX. THE SECOND UNITED STATES FLAG

a. **UNITED STATES   State and national flag; ensign   14 June 1777–30 April 1795 (usual variant)**

b. **UNITED STATES   Used at the Battle of Bennington   16 August 1777 (unofficial variant of national flag)**

c. **UNITED STATES   State and national flag; ensign   14 June 1777–30 April 1795 (infrequent variant)**

a.

b.

c.

Chapter III

THE ORIGINS OF THE UNITED STATES FLAG

SNAKES, STRIPES, AND TREES

As population and commerce developed during the eighteenth century, the British colonies in America grew closer and closer together. To the extent that American aspirations and problems differed from those of the mother country, there arose the need for common local symbols. The necessity was especially acute in time of crisis or war when the very existence of these pioneer commonwealths was called into question. (It should be remembered that long before the Revolution Americans were fighting the French and the Indians who surrounded them to the north and west.)

Until the creation of the first United States flag, the Continental Colors of 1775-1777, a number of symbols competed for the loyalty of the colonists. The earliest such emblem seems to have been the snake which first appears (see p. 45) in Benjamin Franklin's *Pennsylvania Gazette* on 9 May 1754, just before the Albany Congress of that year. The Congress discussed a treaty with the Indians and the possibility of a union of Colonies. This snake, cut into pieces to represent the disunited Colonies, recurs next in November 1765, just before the Stamp Act went

X

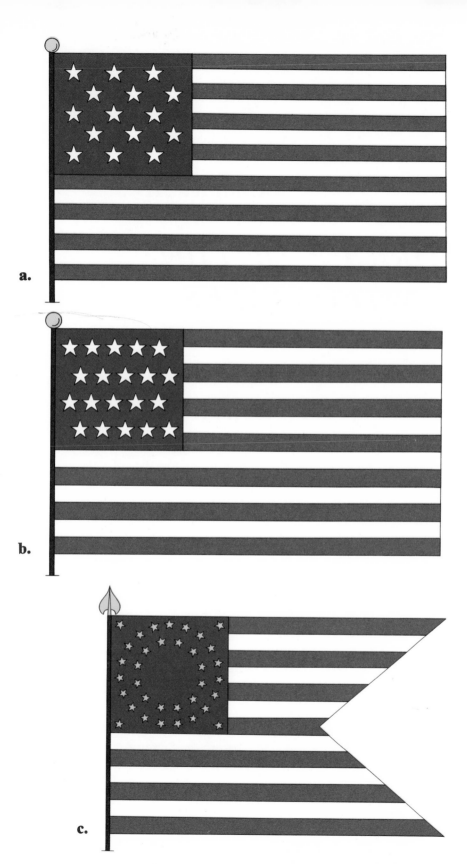

a.

b.

c.

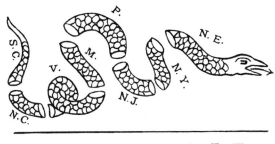

JOIN, or DIE.

COLONIAL SNAKE EMBLEM
(earliest known example; from the "Penn-
sylvania Gazette," 9 May 1754)

into effect. The third and final use of the snake in newspapers extended from June 1774 until August 1776.

It was during this latter period that the first snake flags were used, although unfortunately we cannot date any of them exactly. Three such flags still exist: one is the color of the Fifty-Second Independent Battalion (the so-called Westmoreland County or Proctor's Battalion), which was one of the Pennsylvania volunteer units known as Associators. The other flags are from Rhode Island—the color of the United Company of the Train of Artillery, an independent chartered company from Providence, and the flag carried in 1778 during General Sullivan's siege of Newport. These all bear a coiled rattlesnake and the motto "Don't Tread On Me," indicating a change from the previous period of disunity to a new era of defiance. A similar flag (VII-a), of which no example remains, was flown in early 1776 as the rank flag of the Commander in Chief of the Fleet, a position held by Commodore Esek Hopkins of Rhode Island. Because Colonel Christopher Gadsden presented a copy of this flag to the Provincial Congress of South Carolina, it has

X. NINETEENTH CENTURY AMERICAN FLAGS

a. **UNITED STATES** State and national flag; ensign 1 May 1795–3 July 1818 (variant)

b. **UNITED STATES** State and national flag; ensign 4 July 1818–10 September 1818 (authorized 18 May 1818) Proportions 7 x 12

c. **UNITED STATES ARMY** Cavalry guidon 4 July 1863–3 July 1865 (basic pattern in use 18 January 1862–4 February 1885) Proportions 27 x 41

often, falsely, been called the "Gadsden flag" or the "flag of the South Carolina navy."

Rattlesnakes were also found in the Fifth Pennsylvaina Regiment flag and in the seal of the Army. The most important use made of the serpent symbol, however, was in the flag (VIII-c) which is usually called the "first naval jack."* The flag may possibly have served this function, but contemporary pictures and descriptions suggest that it was simply a variation of the United States naval ensign. Sometimes the white field had six red stripes, sometimes thirteen.

Another popular symbol was the liberty tree or liberty pole. The idea of a great tree under which men gather to make decisions for running the community, for the settling of disputes between citizens, and for conducting other public business is a very old one, and such trees have existed in many countries. In America the tree first became a symbol associated with liberty on 14 August 1765 when effigies were hung from an elm tree in Boston to protest the Stamp Act. Later the revolutionaries known as the Sons of Liberty met under this tree and similar ones in the other colonies; when the British cut down such a tree it was usually replaced by a liberty pole. Often at the top of the tree or pole there was flown a flag with a motto, such as "Liberty, Property, and No Stamps," "The King, Pitt, and Liberty," or "Geo. Rex and the Liberties of America." The flag raised on 21 October 1774 at Taunton (Mass.) was of this type; it bore the words "Liberty and Union." The Sons of Liberty's own flag—nine horizontal stripes, alternately red and white—was also frequently hoisted.

Reference has already been made to the pine tree symbol used in New England and especially Massachusetts. The most common form of the pine tree flag (XXX-a) in use 1775-1777 was officially adopted by the Massachusetts Navy in April 1776. The previous September it flew on the floating batteries which sailed down the Charles River to attack British-held Boston, and unconfirmed references suggest that ships on the Delaware River also displayed it. On 20 October 1775 Washington's military secretary, Colonel Joseph Reed, suggested in a letter that this flag be put into general usage so that American vessels might recognize one another, and there is evidence that it was hoisted by the schooners

---

* This is redundant: jacks are always used by the navy.

later commissioned by Washington. One of these ships, the *Lee* commanded by Captain John Manly, is credited with the first American capture of a British vessel when on 29 November 1775, probably sailing under the pine tree flag, she defeated the brig *Nancy*. On land we find a green military color, possibly used by a company from Newburyport (Mass.) and based on its earlier color (see p. 35), whose white canton bore a green pine tree on a blue circle surrounded with a chain held by thirteen mailed hands issuing from an encircling cloud.

The original pine tree emblem, the New England flag of 1686 (VI-b; p. 38), flew at the Battle of Bunker Hill on 17 June 1775. In Colonel John Trumbull's painting of the battle, "The Death of Warren," the cross of St. George is omitted from this flag. If this variation was in fact used, then the Massachusetts Navy pine tree flag mentioned in the previous paragraph would have been its jack form, just as the St. George's cross and tree flag (VI-c) was the jack of the original New England ensign. Although it is logical to assume that the rebellious Americans might have dropped the English cross at this time, of course that does not prove that it really happened. Certainly Trumbull, like many artists of the Revolutionary War period, allowed his imagination free rein in the matter of depicting details in battle scenes. We do know, however, that the "Bunker Hill flag" with a blue field which is often shown in flag books is definitely incorrect.

CONTINENTAL COLORS AND REGIMENTAL COLORS

The American Revolution, like most revolutions, proceeded in stages, each one characterized by certain goals and tactics which had developed out of the previous stages. Emblems such as the rattlesnake, liberty pole, and the pine tree characterized the formative years of the Revolution from the first protests in 1765 to the outbreak of actual hostilities in the Spring of 1775. They were local symbols having only limited appeal to the nation as a whole and they were conservative symbols which called on the King, Parliament, and Heaven for a preservation or restoration of the rights of Englishmen. The seal of Massachusetts adopted in 1775 (see p. 48) is another good example of these sentiments.

MASSACHUSETTS BAY
Seal
7 August 1775–
13 December 1780

From the Battles of Lexington, Concord, and Bunker Hill (April-June 1775) until the Declaration of Independence in July 1776 there followed a transitional period: Americans were forced to choose sides and to determine just how far they were willing to go in fighting conditions that they felt unjust, while at the same time the British government faced its last opportunities to make amends or to crush the rebellion decisively. It was at this time that the first (unofficial) national flag of the United States (VIII-a), the Continental Colors, was born.

On 3 July 1775 Washington took command of the colonial troops on the Common at Cambridge, just a few miles from Boston. Acting under authority from the Continental Congress, he undertook to transform these irregular forces gathered from many colonies into a unified army. To aid him a committee appointed by Congress and consisting of Benjamin Franklin, Benjamin Harrison, and Thomas Lynch visited Washington in October. That some concern was raised at this time about a flag is evident from the previously mentioned letter written by Colonel Reed; but there is no proof that the committee of three actually designed the Continental Colors as some have claimed. What we are sure of is that on 1 January the new Continental Army became official and that to celebrate Washington had the Continental Colors hoisted "in compli-

XI. FLAGS AND ARMS OF ALABAMA

a. **ALABAMA   Coat of Arms   14 March 1939–present**

b. **ALABAMA (REPUBLIC)   State flag on land (obverse)   11 January 1861–? (not used after 10 February 1861)**

c. **ALABAMA (REPUBLIC)   Reverse of flag b**

XI

AUDEMUS JURA NOSTRA DEFENDERE

a.

INDEPENDENT NOW AND FOREVER

ALABAMA

b.

NOLI ME TANGERE

c.

ment to the United Colonies." The flag was raised on the liberty pole, which formerly flew a red flag, situated on Prospect Hill in nearby Charlestown, now part of the city of Somerville. Since Washington's camp was in Cambridge, the flag has often misleadingly been called "the Cambridge flag." The flag was also occasionally called the "great Union Flag," a name corrupted by later writers to Grand Union.

Copies of a speech recently made by King George, in which he called on Americans to lay down their arms, had just been sent to Washington's camp. Washington—who probably was not present at the flagpole in person as some have assumed—recorded with amusement the reaction of the British in Boston upon seeing the Continental Colors: "behold! it was received in Boston as a token of the deep Impression the Speech had made upon us, and as a signal of Submission . . . by this time I presume they begin to think it strange that we have not made a formal surrender of our Lines . . ." The confusion arose, of course, because of the Union Jack which appeared in the canton of the Continental Colors. Americans undoubtedly saw this Union Jack as a sign of their loyalty to the mother country—the Declaration of Independence being half a year away. The thirteen stripes signified the unity of the thirteen colonies in seeking redress for their grievances. This double symbolism made the flag a popular one with the American patriots.

There are vague references in contemporary sources to "Union flags" and "Continental flags" in use during the fall of 1775 and, while no exact descriptions of them are known, such flags may well have been the Continental Colors. Washington and others do not indicate that the flag at Prospect Hill was new in design. Certainly during 1776 and 1777, spontaneously or by design, the Continental Colors was made and hoisted throughout the colonies, both at sea and on land. Its design was unofficial and variations (as in VIII-b and VIII-c) appeared; yet references in the resolves of the Continental Congress and the Pennsylvania Committee of Safety make it clear that the Continental Colors was universally accepted as a national flag.

In early January 1776 the first regular American fleet, under the command of Commodore Hopkins (whose personal flag has already been described), sailed down the Delaware River from Philadelphia under the Continental Colors. There has long been a dispute about what role John Paul Jones had with regard to the flag at this time. His own statement reads: ". . . it was my fortune, as the senior first lieutenant, to hoist the flag of America the first time it was displayed [on this fleet]." Although he does not describe "the flag of America" and although his lieutenant's commission is dated late December 1775, we do know that the Continental Colors was hoisted on the flagship *Alfred* on 3 December 1775. Thus, if we are to believe him at all, it seems that either Jones was not first lieutenant when he raised the flag or that he was the first to hoist it *officially* as the ships set sail in early January.

Under the Continental Colors a number of other "firsts" are recorded: men of this fleet hoisted the first United States flag over a captured foreign fort (New Providence in the Bahamas, March 1776); the *Lexington* commanded by Captain Barry became the first commissioned American ship to defeat a foreign vessel (the brig *Edward* in April 1776); and the *Andrea Doria* under Captain Isaiah Robinson received the first foreign recognition of the American flag on 16 November 1776. This salute, at St. Eustatius in the Dutch West Indies, was significant for a number of reasons. It provided symbolic recognition of the newly proclaimed independence of the United States, a formal license for American ships to continue purchasing supplies despite the British blockade, and a promise of further help for the American cause from European powers. In revenge for this salute the enraged British Admiral Rodney completely devastated St. Eustatius, carrying off over one hundred million dollars' worth of goods.

Americans flew the Continental Colors over forts and at sea. On land they made use of an array of military colors, most of them locally designed and manufactured. Some of these colors are still in existence and it is immediately evident that in many cases British models have been followed. In some flags even a form of the Union Jack itself appears in the canton, as in the color of the Second New Hampshire Regiment captured at the Battle of Saratoga. Later we find a new union device instead: in the canton appear either thirteen stripes, as in the color of the Second Regiment of Light Dragoons, or thirteen stars, as in the color of the Second Rhode Island Regiment (VII-b). The field of most of these flags is a solid shade and bears a local emblem. The color (VII-c) of the Negro unit known as the Bucks of America is typical of

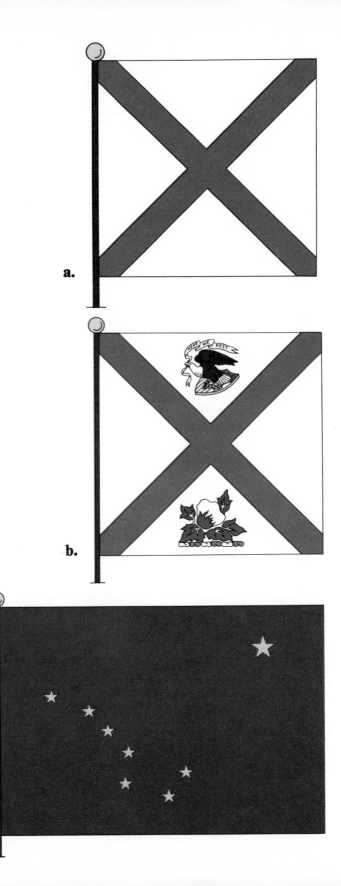

a.

b.

c.

this pattern. It combines the national emblem, a blue canton of thirteen stars,* with the pine tree of Massachusetts, and a buck. On the other hand, there were many military colors during the war having entirely different patterns, such as XVIII-a. Standardization of design for military colors was a luxury the Continental Army could not afford, given the more immediate need for weapons, uniforms, and provisions.

Washington wrote in February 1776 that each regiment and grand division (company) should have its own standard "and that those colours should, if it can be done, bear some kind of similitude to the uniform of the Regiment to which they belong." In May a reminder was sent to the Colonels about choosing designs. Three years later, following changes introduced into the organization of the Army by Baron von Steuben, the company colors were eliminated and each regiment was to be provided with two flags—a single national color, used throughout the Army, and a regimental color, varying from one regiment to the next. The latter was to have as a background the color used in the facings of the State's troops, i.e., white for the Light Dragoons and for the Infantry of Connecticut, Massachusetts, New Hampshire, and Rhode Island; buff for the New York and New Jersey Infantry; red for the Delaware, Maryland, Pennsylvania, and Virginia Infantry; blue for the Infantry of Georgia and the Carolinas; and scarlet for Artillery.

Unfortunately, the existing correspondence does not make it clear what the design was for either the regimental colors or the "national standard." Some have suggested that we can find these two in the seal of the Army (LIX-a); others insist that the national flag was never commonly used by military units until decades later. Adding to our confusion is the fact that very few of the flags of the Revolutionary era still remaining can be precisely dated. Interesting as it would be to know for

---

* The stars are now discolored, but were originally either white or gold.

XII. FLAGS OF ALABAMA AND ALASKA
a. **ALABAMA   Government flag   16 February 1895–present**
b. **ALABAMA   Governor's flag   c1934–5 April 1939**
c. **ALASKA   Government flag 2 May 1927–present   (specifications from 10 March 1959)   Proportions 125 x 177**

sure what the standardized flags of 1779 looked like, it must be kept in mind that few if any were actually used. Despite Washington's plea that "it is essential to the Discipline as well as the Appearance of the Troops that they should be furnished with Colours," as late as March of 1783, a bare seven months before Yorktown, these new colors were still largely undistributed. Older flags (where such existed) had to suffice.

THE FIRST OFFICIAL FLAG

By the summer of 1776 the view that the American colonies should be independent, an idea previously held only by a minority, had become more generally accepted. On 2 July a simple motion was accepted in Congress declaring independence, followed two days later by a public proclamation. In retrospect this event is seen as a turning point in the fate of the continent and indeed of the world, but at the time its impact on the actual course of the war with Britain was slight; European powers still awaited a decisive victory like Saratoga before committing themselves to the rebel cause. Certainly the immediate formal changes in national symbols such as flags, arms, uniforms, and coins which newly independent nations today universally make were absent in America. Even the change in name from United Colonies to United States did not take place until two months after the Declaration of Independence. As in the case of procuring military colors, the leaders of the Revolution were too busy most of the time to concern themselves with any except the most pressing matters of business.

In particular it is not surprising that Congress took no action with regard to a new flag when the Declaration of Independence was proclaimed. Although on that first Fourth of July it did establish a committee to look into an appropriate seal, Congress apparently felt that the Continental Colors adequately served the few commissioned American ships. William Richards, who kept naval stores in Philadelphia and was immediately involved in the supplying of flags, did not agree. We find letters he wrote to the Pennsylvania Committee of Safety, dated in August and October of 1776, complaining that he could not provide the galleys in the Delaware River with flags until a design was established. It may be that protests were already being made by naval men about the retention of the Union Jack in the flag of a nation which claimed to be independent; or it may be that Richards hesitated to invest in flags of one design for fear that another would be favored by the authorities.

In any event the next spring Richards finally got some flags (of unspecified design), as attested by a note dated 29 May 1777 in the minutes of the State Naval Board, recording payment "to Elizabeth Ross for fourteen pounds, twelve shillings, and two pence, for making ship's colours." At least one other demand for flags also arose at this time. On 3 June 1777 the President of the Continental Congress presented that body with three pieces of wampum which he had received from Thomas Green, an Indian, with a request "that a flag of the United States might be delivered to him to take to the chiefs of the nation, to be used by them for their security and protection, when they may have occasion to visit us their brethren."

Whether these requests by Richards and Green were responsible for the adoption of the new flag or not, we do know that Congress finally took its first official action on this question shortly thereafter, on Saturday, 14 June 1777. From the *Journal* of Congress it is evident that the largely routine business of that day's session was within the sphere of the Marine Committee: for example, directions are sought regarding the fleet in the Delaware in case of British attack, and John Paul Jones is appointed as Captain of the *Ranger*.* In between, without a word of comment or explanation, is the terse resolve that "the Flag of the united states be 13 stripes alternate red and white, that the Union be 13 stars white in a blue field representing a new constellation."

Notice of this new design (IX-a) was slow in becoming publicly known. There are a few individual references in July and August, but the *Pennsylvania Evening Post* of 30 August 1777 seems to be the first newspaper to have printed the text of the law. Yet in the same month we still find the Continental Colors being flown on the *General Mifflin* commanded by Captain William McNeil when it was saluted off Brest, France, and over Fort Schuyler, New York, during a British siege. Gradually the news spread and the Union Jack in the old Continental Colors gave way to the first official flag of the United States, the Stars

---

* This resolve prompted one of Jones's biographers to invent and ascribe to Jones the boast "That flag and I are twins, born in the same hour from the same womb of destiny." In fact Jones had received his naval commission months before.

and Stripes. The new flag, like the old one, was used as a national flag during holidays and celebrations and as a state flag on public buildings and forts. At sea it served as the ensign for men-of-war, privateers, and merchantmen, although there is some evidence to suggest that the latter sometimes used the flag of stripes (VIII-b).

The thirteen-star, thirteen-stripe flag, which continued to fly throughout the rest of the war for independence and until 1795 when the present Constitution and form of government were securely established, saw a number of "firsts." There is some reason to believe that it flew in Philadelphia on 4 July 1777 when the first anniversary of American independence was celebrated. John Paul Jones carried a version of this flag with him to France and on 14 February 1778 induced the French Admiral, La Motte Piquet, to render the third salute ever given to an American flag and the first to the Stars and Stripes. He brought further glory to the Stars and Stripes by his capture of the British sloop *Drake* in April 1778 and, a year later, by his heroic defeat of the frigate *Serapis*. The merchantman *Columbia* was the first ship to bear this flag around the world, in a voyage which began in Boston in September 1787 and ended in that city three years and 42,000 miles later.

On land there have been many claims for the honor of the first battle in which the Stars and Stripes was flown, including Assanpink and Middlebrook, New Jersey; Fort Schuyler and Fort Anne, New York; Brandywine, Pennsylvania; Hubbardton, Vermont; and Cooch's Bridge, Delaware. A recently discovered Stars and Stripes is supposed to have been carried by General John Sullivan on Staten Island and in New Jersey and Pennsylvania. None of these claims has been substantiated and some of them are obviously incorrect. Until new research suggested otherwise, the camp flag of a Vermont militia company, known as the

XIII. FLAGS OF AMERICAN SAMOA AND ARIZONA

a.   **SAMOA (KINGDOM)   State and national flag   2 October 1873–28 January 1886; c1888–27 April 1900**

b.   **AMERICAN SAMOA   27 April 1960–present**

c.   **ARIZONA   Government flag   27 February 1917–present   Proportions 2 x 3**

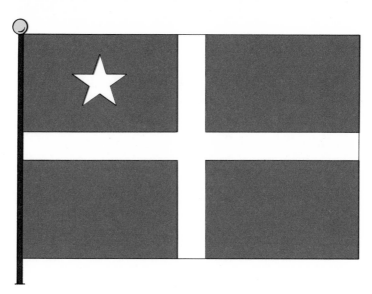

a.

b.

c.

"Bennington flag" (IX-b), was hailed as the oldest Stars and Stripes still extant and the first used on land by American armed forces—supposedly flown on 16 August 1777 during the Battle of Bennington (Vt.). (Fabric analysts believe the flag dates from about 1876, but precise flag dating is difficult.)

The design of the Bennington flag demonstrates rather dramatically how little concern there was in the first decades of the United States for standardized flag patterns. The law of 14 June 1777 gave only the most general description of the flag, and each flag maker liberally interpreted for himself what the Stars and Stripes should look like. Some, like the Bennington flag and the ensign flown in 1779 by the *Alliance,* had seven white and six red stripes like the older rattlesnake ensign (VIII-c). Some had vertical instead of horizontal stripes, a pattern retained in the modern Coast Guard Ensign (LX-c). Jones's flag on the *Bon Homme Richard,* later transferred to the *Serapis,* had stripes of red, white, and blue— something like the Hawaiian flags (XXII-b and XXII-c). Benjamin Franklin and John Adams, the American Commissioners in Paris, described such a flag in a letter to the Ambassador of the Two Sicilies, although the blue stripes never had any official sanction. From contemporary flags and prints we know that the number of points in the stars varied from four to eight.

In describing the stars in the canton as a new constellation, Congress does not appear to have had any particular arrangement in mind. Judging by the examples remaining, the most common patterns set the stars in rows—either of 3-2-3-2-3 stars (IX-a) or of 4-5-4 stars. Another popular variant showed one star in the center and twelve around the edge of the canton. The form which today is most commonly thought of, manufactured, and illustrated in books as the first Stars and Stripes shows the thirteen stars in a circle (IX-c). But this was scarcely ever used in the period 1777-1795, and its widespread use now is a tribute to the popularity of certain nineteenth-century artists. Emanuel Leutze's "Washington Crossing the Delaware," Charles Weisgerber's "Birth of Our Nation's Flag," Archibald Willard's "Spirit of '76," and similar paintings have indelibly impressed the design of thirteen stars in a circle on the mind of the public despite its doubtful pedigree.

THE STRIPES AND THE STARS

The flag in America has always been an everyday object whose design is taken for granted as a heritage from "the founding fathers." Thus in the nation's first century of existence scarcely four slim books on the history of the flag were published, despite the fervent patriotism evoked by the wars of that era. By the time the first scholarly investigations were made on the origins of the flag, it was already too late to obtain first-hand information. The papers of Congress and of prominent men like Washington and Adams; diaries and letters; newspapers, broadsheets, and occasional references in books; even objects like powder horns, wallpaper samples, and scarves: these were and are the materials available for reconstructing the history of the flag. The first attempts in this direction were generally crude, in part because sources were uncovered slowly and in part because the men who did the research were not thorough and unbiased scholars. Although many of the books on the flag in print today are as carelessly prepared as the older ones, there have been a number of important advances in our understanding of America's vexillological history as new facts and new theories have been presented in recent books and articles.

One frequently asked question about the flag regards the source of its stars and stripes. At the very outset it should be pointed out that no definitive answer can now be given and none probably ever will be, although existing evidence and historical reasoning allow us to make surmises with a high probability of accuracy. With even greater certainty we can refute some of the hypotheses that have been put forward and some of those seemingly deathless myths which plague the study of flags.

The reader of this book who began with Chapter I already has the fundamental development of the Stars and Stripes before him. The most familiar flags of the colonial period had been the British Union Jack and the Red Ensign. Both had been slightly modified to represent the colonies in the New England flag (VI-b), the colonial jack (V-b), and other early liberty flags and military colors. When the Revolution was in its first stages, nothing would have been more natural than that the old familiar flags continue to be used, with something added to distinguish the colonies from the mother country. There may seem to be a contradiction in the idea that Americans should war on a people whose flag they displayed. Yet this same borrowing of the general flag design from the country one is revolting against can be found in many instances of colonial liberation, including Haiti, Venezuela, Iceland, and Guinea. Notice is made further on in this book of the first flags of Texas and the Confederacy, which closely resembled those of Mexico and the United States.

If it is granted that the British Red Ensign was the basis for the Continental Colors, the origin of the stripes is still unsolved. Among the earlier interpretations of the stripes the sarcastic suggestion made in 1780 by an English writer that Congress got the idea for the stripes from the thirteen rings on the tail of Martha Washington's mottled tomcat deserves as much serious attention as the claim made later by an American that the stripes derived from the ribbons of military rank worn by Washington and his officers. More to the point some writers, noting that the East India Company flew as a jack and ensign a flag of exactly the same design as the Continental Colors,* have assumed that this ensign inspired the American flag. This seems unlikely, although not impossible, in view of the animosity the colonists had for the Company whose shipments provoked the Boston Tea Party. Moreover, there is very strong evidence that the striped flag of the Company was never displayed in the New World.

Two other ideas advanced in the past appear to be more likely and both perhaps contain substantial elements of truth. One theory claims that the Sons of Liberty flag (p.46) was chosen as the national flag, with a Union Jack added in the canton. The Sons of Liberty were radicals whose flag was probably too partisan in 1775 to have been consciously chosen by conservatives like Washington to represent the whole nation;

---

* The East India Company flag sometimes had nine or eleven stripes, but normally comprised thirteen.

XIV. FLAGS OF ARKANSAS
a. **ARKANSAS   26 February 1913–(February?) 1923**
b. **ARKANSAS   (February?) 1923–4 April 1924**
c. **ARKANSAS   4 April 1924–present**

a.

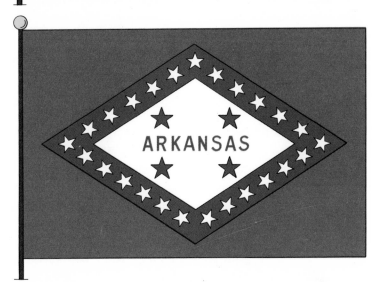

b.

c.

furthermore it had nine stripes, not thirteen. Yet this flag, if not a direct inspiration for the Continental Colors, undoubtedly popularized the idea of stripes as a sign of rebellion. Another theory posits that the colonists copied the striped flags of the Netherlands (see p. 22), a country which aided the Revolution and provided it with many republican ideas. But in fact the Dutch flag never had thirteen stripes and there is no evidence that the normal red-white-blue-striped flag of the Netherlands was ever regularly replaced by one of red and white alone. If the Dutch flags are relevant at all, it is probably only as part of the tradition of horizontally striped flags throughout Europe generally. Such flags in red and white, aside from their use in England, flew in Tunis, Hungary, and the German cities of Wismar and Bremen. Multistriped flags of other colors appeared in Portugal, France (see p. 18), Estonia, Brandenburg, Helgoland, North Africa, Sweden, and some Dutch provinces and cities.

A flag with stripes closer to home is the color of the First Troop of Light Horse, Philadelphia City Cavalry, which is still preserved in that city. We have the original 1775 invoice for the painting of the flag, which has thirteen blue and silver stripes for a canton. But these could not have influenced Washington to choose stripes for the national flag—as has often been suggested—since they were not part of the original design. Underneath the stripes the flag bears the British Union Jack, obviously the original canton. Although this flag has been well known and available for public inspection since it was first made, the existence of the original Union Jack canton was ignored until 1973.

The "Washington arms theory" attempts to explain both stars and stripes by assuming that they were taken from the shield of George Washington (XIX-a). This thesis can be quickly rejected: not only are the two designs unalike in essential respects, but Washington was clearly the kind of individual who would have resisted such an immodest idea. Another suggestion has been advanced concerning the stars, which insists that the "new constellation" mentioned in the law must have been Lyra. This constellation is represented on the American passport of 1820 designed by John Quincy Adams. By conjecture, his father John Adams is presumed to have proposed the same pattern for the flag when he was chairman of the Marine Committee at the time the Stars and

PORTSMOUTH (R.I.)
Town Council seal
c1676–c1683

Stripes was adopted. We know that Adams worked with Benjamin Franklin and Thomas Jefferson to design a United States seal, but nothing is known about any interest he may have had in the flag, nor is any flag known with the stars arranged to form the constellation Lyra.

The theory which carries the origin of the stars furthest back in history surmises that they came to the United States flag from previous use on one or more of the Rhode Island flags which bore thirteen stars—the colors of the First and Second Regiments and of the United Company of the Train of Artillery. Their presence in these flags is then tentatively attributed to the use of stars in the seal of Providence which dates back to at least 1680. In turn this is associated with the very similar Town Council seal of Portsmouth, Rhode Island, used in 1676 (see above). Finally, the possibility is noted that this town took the star from the seal and arms of its namesake city in England (see below; the star and crescent are gold on a blue shield). The English Portsmouth derived its star (and crescent) from King Richard I, who apparently saw it at Constantinople during his participation in the Crusades in the twelfth

PORTSMOUTH
(ENGLAND)
Coat of arms
1194–present

a.

b.

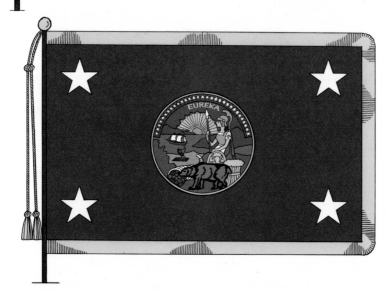

c.

century. It had been adopted as the emblem of that city, long before the Ottoman Turks turned it into an Islamic symbol, when a star representing the Virgin Mary was added to the crescent of the pagan goddess, Diana. This occurred around 330 A.D. when Constantine renamed the city of Byzantium after himself and forced its conversion to Christianity. The proponent of this theory has, wisely, not insisted that it be accepted as any more than a plausible line of development. One of its chief weaknesses is our inability to date precisely the starred flags of Rhode Island: if they preceded the Stars and Stripes they may have inspired it, but it is as easy to believe that they postdated the national flag and took their stars from its precedent.

BETSY ROSS AND FRANCIS HOPKINSON

In addition to these hypotheses we are confronted with a number of flags, existing or supposed to have been in existence, which demand some explanation. The "Hulbert flag" and "Easton flag" are interesting relics of American history, with claims of being authentic Stars and Stripes flags dating from 1775 and 1776, respectively. Unfortunately, the implausibility that either of these flags or the "Montgomery flag" was made before the flag resolution of 1777 has never been overcome by any substantial facts. The "General Schuyler flag" lacks contemporary references to its supposed use during the summer of 1777. Other vexillologists have already shown that there is no reason to believe the legend about the flag supposedly made in Portsmouth, New Hampshire, for John Paul Jones and hoisted on 4 July 1777 by him on the *Ranger*. The so-called "Stafford flag" which was reputed to have been saved from Jones's ship *Bon Homme Richard* and presented to James Stafford has also been convincingly discredited.

XV. FLAGS OF CALIFORNIA

a. **CALIFORNIA REPUBLIC (BEAR FLAG)   State flag on land   14 June 1846–9 July 1846 (unofficial)**

b. **CALIFORNIA (BEAR FLAG)   Government flag   3 February 1911– present   Proportions 2 x 3**

c. **CALIFORNIA   Governor's flag   8 June 1957–present   Proportions 5 x 8**

Perhaps the most famous early Stars and Stripes is the one which generations of school children have learned was "made by Betsy Ross for George Washington." The flag, if it ever existed at all, is long since gone and the conjectural reconstruction of it usually made (IX-c), with the stars in a circle, is pure fantasy. The story of its making has so far not been definitively treated, but a tally of books about the flag by scholars is revealing. Fifteen reject the Betsy Ross legend, five more conclude that it is unproven, and only two support it as believable history. Certainly the story strains the imagination, at least when examined in the light of known facts. The questions raised cannot be dealt with fully here; an outline of the story and criticisms made of it will have to suffice.

The first public knowledge of any role that Betsy, Mrs. Elizabeth Griscom Ross Ashburn Claypoole, may have had with regard to the flag only came ninety-four years after the events in question. One of her grandsons, William J. Canby, told the Pennsylvania Historical Society in 1870 that his grandmother—who died at age eighty-four, when he was eleven years old—had related the following story to him many times. "Colonel [George] Ross [uncle of Betsy's late husband, John], with Robert Morris and General Washington, called upon Mrs. Ross, and told her they were a committee of Congress, and wanted her to make the [new] flag [they intended to present to Congress for adoption] from the drawing, a rough one, which, upon her suggestions, was redrawn by General Washington in pencil in her back parlor. This was prior to the Declaration of Independence." This flag, which would have had to have been made in early June 1776 when Washington was in Philadelphia, thus pretends to the title of the first Stars and Stripes.

After presenting his paper, Canby secured affidavits from aunts who also claimed to have heard the story from Mrs. Ross's lips. They added certain details: that the flag was only one of a number of models made by various women to be presented to Congress; that the changes suggested by Mrs. Ross were to make the flag rectangular instead of square and to give the stars five points instead of six; that the flag was adopted by Congress shortly thereafter; and that Mrs. Ross immediately received an order to manufacture as many flags as she could for government use. Since that time the story has been elaborated in countless books and interpreted in paintings many times, and the house in which Mrs. Ross is claimed to have lived ranks as a popular tourist attraction

Since 1870, however, the only really new piece of evidence uncovered is an original portrait of Mrs. Ross found in 1963.

Briefly summarized, the chief arguments against the Betsy Ross story are as follows: There is no contemporary reference in any known letter, newspaper, government document, or other source to the existence of a "flag committee," of the acquaintance of Washington and Mrs. Ross, of the adoption by Congress of any flag before 1777, or of any other detail in the story. Although Trumbull and Peale show thirteen-star flags in paintings of battles which occurred early in 1777, the paintings themselves were made years afterward when patriotism was likely to have overruled historical accuracy by insisting that the Stars and Stripes be shown in preference to the Continental Colors with its Union Jack. Moreover, aside from these secondhand instances we have no indication of any kind that the Stars and Stripes was in use until after its official adoption in 1777. The first known usage of this flag comes just at the time when the Continental Colors ceased to be used, during the Summer of 1777. More positively, Richards' letters cited above show clearly that this man, living in Mrs. Ross's own city and vitally concerned with flags, had no knowledge of any new design in August or October of 1776.

We are entitled to ask a number of questions about the Betsy Ross account. Would Washington be likely to have a flag made which clearly asserted American independence at a time when independence had not been proclaimed by Congress? If on the other hand a secret Congressional committee had gone to the trouble of soliciting patterns for flags and having samples made in anticipation of the declaring of independence, would it then ignore the whole flag question for a year? Indeed would either the Commander in Chief of an army at war or a committee of Congress take off an afternoon to visit the shop of a common upholsterer and accept advice regarding a design for the national flag from a young woman who had never even made a flag before? Is it not more than a coincidence that most new nations eventually "discover" some simple but devoted patriot who, during the darkest days of the national war of liberation, designed or made the first flag at the request or for the use of the founding father of that country? (See, for example, similar stories on pp. 190, 206, and 266.) And, finally, when so many strong arguments have been produced against the story, why do so many Americans continue to insist on its absolute validity?

The question invariably asked by someone who has previously believed in Betsy Ross is, who did make the first flag? Our answer cannot be simple. If the query means, who designed the first flag, or rather who modified the Continental Colors into the Stars and Stripes, the answer may be several people, including Francis Hopkinson. (In any event this honor has never been claimed for Mrs. Ross; at best she slightly amended the new design and sewed the first copy.) Active in several government posts including the Naval Board, Hopkinson made the only contemporary claim to the honor of having designed the flag. In 1780 he asked Congress for a quarter of a cask of wine for having suggested patterns for the American flag, several seals, and certain coins. Later he indicated he thought the flag design was worth $1440 in paper money —or $24 in hard cash. Congress did not deny his claim, as it probably would have if it were false; but they refused to pay him because they said others had also been involved in the designing.

All this is not to suggest that the Betsy Ross myth is an intentional hoax. We do know that Mrs. Ross made flags for the government; the invoice from May 1777 (see p. 55) hints that she may even have made some of the first Stars and Stripes flags just prior to their adoption. But the popular image of the young girl in her shop showing Washington how to cut five-pointed stars in one snip undoubtedly began in the faulty recollections of an elderly lady and the impressionable mind of her young grandson. No useful purpose is served in perpetuating such false or highly doubtful tales; nor is honest and scholarly historical criticism unpatriotic or otherwise reprehensible. The true story of the flags of the United States, at peace and in war, on land and at sea, is more than adequate to stir the minds and hearts of men.

XVI. FLAGS OF THE CANAL ZONE

a.   **PANAMA CANAL COMPANY   Distinguishing flag for ships   c1915– present**

b.   **CANAL ZONE   Governor's flag   8 June 1915–present   Proportions 4 x 5**

c.   **CANAL ZONE   Government flag on land, jointly with the U.S. flag 21 September 1960–present (state and national flag of Panama) Proportions 2 x 3**

a.

THE LAND DIVIDED THE WORLD UNITED

b.

c.

Chapter IV

THE UNITED STATES
FLAG SINCE 1795

FROM FIFTEEN STARS TO FIFTY-ONE

From 1777 to 1795 the first Stars and Stripes served the United States in war and peace. By that time the flag no longer accurately represented the federal Union, since in 1791 and 1792 Vermont and Kentucky were joined to the original thirteen States. Therefore in 1793 a motion was introduced in the Senate, providing that on 1 May 1795 the flag be changed by the addition of two stars and two stripes. The bill passed, but in the House it was strongly opposed by a number of members. Surprising as it may seem today, the reason they objected to the proposal was that they considered it, as Representative Thatcher of Massachusetts put it, "a consummate piece of frivolity." If one began to change the flag for each new State, as another man with some foresight pointed out, there would be no telling when it would end. Representative Smith of Vermont, overlooking the honor involved for his own State, objected that it would cost $60 apiece to change the flags for each merchant ship in the nation.

Despite the criticisms raised, a new flag (X-a) was adopted which was to serve for the following twenty-three years. It flew when the United States engaged in an unofficial war with France in 1798 and

a.

b.

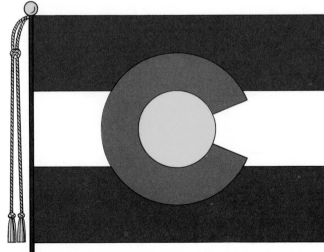

c.

during the War of 1812 with Britain. In between, the country undertook to end the piracy on American and European ships which had long been carried on by the Arab states of the "Barbary Coast," i.e., North Africa. It was during this war that Americans first raised their flag in military victory over a fort in the Old World: on 27 April 1805 the fortified city of Derna, Tripoli, fell to the U. S. Marines.

The most famous incident involving the flag of fifteen stars and fifteen stripes was undoubtedly its display over Fort McHenry, Maryland, during its bombardment by the British on the night of 13-14 September 1814. A Washington lawyer named Francis Scott Key was in custody on a British ship that night because he had gone to seek the release of a friend. He and his companion, Colonel John Skinner, watched fearfully as the fort was subjected to the rocket attack. In his joy the next morning at seeing the flag still waving defiantly, Key wrote "The Star-Spangled Banner." Sung to the tune of an English drinking song, "Anacreon in Heaven," the new poem became very popular and finally in 1931 it was adopted as the national anthem of the United States. The name "The Star-Spangled Banner" has also remained in common usage for the flag. A flag from the fort, possibly the Star-Spangled Banner itself, now hangs as the central exhibit in the History and Technology Building of the Smithsonian Institution in Washington, D.C. It has been restored to show its original thirty by forty-two foot size.

In 1796, a little over a year after the third United States flag was established, Tennessee joined the Union. Seven years later Ohio became a *de facto* State, although final legal confirmation of its Statehood was not made until 1953. In 1812, 1816, and 1817 Louisiana, Indiana, and Mississippi increased the total to twenty States. During this time many

XVII. FLAGS OF COLORADO

a. **COLORADO** Government flag 9 April 1907–5 June 1911 (reconstructed)

b. **COLORADO** Government and general usage flag 5 June 1911–31 March 1964 (official) Proportions 2 x 3

c. **COLORADO** Government and general usage flag 31 March 1964–present (unofficial from 5 June 1911) Proportions 2 x 3

national flags unofficially reflected the admission of new States by showing additional stars and stripes. Similarly, the Coast Guard ensign created in 1799 (LX-c) had sixteen stripes and the Vermont State flag of
1804 (LIV-a) had seventeen stars and seventeen stripes. There was no
government action on the question of a new flag, however, until Representative Peter Wendover of New York induced Congress to set up a flag
study committee in 1816.

On 2 January 1817 Wendover's committee reported on the question of the new States. Noting that the existing flag was well received by
Americans, the committee recommended that no fundamental changes
be made. While new States deserved to be included in the flag, it was
pointed out that the frequent adding of stripes would decrease the distinctiveness of the flag, especially at sea. It was proposed, therefore, "to
reduce the stripes to the original thirteen, representing the number of
States then contending for, and happily achieving, their independence—
and to increase the stars to correspond with the number of States now in
the Union—and hereafter to add one star to the flag whenever a new
State shall be fully admitted." This stroke of genius thus preserved the
essential appearance of the flag, while guaranteeing that the continuing
growth of the country would be symbolized. The bill was accepted the
following year in this form:

> *Section 1. Be it enacted, &c.,* That from and after the fourth day of
> July next, the flag of the United States be thirteen horizontal stripes,
> alternate red and white; that the union have twenty stars, white in a blue
> field.

> *Section 2 And be it further enacted,* That on the admission of every
> new State into the Union, one star be added to the union of the flag; and
> that such addition shall take effect on the fourth of July next succeeding
> such admission.

The new law, which continued in force until 1947,* specified that
the stripes should be horizontal but it gave no clue as to the arrangement
of the stars. We know from correspondence between Wendover and
Captain Samuel Reid that the latter had in mind to distinguish between
the flags of warships on the one hand and, on the other, merchant ships,

---

* While the original law was repealed in 1947 its essential provisions were
reenacted and continue in force today.

government buildings, and private citizens. The naval ensign would have had the twenty stars of the new flag in the usual rows; the state and national flag would have had one large star composed of twenty small stars. But the Navy Commissioners did not concur in this idea when they issued specifications for the flag on 18 May 1818: the only flag approved by them was to have four staggered rows of five stars each (X-b). The size of the flag was fourteen by twenty-four feet; the canton was one third the length of the flag and extended down as far as the eighth stripe. On 10 September of the same year these specifications were modified slightly at the order of President James Monroe, who required that the rows of stars be one over another instead of in staggered form.

Despite the existence of these and subsequent clear-cut specifications, there was very little uniformity in American flag design until the late nineteenth century when the mass production of flags became common. Before the Civil War especially, flags were made to taste by each individual since hand-stitching was then the common mode of manufacture. Variations can be found, in pictures and actual flags, with respect to the arrangement of the stars, their sizes, and the number of points in each; the shades of red and blue; the number of stripes; the size of the canton and the proportions of the flag as a whole; and, of course, the kinds of material used. Government flags were as irregular as ones used by private citizens. During the Civil War, for example, it was common practice in military colors like the cavalry guidon (X-c) to employ gilt stars instead of white ones. Even today specifications are regularly ignored; the most common proportions currently made by manufacturers for United States flags are not the legal 10:19, but either 2:3 or 3:5.

One very popular form of the Stars and Stripes used from the time of the Revolution through the Civil War placed the coat of arms of the United States in the blue canton, surrounded by the stars. These arms have been subject to extensive artistic modification over the years, although the present form (Frontispiece) has been in use since 1885. The seal of the United States is similar, except that it appears within a circle. The seal also has a reverse (see p. 76) which is familiar only because it is part of the design on the reverse of the one-dollar bill; it has never been cut as a seal. The unfinished pyramid topped with an all-seeing eye is of Masonic inspiration. The mottoes read "A New Order Of the Ages" and "He [God] Has Favored [Our] Undertakings."

UNITED STATES
Seal (reverse)
20 June 1782–present

The obverse of the seal has the Latin motto "E Pluribus Unum" ("One Out of Many"), which is suggested by the constellation formed of thirteen stars serving as a crest above the eagle's head. The shield has often been mistakenly shown with stars on it; it is in fact quite distinct from the flag and has never had stars, nor horizontal stripes, and the red has always been placed on the white instead of vice versa. The eagle is an ancient emblem of sovereignty which, in one form or another, has been used by Imperial Rome, Byzantium, the Holy Roman Empire, Russia, Germany, Austria, Italy, Spain, and many other countries. The bald-headed eagle as a symbol is, however, unique to the United States. The seal was created by William Barton and Charles Thomson at the request of a Committee appointed by Congress. The design was approved on 20 June 1782 and has been recut in brass or steel seven times. The eagle first gained usage in American flags right after the Revolution when it appeared on military colors, usually against a blue background (similar to XXXVIII-a). From there its use gradually spread to other flags, e.g., the President's standard (LVIII-a) and certain State flags.

XVIII. FLAGS OF CONNECTICUT AND DELAWARE

a. **CONNECTICUT** Color of the 2nd Battalion, 2nd Regiment c1775
b. **CONNECTICUT** Government flag 3 June 1897–present (authorized 4 July 1895; specifications from 11 April 1957) Proportions 26 x 33
c. **DELAWARE** Government and general usage flag 24 July 1913–12 February 1953; 13 June 1955–present

a.

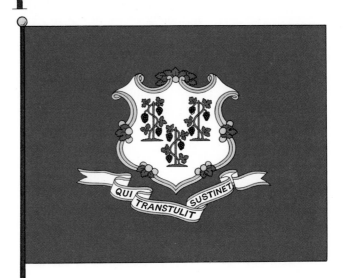

b.

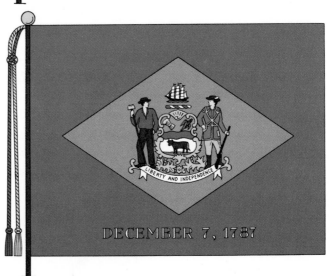

c.

Since 1818 no fundamental change has been introduced into the design of the United States flag. The admission of new States, which has caused new stars to be added twenty-four times in accordance with Wendover's law, gives the United States an unparalleled record of twenty-eight national flags in the course of its history. (Complete details for each of these flags will be found in Appendix I.) Of course the greatest number of alterations was made in the last century, the twentieth century having seen the creation of only four new designs to represent Oklahoma (forty-six stars), New Mexico and Arizona (forty-eight stars), Alaska (forty-nine stars), and most recently Hawaii (fifty stars). The forty-eight-star flag holds the record for the longest use, flying over the nation during forty-seven years from before the First World War until just before the Vietnam war. On 4 July 1960 the present flag (Frontispiece) superseded the previous one, which had served only one year.

Whenever a new State seems imminent, millions of Americans try to guess what the new design will be like and many send their ideas to the Government. Actually, fairly rigid "laws," based on traditions established over the course of two centuries, limit the possibilities to a few choices. The rows of stars seem irreversibly set as a basic pattern, despite the circles of stars and other patterns favored by a few would-be designers. A historical and mathematical study based on such factors was carried out by the author in 1963; it shows that there is only one likely pattern for the national flag should it ever be increased to fifty-one stars. The new arrangement would have six rows, alternating between nine and eight stars.

MAKING AND HONORING THE FLAG

A United States flag, flying in the wind, displays a strong, harmonious design that is very arresting. This is actually somewhat surprising, since the flag (not including its heading, halyards, and other accessories) is composed of sixty-four separate elements. In contrast the flags of eighty-six other nations, including France, Italy, Canada, Japan, and the Soviet Union, can be made with four or fewer pieces of material each. Despite the amount of work that is involved in making an American flag, whether it is printed, dyed, sewn, or embroidered, mass-production techniques have been perfected to such an extent, and flag sales are so high, that the cost of a large flag for display on home or business building is very reasonable. The owner of such a flag should be aware not only of its meaning and history but also of its design and the correct way to use the flag.

While general specifications have existed since 1818, it was only in 1912 that detailed standards were approved by President Taft for making of the flag. Since that time Executive Orders have been issued by Presidents Wilson and Eisenhower, modifying certain points. The current table of official porportions, shown on p. 81, provides for a flag almost twice as long as it is wide. The canton is two fifths the length of the flag and extends down to the top of the eighth stripe. The size and placement of the stars are precisely fixed. Flags made of bunting, for outdoor use, do not have any fringe, but it is the custom to add a gold fringe to a silk or rayon flag used indoors or carried in a parade and to decorate its staff with gold cords and tassels. This custom, probably derived from military tradition, is neither required nor forbidden by law. Official color shades were specified for the flag in 1934 and were slightly modified in 1960. The blue is very dark and the red is a cardinal red rather than a Chinese red, although the appearance of the colors varies depending on the type of material and dye used, the lighting conditions, and the age of the flag.*

During the late nineteenth and early twentieth centuries the flag has been subjected at times to considerable abuse, some of it intentional and even malicious, much of it simply from carelessness or ignorance. Individuals have often left flags out in bad weather or have allowed the flag to become dirty or torn or have forgotten to treat it respectfully in other ways. In the 1960's the flag, long used as an object in art (see p. 86), came into prominence in the works of certain painters, sculptors, and playwrights in situations ranging from simple poor taste to flagrant desecration. The flag has also long been exploited by business firms to promote their own goods and services, often under the guise of patriotism. Since the flag has always been the chief symbol of the United States,

---

* The exact shades of blue and red are numbers 70075 and 70180 in the *Standard Color Card of America* published by the Color Association of the United States.

its misuse brings protests from many sides, including veterans' and civic organizations.

During the periods of hysterical anti-Communism in the 1920's and after World War II, many Americans campaigned with an almost religious zeal to persuade the Government to adopt strict laws regulating flag display. In the first period State laws were adopted, providing penalties for abuse of the national flag and outlawing the display of black and red (anarchist and communist) flags. In 1923 a code of flag etiquette was drafted at the national level by the American Legion, the Daughters of the American Revolution, and similar groups. This subsequently gained acceptance throughout the country and in 1942 was adopted by Congress as a "Joint resolution to codify and emphasize existing rules and customs pertaining to the display and use of the flag of the United States of America."

No penalties have been established for breaches of this etiquette code and indeed its preamble and other wording make it clear that it was originally intended only as a set of suggestions. Contrary to this spirit and to the tradition of toleration for variations of flag display dating back to the earliest days of the republic, some have taken the code provisions as absolutely binding in all cases. Moreover, they have campaigned for laws making "desecration" of the flag a criminal offense and have initiated court cases against those who have used the flag to express unpopular political ideas.

During the period from about 1967 to about 1972 Richard Nixon and other conservatives attempted to associate the Stars and Stripes exclusively with their own political philosophy. A combination of factors, including the willingness of civil libertarians to take cases through to the Supreme Court and the eventual divulgence of the political and moral bankruptcy of those who had promoted themselves as defenders of the flag, established certain basic principles for American flag usage. Fundamentally, the United States flag belongs to the people, and even when their good taste or common sense is deficient in protecting it from improper display, it is not the function of government to compel adherence to its own standards of propriety, least of all through the threat of punishment. Specifically, in instances of political protest where, for example,

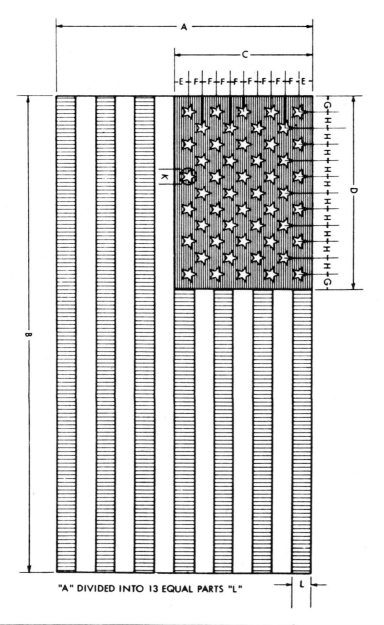

"A" DIVIDED INTO 13 EQUAL PARTS "L"

STANDARD PROPORTIONS									
HOIST (WIDTH) OF FLAG	FLY (LENGTH) OF FLAG	HOIST (WIDTH) OF UNION	FLY LENGTH OF UNION					DIAMETER OF STAR	WIDTH OF STRIPE
1.	1.9	.5385($\frac{7}{13}$)	.76	.054	.054	.063	.063	.0616	.0769($\frac{1}{13}$)
A	B	C	D	E	F	G	H	K	L

FLAG OF THE UNITED STATES Official specifications 4 July 1960–present

the flag is flown upside down or burned or decorated with an inscription or symbol, it is a contradiction of the very freedom which the Stars and Stripes stands for to insist that such flag usage is illegal simply because it is disapproved of by the majority. (It is also hypocritical, since commercial exploitation of the symbolism and design of the flag, which the original flag desecration laws were intended to prevent, has flourished without challenge.)

The flag code, now a half century old, contains a number of ambiguous sections and some subjects are not treated at all. Various private institutions, including the Flag Research Center, have tried to deal with these in the spirit of preserving the flag as a symbol of national dignity and of encouraging its widespread use, rather than inhibiting people from flag display through the elaboration of rigid and complicated etiquette procedures. For example, the code says that "the flag may be displayed at night on special occasions when it is desired to produce a patriotic effect." Some have taken this as an injunction against its use at night except on special occasions or in special places, and indeed a number of sites of historic importance have sought and received Congressional or Presidential approval to fly the flag day and night. Since the work of the nation goes on twenty-four hours a day, these restrictions seem unnecessary and floodlighting of the flag, while desirable, is not legally required. The durability of modern flags, moreover, suggests that light rain or wind is not reasonably the kind of "inclement weather" in which the code specifies the flag should be lowered.

While the original code of 1942 (as amended by Presidential proclamations in 1954 and 1969) specified the number of days that the flag should be flown at half-staff as a mark of respect following the death of a major official, it is common practice to lower the flag as well for state and local dignitaries who have died. While it would be more proper to lower a different flag—the municipal flag, for example, if a city official has died—the popular practice is not illegal. Another custom which has existed for decades but has come into special prominence since the late 1960's is the wearing of a small replica of the flag particularly on military and other (scout, police) uniforms, or the incorporation of the design and colors of the flag in other forms of clothing. While many find the latter objectionable, they rarely protest the former usage, and in a landmark civil rights case of 1974 the Supreme Court struck down as unconstitutional a Massachusetts law which had been used in the conviction of a young man who used a small flag to patch a hole in his pants. There is no doubt that the majority of Americans found that action repulsive— although many saw a higher form of desecration in the flag's use during the unconstitutional American invasion of Cambodia in 1970—yet it is scarcely surprising that fundamental political disagreements within the society should be reflected in its leading symbol.

Those who wish to pay proper respect to the flag will not welcome complicated and restrictive government regulations, which at times threaten to turn the flag into a fetish and its display into a civil religion. Keeping in mind that the purpose of a flag etiquette code is to maintain dignity and respect without hindering the extensive use of flags, the average citizen will generally find no better guide to etiquette than his own common sense.

The flag is formally honored by the "Pledge of Allegiance" and by Flag Day, 14 June, which commemorates the adoption of the first Stars and Stripes. The Pledge was devised in 1892 by Francis Bellamy and published in *Youth's Companion* whose circulation chief, James B. Upham, was promoting a patriotism campaign. Through their efforts school children bought American flags for thirty thousand schools and the Pledge of Allegiance to the flag became a regular feature of the school day across the country. The Pledge became part of the Flag Code in 1942 and in 1954 the phrase "under God" was added to it. In 1943 the Supreme Court ruled that State laws making the Pledge obligatory on students, rather than a voluntary exercise, are contrary to the First Amendment and to the very principles of freedom for which the flag stands. Flag Day had been observed, especially in schools, ever since 1877 before it achieved national recognition from Congress in 1949. (It is not, however, a legal holiday.)

a.

b.

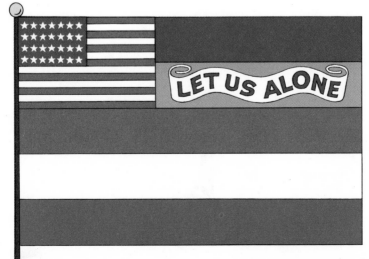

c.

THE UNITED STATES FLAG TODAY

So far this book has dealt with formal aspects of the United States flag and historical events in its development. The greatest significance of this flag, however, lies in the influence which it has in the hearts and minds of millions of men and women. The power of any flag as a national symbol may be very great but it is also difficult to define and measure. Perhaps the best indication we have of the significance of such a flag is the degree and manner in which it enters into the everyday life of the people. In this respect the flag of the United States has scarcely any equal.

This flag will be found where flags always have been displayed: over forts, arsenals, war memorials, and important public buildings, in parades and military reviews, on merchant and warships. But the display is not limited to these official and necessary occasions, as is true in some countries. Small flags decorate graves, store windows, and street name-posts. Public and private schools not only fly the flag outside daily, but generally each classroom has a flag of its own. Every court, post office, and minor government building from the federal to the township level has a flag either on a pole outside or inside on the wall or on a staff. The flag appears at almost all public gatherings and in many private association and club meetings; although some cities require flags to be used when public outdoor speeches are made, the laws are hardly necessary to insure the presence of the flag. Toll-road ticket booths, airports, churches, parks and commons, and sports stadia are ready excuses for hoisting the flag. New buildings are "topped off" with a flag, desk flags are presented to business executives, military caskets are draped with the flag, bank openings and ship commissionings are occasions for decorat-

XIX. EMBLEMS OF THE DISTRICT OF COLUMBIA AND FLORIDA

a. **GEORGE WASHINGTON   Personal coat of arms**

b. **DISTRICT OF COLUMBIA   Government and general usage flag   15 October 1938–present   Proportions 10 x 19 but variable**

c. **FLORIDA   4 July 1846–3 July 1847   (reconstructed; basic design authorized 27 December 1845)**

ing with the flag. Explorers of the modern era—whether in deep-sea diving equipment or astronauts' uniforms—carry the flag. Most significantly, private persons without any particular interest in flags in general, without partisan or ideological or even hyperpatriotic inspiration, and certainly without any official or unofficial coercion, buy flags and display them outside their homes. And it is not thought necessary that such display wait for a holiday or other special occasion.

The United States flag is also a common feature in art and literature. Countless poems, songs, speeches, sermons, short stories, and novels have used the flag as a theme. Folk art features the American flag and frequently the coat of arms as a motif for bedspreads, pillow covers, tapestries, pictures, outdoor wall decorations, toys, silverware, chinaware, jewelry, and clothing, although flag desecration laws have eliminated much of what was formerly considered sincere and respectful use of the flag in everyday objects. Graphic art for all purposes (advertising, decoration, postage stamps, etc.) similarly recognizes the appeal of the flag. Often the flag design is hinted at by the use of a few stars and a few stripes, rather than being represented in full.

The flag also figures prominently in American folk history. Numerous examples from almost every war fought by the United States could be cited where the defense of the flag constitutes a central theme. This makes it very difficult to separate history from legend and myth; the Betsy Ross story, even if it is someday proven completely erroneous, has a deathless quality because of the way it links a Founding Father, the Flag, and a Patriot Widow. Among the misconceptions that have grown up about the flag is the idea that each State is represented by a particular star, according to its order of admission to the Union. Not only is this pure fantasy, but the idea that the thirteen stripes should be considered to represent only the original thirteen States was explicitly rejected by the committee of 1818 which fixed the basic flag law.

We must also recognize that popular interpretations of the meanings attributable to the red, white, and blue colors of the flag have no official standing. White may suggest to us liberty or purity, red valor, and blue justice, loyalty, and perseverance; but in fact the colors were simply derived from British flags familiar to the men who made the first American flags. The quotation ascribed to Washington ("We take the stars from heaven, and the red from our Mother Country, separating it by white stripes . . . and the white stripes shall go down to posterity representing liberty") is a pretty piece of imagery, but has absolutely no standing in history despite its repetition in Government publications.

If we are to reject false history, we can still find much in the true story of the flag that evokes the highest admiration. It has waved over the unparalleled progress of a nation in developing democratic political institutions, scientific and technological knowledge, education and culture, commerce and industry, and countless other advances. It has served as a beacon for millions of poor and oppressed refugees from abroad and stands as a promise that the underprivileged within the country are not forgotten. Its influence throughout the world is inestimable. Even in the simple aspect of design, we note that the United States flag has set a pattern copied in the flags of many States, Puerto Rico, Cuba, Chile, Uruguay, Liberia, several Brazilian states, and others. Before the adoption of the American flag of 1777, stars, now used in many flags, were an unknown element in national banners. The United States made the star a symbol of independence and sovereignty. Its use spread from the national flag to the arms and flags of the States—beginning with the arms adopted in 1780 by Massachusetts—and then to the Southern banners of 1860-1861 and the flags of dozens of foreign nations. American vexillology has also contributed heavily to the concept of the flag as the chief national symbol.

What is the meaning of the United States flag? There can never be a single, definitive answer to that question. Today the American flag is reviled in many parts of the world as a symbol of imperialism, yet in 1864 Karl Marx himself wrote, concerning the Civil War, that "the working men of Europe felt instinctively that the star-spangled banner carried the destiny of their class." The paradoxes implicit in these and similar views of the flag have been resolved by President Woodrow Wilson. "This flag," he said, "which we honor and under which we serve, is the emblem of our unity, our power, our thought and purpose as a nation. It has no other character than that which we give it from generation to generation. The choices are ours."

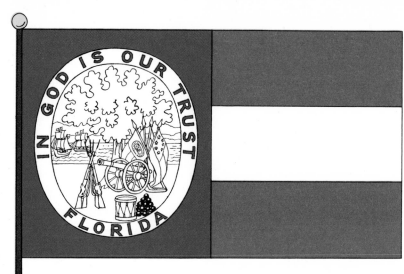

a.

b.

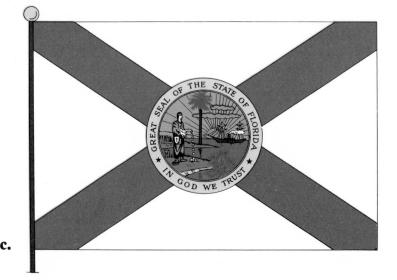

c.

Chapter V

FLAGS OF THE STATES AND TERRITORIES

THE DEVELOPMENT OF STATE FLAGS

The United States is unusual among the great powers of the world in the degree of autonomy which it recognizes, both in theory and in actual practice, for its constituent parts. Most countries are subdivided into provinces or districts for administrative purposes, but these units generally do not control such areas as taxation, military forces and police, education, and welfare systems, nor do they determine their own local constitutions and governments. Despite the growth in the power of the federal government in the United States, especially since World War II, the strength of the fifty States in dealing with important political matters often amazes individuals from other countries.

XX. FLAGS OF FLORIDA

a. **FLORIDA   13 September 1861–? (authorized 8 February 1861)**

b. **FLORIDA   6 August 1868–6 November 1900   Proportions 12 x 13**

c. **FLORIDA   8 November 1966–present (basic design authorized 6 November 1900)   Proportions 2 x 3 but variable**

Local autonomy has had considerable influence on flags and other symbols in at least two respects. American States show widely diverging attitudes in the designs and uses of their flags; the statements that can be made which apply to all State flags are few and very general. In contrast we find, for example, that the Venezuelan state flags are indistinguishably alike as are the standards of state Governors in India, except upon very close examination. The flags of the subdivisions of Liberia, Australia, the Soviet Union, and some other countries are not quite so similar, but they do have certain major characteristics in common. Even more fundamentally, it is important to note that the States of the Union *have* their own flags: the principal subdivisions of Mexico, Argentina, New Zealand, Italy, China, India, and most other countries do not. State flags have been abolished or prohibited in Nigeria, Uganda, Brazil, and Germany at one time or another in this century. Even in the United States State flags have not been used from the beginning nor have they always been adopted without objections (see p. 142).

There are four phases which can be distinguished in the development of American State flags. The first ran from the Revolution to the Civil War (1775-1860); the second lasted roughly until the end of the century (1860-1900); the third, overlapping the second, began with the Centennial Exposition and ended with World War II (1876-1945); the fourth period continues to this day. The phases differ from one another in the conceptions popularly held of State flags, in their modes of construction and usage, and in their designs and designers. While the individual articles on the flags of each State will make these points clear, it may be useful here to summarize these changes.

Before the Revolution few local symbols are known to have been used. The Puritans of Massachusetts Bay modified the English flag (see p. 36) not so much to set themselves apart, but to express their religious convictions. The Maryland flag (see p. 150) was, strictly speaking, the family banner of the Proprietors and might properly have been flown in their colony of Avalon (Newfoundland). Use of a beaver flag by New York is unproven. Thus the only distinctive prerevolutionary flag, other than military colors, seems to have been the New England flag, which represented a whole region rather than one State. This situation changed radically in the years 1775-1780. Connecticut, Rhode Island, New

York, Delaware, South Carolina, and possibly others, created flags which identified their troops and eventually provided the basis for the State flags of today. Massachusetts and South Carolina adopted official state flags. From time to time after the Revolution further flags were created as the need arose for State military colors, but more significant in the long run was the creation in this period of State seals and coats of arms. Even when unused at the time on any banner, the emblems and mottoes of the seals were often incorporated in flags later on.

From the modern standpoint these early flags are striking in several ways. Their lack of uniformity in design has already been noted: it reflects the unofficial character of most of the flags. In many cases only a single flag of any one design was ever made, for not only was mass production unheard of, but quite simply there were only a few situations in which early Americans thought it appropriate to display a flag. Thus mention of a State flag in this era does not refer to a flag that was extensively used on ships, public buildings, meeting halls, business establishments, and private homes; it means rather that the particular military color in question had a local rather than a national design. This limited symbolism predominated in the second period as well.

The start of the Civil War encouraged for the first time on a wide scale the display of the national flag. It also stirred local patriotism as thousands of men joined the Union and Confederate armed forces. The first real State flags appeared at this time in the South when substitutes became necessary for the United States flag, although these were short-lived because they were soon replaced by the flags of the Confederacy. More prevalent in both parts of the country were the new regimental colors identifying the State troops. In the North their form, almost without exception, consisted of a field of national (i.e., dark) blue with the coat of arms of the State in the center. These silk* colors were painted by local artists or embroidered by soldiers' wives with the fancy scroll-work, floral decoration, inscriptions, and other artistic touches favored by the style then current. The impact of the Civil War on the lives of all

---

* Since leaded silk was used, these flags are now generally in poor condition. In contrast the linen and unleaded silk flags of the Revolution tend to be in much better repair, although there are fewer of them in existence.

Americans is evident in the blue flags with coats of arms attributed to every State and Territory (except Massachusetts which has a white field) in the first illustrated collection of State flags.* While this uniformity is certainly an exaggeration—such traditional flags as those of Texas and South Carolina were well known—it is indicative of the conception of State flags then current.

Very slowly this situation changed. The United States fought only one major war, the Spanish-American, in the period between 1865 and 1917, and the need for military colors was correspondingly low. At the same time the spread of wealth and industry, the pushing back of the frontier, and the growth of urbanization, literacy, and communications all contributed to increased national self-awareness. The desire for a general-purpose State flag, vaguely felt at first, gained impetus from such things as the building of State capitols and the participation of individual States in fairs and exhibitions. At the time of the national Centennial in 1876 only nine of the thirty-eight members of the Union (Florida, Georgia, Louisiana, New York, South Carolina, Texas, Vermont, Virginia, and Wisconsin) had true State flags; a quarter century later there were nineteen out of forty-five; in 1914 the number was thirty-five out of forty-eight; and by the Sesquicentennial in 1926 all the States had flags. To be sure, in many cases the legislature had simply declared an old regimental color to be the State flag, sometimes even specifying that the flag be made of silk, four feet four inches by five feet six, in accordance with army regulations. But for flags flown outdoors bunting soon replaced silk and proportions of 2:3 and 3:5 gradually became standard.

* In *Flags of all nations*. Richmond: Allen and Ginter, 1888.

XXI. FLAGS OF GEORGIA

a. **GEORGIA** General usage and military flag 17 October 1879–22 August 1905

b. **GEORGIA** General usage and military flag 17 August 1914–1 July 1956

c. **GEORGIA** Government and general usage flag 1 July 1956–present (authorized 13 February 1956) Proportions 2 x 3

a.

b.

c.

The designs of this "first generation" of State flags, particularly those adopted after 1914, were less and less based on the military stereotype. Memories of the Civil War, and even of its veterans who carried the old colors on parade, were fading when interest in flags again surged during World War I. Furthermore the armed forces were no longer organized on the old basis where men from one State served together; their colors, therefore, bore national rather than State emblems. In many States the campaign to adopt an official State flag was undertaken by patriotic organizations, such as the Daughters of the American Revolution, who proposed original designs uninfluenced by the old traditions. This trend towards more distinctive flags was followed by the Territories when they created flags for themselves.

Since the end of World War II there have been further developments which are still in progress. Although the need for a State flag had been generally recognized decades before, it was still true in 1945 that very few States made much use of their flags other than on the capitol building and in the office of the Governor.* Now State flags are appearing more and more frequently on all kinds of public buildings, in parades, in banks and other business buildings, and at schools. In Massachusetts the largest manufacturer, a State prison, sells thousands of State flags every year. During the wars in Korea and Vietnam many requests were received in every State capital from servicemen who wished to fly their own State flag. Even new types of State flags for special uses have been created, e.g., in Kansas, Maine, and North Dakota, and flags have been created for many Governors and Adjutants General.

An important factor favoring the more extensive usage of State flags is the improvement in materials and manufacturing techniques. The use of synthetic fibers, and especially of wool-nylon combinations, has produced flags which are lightweight, durable, colorfast, and which fly well. The tedious hand-painting and embroidering of the past, which made flags fragile, have been largely replaced by printing, dyeing, and appliqué. Costly double-sided flags have now been abandoned, except by Oregon. At the same time budget-conscious State governments

---

* In 1937 the local Flag Committee of one western State found only twenty flags existing in the whole State.

have begun to produce specification sheets giving the exact details of design and manufacture which must be used for the State flag. This standardization helps to guarantee that the highest symbol of the State will not be subject to abuse or whim and that well-made flags will be available to the public cheaply. Unofficially, standardization has long been carried on by manufacturers themselves; for reasons of cost and uniform appearance, it is customary for them to make all State (and other) flags in standard color shades and proportions of 2:3 and 3:5, regardless of the legal requirements.*

While it is not the purpose of this book to present a thorough history of the seals and coats of arms of the United States, in dealing with State flags it is inevitable that questions arise about American heraldry and sphragistics (the study of seals). Both the Communist world and the nations of the New World are within the general European tradition of symbolism, but they have evolved styles, ideas, and practices of their own which reflect the needs, culture, and environment of the people. Several American contributions to symbolism have already been mentioned, including the flag as a truly national symbol, the star as a symbol of sovereignty, a certain number of stripes or stars as an indicator of the political structure of the country, and the extensive use of fringe, cords and tassels, and special pole finials. Two other characteristics, especially evident in the flags of States, are the use of words on flags and the landscape which serves both as a seal and a coat of arms.

Words on arms and flags have long been opposed by heraldists for a number of reasons. The principal one is that the purpose of a seal or arms is to symbolize graphically a political unit or person or corporation; to use verbal symbols, or words, for the same purpose is unnecessarily repetitious. Words also tend to work against one of the other objectives of heraldry, which is to represent something in a simple, striking, and easily recognizable form. In practical terms words are objectionable on flags for two reasons. At any distance or in a breeze they tend to be hard to decipher, thus defeating the purpose of identification which the flag is

---

* Professional norms for flag standardization have been evolved by the Flag Research Center (Winchester, Mass.), working in cooperation with the North American Vexillological Association. The Flag Research Center provides assistance to State governments in drafting new flag laws or defining old ones more precisely so that the standardizing of flags will have proper legal backing and not just the sanction of common usage.

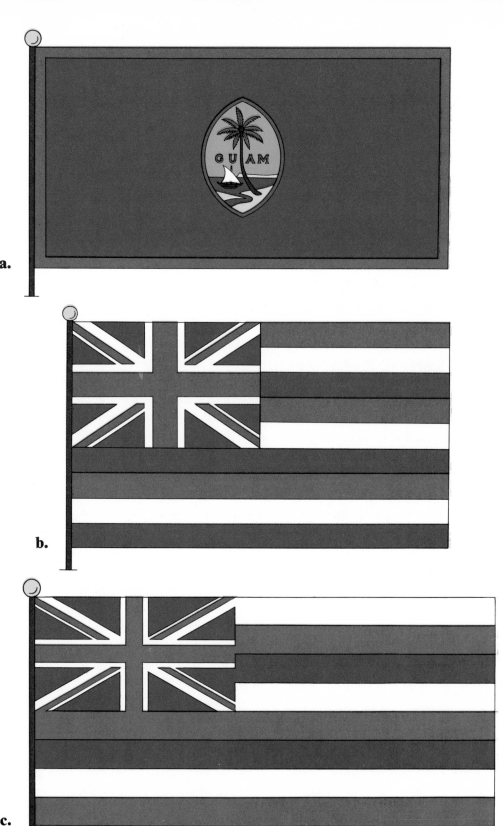

a.

b.

c.

supposed to serve. Also it greatly increases the cost and decreases the life-span of a flag to have inscriptions appliquéd or embroidered on it.

The landscape as a symbol, which is found in thirty-two of the fifty-eight American State and Territorial seals, is criticized for the same general reasons. Rivers, mountains, railroads, trees, men plowing fields, etc., do not symbolize a State, they present it to the viewer as a picture-postcard might. They do not adequately distinguish between different States in which the scenery or occupations are similar. Even more so than inscriptions, complicated pictorial emblems are hard to see at a distance and expensive to reproduce. Nor do they conform to the traditional rules of heraldry. In theory, a coat of arms consists of a shield, not a circle; it has one background color, not a detailed view of scenery; it has one or more figures placed on this background, but these are stylized and are never shown in perspective; the number of colors is ideally limited to two or three, but in no case are shades of color shown; except as a motto written on a ribbon below the shield, words are avoided as much as possible.* Examination shows that only fourteen States, including seven of the original thirteen, have true coats of arms, while another seven would have coats of arms if their present emblems were slightly modified.

To put such criticism in the proper light, a number of points should be considered. State symbols have had at most two centuries of development and in many cases only one century, in contrast to the eight hun-

---

* The American use of words is undoubtedly a reflection of the high degree of literacy existing when the seals and arms bearing them were devised; in feudal Europe words could not be used on shields because very few people, even of high social standing, could read. The redundant use of the seal and the name of the State on a flag may also be a reflection of American lack of subtlety.

XXII. FLAGS OF GUAM AND HAWAII

a. **GUAM Government and general usage flag   4 July 1917–present**
     Proportions 21 x 40

b. **HAWAII (KINGDOM) State and national flag; ensign   1816–25**
     February 1843; 31 July 1843–20 May 1845 (variant)

c. **HAWAII Government and general usage flag   20 May 1845–1 February 1893; 1 April 1893–present (official since 3 July 1894, specifications from 8 April 1896)   Proportions 1 x 2**

dred years over which many European symbols have evolved. At the same time the practical need for a seal, for a military color, or for a State flag has often been immediate. Thus in a number of instances we read of makeshift emblems being pressed into service*; once such a symbol is in use, it has often proved difficult to convince the State to alter it to a more suitable form. In other societies the control of all important symbols has been a jealously guarded prerogative of royalty, nobility, and other established classes absent from the American social structure. This has meant that symbols in the United States, generally created by elected government officials or by patriotic organizations, have reflected the taste of the average citizen.

In the nineteenth century, when most American seals and arms were designed, there was much exuberant national self-confidence and a belief in Manifest Destiny. The pioneer farmer or miner was looked on as a hero helping to push forward "the Frontiers of Civilization." Reliance on what were known as husbandry and the mechanic arts, a naïve faith that America was God's chosen land, the impressiveness of thousands of square miles of untamed plain and forest, and pride in being part of a great and democratic nation were all close to the everyday lives of the people. Given these concerns and the prevailing Victorian canons of art, it was perhaps inevitable that the designs looked the way they did. Certainly the use of inscriptions and the love of cluttered scenes from nature were not exclusively American; the seals of British colonies, which later developed into flag badges, show similar traits.

It would be a mistake to insist, as some have, that symbolism in the United States must conform to the traditional laws of heraldry. The historical bases from which heraldry derived in medieval Europe never existed in America; even personal coats of arms originally granted in Europe are artificial and anachronistic when used by families now living in the United States, given the social context of the twentieth century. Moreover, many societies have shown that it is possible to develop rich, sophisticated, and diverse forms of symbolism which have little or no relation to classical heraldry. Ancient Egypt, feudal Japan, the Ashanti nation in Ghana, and modern Communist states are all examples. Flags

* For example the original seal of Texas was simply a coat button bearing a flower pattern.

in particular provide a case of a symbolic medium flourishing quite separately from the formal limitations set by the laws of heraldry. In the United States there is more concern for commercial trademarks and logotypes than public seals and arms; nevertheless there are many excellent American symbols, of both heraldic and nonheraldic inspiration. Much credit for vigorous and imaginative work in creating symbols, particularly in the military, belongs to the Institute of Heraldry of the United States Army.

ALABAMA
Seal
1939–present

ALABAMA

In the history of the symbols of this State 1939 was a very important year. The flag which had flown during the period when Alabama was independent was returned from Iowa where it had been taken after the capture of Montgomery by Union troops in 1865; the seal adopted in 1868 was abolished and the original design of 1817 was reestablished; and Alabama became one of the very few States to have a coat of arms which differs significantly from its seal.

The first State emblem had been a seal, cut in 1817 at the order of Governor William W. Bibb; it bore a map of the then Territory with all of its rivers. This is basically the same seal that is currently used (see above), the chief difference being in the inscription which originally read "Alabama Executive Office." This seal pattern was replaced after the Civil War by one (see XII-b) including the American eagle and shield and the motto "Here We Rest." These words are the translation, now discredited, once given to the Indian word *alibamo* from which the State's name derives.

The coat of arms of Alabama (XI-a) was designed by B. J. Tieman at the request of Mrs. Marie Bankhead Owen, Director of the State Department of Archives and History. It comprises in its shield the flags of France, Spain, Great Britain, and the Confederate States—all surmounted by the shield of the United States. (The British flag is historically inaccurate in that it includes the saltire of St. Patrick; see p. 31.) The supporters are American bald eagles. The motto "Audemus Jura Nostra Defendere" translates as "We Dare to Defend Our Rights." The crest is a ship of the type in which the French under Pierre and Jean Le Moyne arrived in 1702 to create the first European settlement in the area.

From 11 January until 8 February 1861, while Alabama was the independent Republic of Alabama, the only flag it had was one (XI-b and XI-c) which was officially approved to be "raised upon the Capitol, as indicative whether the Convention shall be in open session." This flag, of which it appears only a single copy was ever made, had been painted by some young women of Montgomery for presentation on the day when Alabama seceded from the Union. On the obverse the Goddess of Liberty bears a sword and a single-starred flag (see p. 265). On the reverse, in the words of a contemporary commentator, "is a cotton plant to indicate the source of our national wealth and beneath it is a rattle snake coiled to manifest our determination to defend our rights." The motto "Noli Me Tangere" ("Dare Not Touch Me") expresses the same idea. The Executive Office seal appeared to the left, above the cotton plant (unfortunately not shown in XI-c, as it should have been).

XXIII. FLAGS OF HAWAII AND IDAHO

a.   **HAWAII (KINGDOM)   Royal standard   c1874–c1891 (variant)**

b.   **HAWAII   Governor's flag   c1959–present (unofficial)   Proportions 25 x 36**

c.   **IDAHO   15 March 1927–present (unofficial from 1907; specifications from 1 March 1957)   Proportions 26 x 33**

a.

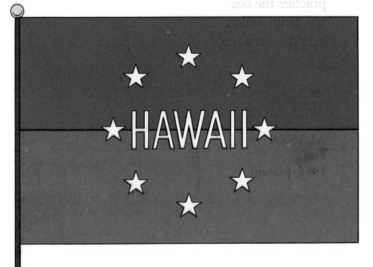

b.

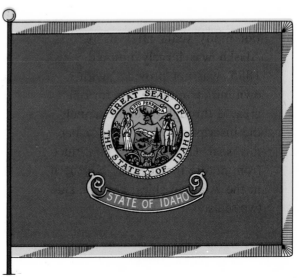

c.

The present State flag (XII-a) was adopted by the Legislature on 16 February 1895 in accord with a motion introduced by Representative John W. A. Sanford, Jr. It is described as having a "crimson cross of St. Andrew," although St. Andrew's saltire has in fact always been white (see p. 27). The proportions are not specified, but since the intention of the creator was to suggest the Battle Flag of the Confederacy (LXV-a), the flag should be made square in shape.

The Governor had a personal flag designed by Hartley A. Moon (XII-b) for at least five years before the present design became official in 1939. The Governor's flag today is the same as the State flag, except for two additions. The law requires that the seal *or* the coat of arms—in practice the coat of arms is used—be added above the arms of the saltire, the State military crest below. This crest shows a cotton boll on a heraldic wreath of the State colors, white and red.

ALASKA
Seal
1960–present

ALASKA

For many years after its purchase from Russia by the United States, Alaska was largely ignored. The first civil government, established in 1885, was not provided with a seal and therefore the Governor on his own initiative made one for official business. Finally, in 1910, a seal was created through official channels for Alaska. Except for modifications in the inscription when Alaska became first a Territory and then a State, this seal (above) has continued in use since that time. The scene from nature includes the Northern Lights, a striking phenomenon visible in the Alaskan skies. On one side of the seal is a fish and on the other two seals.

Although there had been a special flag flown in the area when it was subject to the Russian-American Company (III-c), Alaska under United States administration did not select a flag until 2 May 1927. This design (XII-c) has been used by the Territory and, since 1959, the State of Alaska. Official specifications for manufacturing purposes were adopted by law on 10 March 1959. The blue, as in the case of certain other State flags, is the same shade as in the flag of the United States. The stars are supposed to be the color of "natural yellow gold."

The inspiration for the blue field, standing for the Alaskan lakes and sea, and the stars of gold came from an Indian, Benny Benson. At the time (in 1926) he was a thirteen-year-old student at the Mission Territorial School near Seward. A contest to create a flag had been sponsored in the schools by the American Legion after Governor George A. Parks discovered that Alaska's lack of a flag meant its exclusion from a flag display in the Post Office Building in Washington, D. C. Designer Benson, who later became a fisherman, was given $1000 by the grateful Territorial Legislature to further his education.

In explaining his concept of the flag, Benson referred to the blue of the Alaskan sky and the forget-me-not flower. The Great Bear, or Big Dipper constellation, was to symbolize strength, and the North Star stood for the future State of Alaska, the most northerly State of the Union. His sketch and the original flag made from it are now in the Alaska Historical Museum, Juneau.

In 1955 the poem "Alaska's Flag" by Marie Drake with a musical accompaniment by Mrs. Elinor Dusenbury was adopted as the official song of the State. The poem reads:

Eight stars of gold on a field of blue—
Alaska's flag. May it mean to you
The blue of the sea, the evening sky,
The mountain lakes, and the flow'rs nearby;
The gold of the early sourdough's dreams,
The precious gold of the hills and streams;
The brilliant stars in the northern sky,
The 'Bear'—the 'Dipper'—and, shining high,
The great North Star with its steady light,
Over land and sea a beacon bright.
Alaska's flag—to Alaskans dear,
The simple flag of a last frontier.

AMERICAN SAMOA

For centuries there was no centralized Samoan government and there-fore no national or royal flag, although totemic emblems were frequently used by the Samoans. During the nineteenth century many Western con-cepts were introduced and various flags came to be used. Concerning some of these we have only vague references, while others are well known to the vexillologist. The earliest of these flags was like the modern flag of Turkey, although the white crescent and star on red certainly were not symbols of Islam as they are in the Turkish flag. This flag was in use about 1858.

In 1872 Commander Meade of the U. S. Navy is reported to have designed a flag for use by the chiefs of Tutuila which consisted of "vari-colored stripes symbolizing the large and small islands of the Samoan group; two crescent moons were arranged to approximate the letter 'S'." This was replaced on 2 October 1873 with a new flag (XIII-a) which, except for two years, flew as long as Samoa was independent. Its red and white colors and cross were common in other flags of Pacific nations during the nineteenth century as well. The only change made in the Samoan flag was under King Tamasese who was sponsored by the Ger-mans. To show the German influence, a black cross (as in the German naval ensign) was superimposed on the white cross of the flag after 28 January 1886. This cross was omitted when Tamasese lost power in 1888.

American interest in the islands, especially the harbor at Pago Pago, steadily increased in this era. In 1886 the American Consul pro-

XXIV. FLAGS OF ILLINOIS AND INDIANA

a. **ILLINOIS   6 July 1915–1 July 1970 (alternatively with emblem in black instead of in color)**

b. **INDIANA   General usage flag   9 March 1901–3 July 1908   Propor-tions 19 x 36**

   UNITED STATES   State and national flag; ensign   4 July 1896–3 July 1908

c. **INDIANA   Government flag   31 May 1917–present (for Indiana, gen-eral usage flag since 4 July 1960, see Frontispiece)   Proportions 26 x 33**

a.

b.

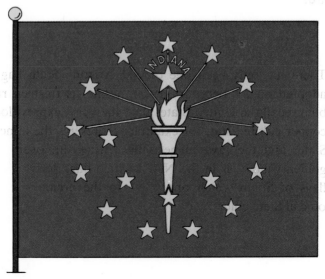

c.

claimed a United States protectorate over Samoa, but this claim was not accepted by the government. In 1899 Britain, Germany, and the United States agreed to a partition of the islands, and on 27 April 1900 the flag of the United States was first hoisted officially. After this time, of course, the German and British segments of Samoa developed a separate flag history. Today both are part of the Independent State of Western Samoa which flies its own national flag.

For a long time no action was taken on a distinctive symbol for American Samoa. Even the Governor for his official papers used only a circle with the words "Governor of American Samoa—Seal" written on it. Then in the 1950's the Office of the Governor solicited ideas for a flag from the local citizens. These were screened by the traditional leaders in Executive Council and a final design (XIII-b) was worked out by the Institute of Heraldry of the U. S. Army. It was first officially hoisted on 27 April 1960, the anniversary of the hoisting of the United States flag and the day when the new Constitution of American Samoa was promulgated.

In addition to the old Samoan red and white, dark blue was included so that all three American colors would be in the flag. The bald eagle, long a symbol of the United States, appears in flight bearing two Samoan emblems. The right claw holds a *fue*, the staff used by Samoan chiefs, as a symbol of the traditional wisdom of the Councils. In the left claw is a *uatogi,* or war club, suggesting the power of the state. Together they represent peace and order, under American direction. The Governor of the territory formerly flew the Union Jack (LVIII-c) as his standard.

ARIZONA

There has only been one official Arizona State flag (XIII-c), the one adopted on 27 February 1917. While its thirteen rays, star, and dark blue recall the United States flag, they also express local symbolism. The copper-colored star, for example, represents the mineral resources of the State, and the rays suggest the setting sun over the desert. Red and golden yellow, as in the New Mexico flag, derive from the colors of the flags of Spain which once flew in the area. Blue and yellow are the official State colors.

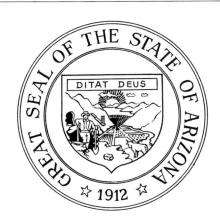

ARIZONA
Seal
1911–present

The design of the flag was created by Colonel Charles W. Harris in 1911 when he was Adjutant General of the Territory of Arizona. (It has been suggested that the thirteen rays behind the star stood for the then thirteen counties of Arizona, but this has not been proven.) The occasion was the participation of the Arizona National Guard rifle team at a national match in Ohio. Colonel Harris, as captain of the group, wanted to be sure that Arizona was represented by a flag. He took his pattern to Mrs. Carl Hayden, who made the first copy. Mrs. Hayden's husband, then a member of the rifle team, served as a Representative and Senator from Arizona from its admission to the Union in 1912 until 1968.

In 1915 a motion to make this flag official failed to pass the Legislature, but in 1917 the measure was approved after some debate. A number of alternative proposals were made in that session, including flags bearing the seal of the State, the word "Arizona," an eagle, and a local lizard, the Gila monster. One group championed the forty-five-star United States flag which had been carried by the Arizona Squadron, First U. S. Cavalry ("the Rough Riders") in the Spanish-American War. Objections were raised to the design of Harris's flag by some who said that it too closely resembled the Japanese naval ensign (XLIV-c). In the end, however, only very slight modifications were made in the flag before its adoption. One of the first flags made was presented to the battleship *Arizona,* which was later sunk at Pearl Harbor.

The seal of Arizona (above) was drawn in 1910. It replaced a number of earlier seals that had been used by the Territory. The earliest form (1863), from which the mountains and the miner with his pick and

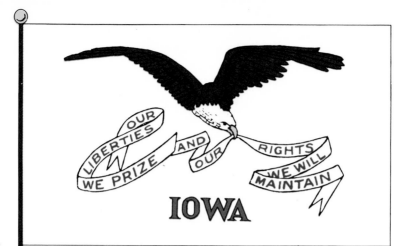

a.

b.

c.

shovel of the present seal derive, was derisively called "the baking-power seal." This was due to its striking similarity to the trademark label used on Bovee's Pioneer Brand Baking Powder. The same motto—"Ditat Deus," "God Enriches"—has been used on all the seals of Arizona.

ARKANSAS
Seal
23 May 1907–present

ARKANSAS

During the national Centennial Exposition in 1876 at Philadelphia, Arkansas was represented by a red flag with its seal in the center. In 1911 the Federation of Women's Clubs in the State tried to get official approval of their own proposed flag design, but no action was taken. Finally, on 26 February 1913 the Legislature approved the flag (XIV-a) sent to it by a commission which had been set up by the Secretary of State.

The design, selected from among sixty-five drawings, had been the idea of Miss Willie Hocker, a member of the Pine Bluff Chapter of the Daughters of the American Revolution. This was the very group which had suggested to the Secretary of State the necessity of a State flag, for presentation to the battleship *Arkansas*. The only modification made by the commission to Miss Hocker's flag was the addition of the name of the

XXV. FLAGS OF IOWA AND KANSAS
a. **IOWA   c1917–1921? (semi-official)**
b. **IOWA   "State banner"   Government and general usage flag   29**
     March 1921–present
c. **KANSAS   "State banner"   Government and general usage flag   27**
     February 1925–30 June 1953   Proportions 3 x 4

State. The colors of the flag are those of the nation; the diamond pattern symbolizes the fact that Arkansas is the only diamond-producing member of the Union. The two parallel blue stars at the bottom of the diamond stand for Arkansas and Michigan which are "sister States," having been admitted simultaneously to statehood in 1836. The 25 stars in the frame of the diamond indicate the order of admission of Arkansas into the Union.

The three central blue stars in this flag could be interpreted in three ways. They were for the three nations that had ruled the area (France, Spain, and the United States); the year 1803 in which the Louisiana Purchase was made; and the fact that Arkansas was the third State to be created from the Louisiana Territory. In 1923 the Legislature, feeling that the association of Arkansas with the Confederate States of America should be commemorated, added a fourth blue star to the flag (XIV-b). In doing so, it destroyed the symbolism of the three stars and objections were raised to this pattern by Miss Hocker and others. Consequently, on 10 April 1924 the present arrangement (XIV-c) was made official, the star representing the Confederacy being placed alone at the top of the diamond. The official pledge to the State flag, approved by the Legislature in 1953, states: "I salute the Arkansas Flag with its diamond and stars. We pledge our loyalty to thee."

The seal of Arkansas has been changed a number of times since the basic design was established in 1820 by Judge Samuel C. Roane. The most recent form (see p. 109) was fixed on 23 May 1907, when the former motto "Regnant Populi" ("The Peoples Rule") was altered to "Regnat Populus" ("The People Rule"). The different elements of the emblem appear to have been copied from other seals: the figure of Liberty with her wreath and pole come from North Carolina, the boat and plow from Tennessee, the thirteen-star crest and eagle from the national seal, and the tripartite shield from Pennsylvania. In addition on the Arkansas seal may be found the Angel of Mercy, the Sword of Justice, and a beehive.

CALIFORNIA

Relations between Mexico and the United States in the mid-nineteenth century were strained by the presence of American settlers in borderlands between the two countries, particularly in Texas and California. After a long struggle, Texas broke away from Mexican rule and, after several years as an independent country, annexed itself to the United States. This was one of the immediate causes of the Mexican-American War in which California was one of the battlegrounds.

Dissatisfied with Mexican rule in 1846, a group of American settlers in California followed the example of the Texans: they seized the area around Sonoma and proclaimed an independent California Republic. Their flag (XV-a) was hoisted on 14 June 1846 and flew until 9 July when American troops occupied the area and declared it part of the United States. Although there is some question about the seriousness of the so-called Bear Flag party's actually wishing to establish a separate nation, their action did guarantee that the United States would acquire California as part of the spoils of the war with Mexico.

The original flag, crudely painted by William L. Todd, had a large star, presumably symbolizing independence. The native grizzly bear, now extinct, was added at the suggestion of Henry L. Ford. Legend indicates that the red and white material came from women's dresses and that the star and bear may have been painted in berry juice. There has been some dispute about the exact details of the flag, however, because the original was lost in the San Francisco fire of 1906, and the contemporary accounts differ in minor respects.

Pride in this historic flag was promoted in the 1890's by the Native Sons and Daughters of the Golden West, who made a number of replicas. In 1909 a member of the organization, R. D. Barton, suggested that the State should adopt the design as its official State flag. On 3 February 1911 a bill to this effect was signed by the Governor. The exact form approved (XV-b) was more artistic than Todd's version, yet over the years it, too, suffered from lack of official precision in details. Therefore on 2 June 1953 a new law went into effect which designated the exact style of all the elements in the design and the correct proportions and color shades for manufacturing purposes. The specifications now issued by the State government run to fourteen pages.

The State also has numerous other symbols. In 1951 the Legislature made blue and gold the official State colors. The flag of the Governor (XV-c) was first used at the beginning of the twentieth century and then legalized in 1957. The seal in the center is not the seal of the Governor—which pictures the State flag, a rising sun, and the golden poppy which serves as the State flower—but a modified version of the State seal. The correct State seal, which differs only slightly, was created in 1849, the year before Statehood was granted. On this seal the Goddess Minerva (who, according to legend, sprang full-grown from Jupiter's forehead) symbolizes California, which became a State without first having been a territory. The ships in the harbor and the miner digging for gold were characteristic of the period, as was the grizzly bear. The stars, as in other States, indicate the order of admission to Statehood. The Greek motto "Eureka" means "I Have Found It."

CANAL ZONE

In order to build a canal through the Isthmus of Panama, the United States signed a treaty with the newly established Republic of Panama in 1903. The treaty provided that a certain strip of territory, which cuts the Republic into halves, should be granted to the United States in perpetuity, although Panama was to retain an undefined titular sovereignty. Since then the exact nature of Panamanian rights over the Canal Zone has been disputed between the two countries. Symbolically, the most significant claim put forward by Panama has been that her flag (XVI-c) should fly inside the Zone.

After riots on the flag question broke out in 1958 and 1959, a joint flying of the United States and Panamanian flags ordered by President

XXVI. FLAGS OF KANSAS

a. **KANSAS   "State banner"   Government and general usage flag   30 June 1953–present   Proportions 3 x 4**

b. **KANSAS   "State flag"   Government and general usage flag   23 March 1927–30 June 1963   Proportions 72 x 113**

c. **KANSAS   "State flag"   Government and general usage flag   30 June 1963–present   Proportions 3 x 5**

a.

b.

c.

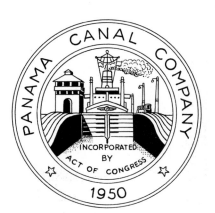

**PANAMA CANAL
COMPANY**
Seal
1950?–present

Eisenhower began in one selected spot in the Zone on 21 September 1960. In October of 1962 the dual flag display was extended to other areas of the zone, the United States flag always being in the honor position. On 31 December 1963 Zone Governor Robert J. Fleming issued an order, effective 2 January 1964, forbidding the display of the United States flag on any nonmilitary public building except in conjunction with the Panamanian flag. A few days later the teen-age children of American citizens living in the Zone hoisted the United States flag at a school with the implicit approval of their parents. When Panamanian students tried to raise their own flag alongside it was torn, and in the four days of rioting which followed more than twenty persons were killed. Since then the two flags have flown together peacefully throughout the Canal Zone.

The Canal Zone itself has never had a distinctive flag except for the signal (XVI-a) flown by ships of the Canal Zone Government. There is a flag, however, which was prescribed on 8 June 1915 by President Woodrow Wilson for use by the Governor of the Canal Zone. This flag (XVI-b) shows the central emblem from the seal of the Zone—an anachronistic picture of a fifteenth century Spanish galleon passing through two heads of land apparently meant to suggest the canal. The Panama Canal Company also has its own seal (above).

COLORADO

For several years a flag made by Mrs. J. J. Hagerman of Colorado Springs hung in the office of the Governor of Colorado. It was dark blue with the coat of arms of the State; gold cord bound the two long sides of the flag, which was hung from a horizontal pole. The bottom edge was fringed in gold. In early 1907 a bill was introduced into the Legislature which designated this general design (XVII-a) as the State flag, although its vertical position and gold fringe were not mentioned. The bill became a law on 9 April 1907. The original flag continued to be displayed in the office of the Governor until the late 1950's when for safekeeping it was transferred to the State Archives. It has been proposed that this design, on a square flag and with the arms surrounded with a circle of thirty-eight stars to indicate that Colorado was the thirty-eighth member of the Union, be adopted as a flag for the Governor. So far no official action has been taken.

The arms appearing on the first State flag had been adopted in 1877, the year after Statehood was obtained; they formed the central portion of the new seal. The eye which serves as a crest appears to be derived from the reverse of the seal of the United States (see p. 76); the Latin motto means "Nothing Without the Divinity." The traditional miner's badge of pickaxe and hammer signifies the State's mining activities.

In 1911 a new State flag (XVII-b) was approved by the Legislature on 5 April and filed in the office of the Secretary of State on 5 June. This flag was designed by Andrew Carlisle Carson, who appears to have been inspired by the blue, gold, and white of the State flower, the Rocky Mountain columbine. These colors, plus red for Colorado itself—since *colorado* is the Spanish word for red—were incorporated in this design. Red, white, and blue are also the national colors and gold and silver were to recall the mining of these precious metals in Colorado. Carson gave other explanations to the colors as well. The letter C stands for Colorado which is both the "Columbine State" and the "Centennial State," because of its admission to the Union in 1876. The law specified that the flag should be decorated with cords and tassels of intertwined gold and silver strands.

The legal description of the flag as approved in 1911 was faulty in two respects. The designer had intended to have a large C, somewhat off-center, but the proportions actually adopted produced a much smaller pattern set quite near the hoist. Moreover, the color of the top and bottom stripes was unspecified. This latter error was corrected in a new law passed in 1929, when the two stripes were designated as being of the same shade of blue as in the national flag. On 31 March 1964 the other question was dealt with and the size and placement of the C altered (XVII-c). However, the flag still does not exactly correspond to the design which Carson had intended: that pattern shows the end points of the outer margin of the C exactly coinciding with the lines between the blue and white.

CONNECTICUT
Seal
c1644–1687

CONNECTICUT

The early settlers of the eastern colonies were highly motivated by religious beliefs and evidences of their faith abound in the symbols they adopted. Thus the motto which Connecticut has used (in Latin) since at least 1647 reads in English "He Who Brought Us Over Will Sustain Us." This appears to have been inspired by part of the 80th Psalm: "Thou

XXVII. FLAGS OF KENTUCKY AND LOUISIANA

a. **KENTUCKY Government flag 26 March 1918–present (specifications from 14 June 1962) Proportions 10 x 19**

b. **LOUISIANA 11 February 1861–?**

c. **LOUISIANA Government flag 1 July 1912–present (unofficial since the 19th century) Proportions 2 x 3**

a.

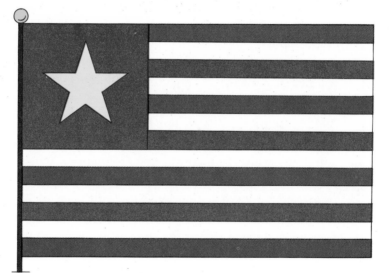

b.

c.

CONNECTICUT
Seal
24 March 1931–present
(basic design authorized
25 October 1711)

hast brought a vine out of Egypt; Thou hast cast out the heathen, and planted it." This impression is reenforced by the design of the seal itself (see p. 116), which shows the hand of God issuing from a cloud, blessing a vineyard of fifteen vines.

In later seals the number of vines is reduced to three and the hand and cloud are missing. It has been suggested that the three fruited vines may represent either the three towns (Hartford, Wethersfield, and Windsor) which formed the first Colony of Connecticut in 1639, or the colonies of Connecticut, New Haven, and Saybrook, which were united to form the area of the present State of Connecticut. Whether or not this is true, from time to time there have been certain minor artistic modifications in the seal, as when the inscription around the edge was changed in 1784 to read (in Latin) "Seal of the Commonwealth of Connecticut." This form of the seal (above) is still in use today. The coat of arms, which is closely modeled after the seal, was standardized in its present form in 1931.

As a colony Connecticut considered it necessary that her local militia have their own distinctive colors. The oldest patterns are unknown to us, but there is a flag extant dating from the time of the Revolution (XVIII-a) which has a field of solid red with the arms on the obverse. The reverse inscription is "II. Bat: II. Reg: Connecticut Raised 1640." A similar flag was carried by Connecticut troops at the Battle of Bunker Hill in 1775. The military regulations of 1775 established as the proper background shades for the colors of the First through the Eighth Regiments yellow, blue (later changed to green), scarlet, crimson, white, azure, blue, and orange. Further regulations issued in 1780 stated that, "If the ground of two colours should be so alike as not to be distinguishable [at] 3 to 400 yards, a small field of 13 stripes in the Lower Quarter on one of them may serve as a distinction."

During the nineteenth century Connecticut followed the pattern of most States by displaying its arms, joined in the Civil War period with the national arms, on a field of blue. Since this was the Connecticut flag most familiar to soldiers and civilians alike, it is not surprising to find the Legislature adopting the following resolution on 4 July 1895: "The flag which has up to the present time been generally accepted as the flag of this state ought to be officially and formally designated as such." The Adjutant General prepared a brief report on the various designs in actual use at the time. Aside from strictly military colors, he found that the Governor displayed a square blue flag with the coat of arms in the center and that a similar flag flew over the Capitol during sessions of the Legislature.

An exact pattern was finally selected and adopted on 3 June 1897 (XVIII-b). The military tradition is evident in the nearly square shape which is today, in practice, ignored in favor of the more common 2:3 or 3:5 proportions. In 1957 the Purchasing Division of the State Department of Finance and Control issued a set of specifications for the manufacture of the flag. These included exact color shade references, based on the official illustration of the coat of arms found in the office of the Secretary of State.

DELAWARE

On 24 July 1913 the present State flag of Delaware (XVIII-c) became official. The flag was readopted on 13 June 1955 after it was discovered that the law describing it had been left out of the 1953 Delaware Code. The tradition of a State flag, however, goes back long before this. The troops of the State during the Civil War carried blue flags with the State arms. At the Centennial Exposition in 1876 at Philadelphia, the Delaware Building flew a pennant of white with the name of the State in blue

a.

b.

c.

letters. A flag bearing the arms was displayed in 1907 at the Jamestown Exposition and in 1910 on the battleship *Delaware*. The form of the flag as finally adopted was determined by a legislative Commission.

The date appearing below the diamond indicates when the State ratified the Constitution, Delaware being the first State to do so. The principal colors of the flag are "colonial blue and buff," recalling the colors of Revolutionary War uniforms. These were given precise definition in the law of 1955. This law also specified that the cords and tassels of the flag should be blue and gold, although the official description of the flag does not mention the use of this accessory. Blue and gold were the colors of the flag (III-b) which flew over the colony of New Sweden, located in what is today the State of Delaware, but there is no indication that the designers of the State flag had this color tradition in mind.

The Governor of Delaware has a personal standard which is basically the same as the State flag. Added to the flag are a fringe of gold and, at the top of the pole, a representation of a "Blue Hen's Fighting Cock." The Blue Hen chicken is the official State bird and has been used as a nickname or emblem by various groups in Delaware since the Revolution. The Governor issued an Executive Order in 1955 specifying the correct use for the State and Governor's flags.

The arms of the State were adopted in 1777, which accounts for the presence of a colonial soldier as one of the supporters. The other supporter is a farmer, the agricultural theme further being carried out in the shield which includes an ox, a sheaf of wheat, and an ear of Indian corn. The corn and wheat had been used in the seals of Kent and Sussex Counties, respectively, as crests over the shield of William Penn, who was their Proprietor in 1683. The seals of New Castle and Kent Counties were used by the State government from 1776 until the new seal was ready in 1777. There were minor modifications in the seals cut in 1793 and 1847.

XXVIII. FLAGS OF MAINE

a. **MAINE   21 March 1901–24 February 1909 (reconstructed)**

b. **MAINE   Government flag   24 February 1909–present   Proportions 26 x 33**

c. **MAINE   "Merchant and marine flag"   General usage flag at sea   21 July 1939–present**

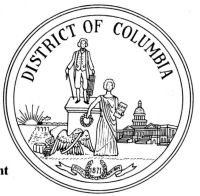

**DISTRICT OF
COLUMBIA
Seal
3 August 1871–present**

DISTRICT OF COLUMBIA

Like other parts of United States territory not having local self-government, the District of Columbia was slow to develop symbols of its own. The first emblem to be adopted was the seal (above), created in 1871 by the Legislative Assembly of the District. In addition to the Capitol Building and an American eagle, it includes a number of symbols. The figure of Justice places a wreath before a statue of George Washington, while her other hand bears a tablet reading "Constitution." Agricultural produce and a train heading over the Potomac toward Virginia fill in the left side. The motto "Justitia Omnibus" ("Justice to All") frames the date of the seal's adoption.

In at least two instances we have record of unofficial flags bearing the District seal. Other emblems associated with General Washington or the city named for him also appeared on military flags. Thus the first headquarters flag of the District of Columbia Militia showed, surrounded by scrolls with inscriptions, the hatchet which Washington used as a boy to cut down the cherry tree in Parson Weems's famous legend. The field of the flag was blue and swallow-tailed. Later the swallow-tails disappeared and the hatchet was replaced by the dome of the Capitol Building on a heraldic wreath and in front of a rising sun.

Finally, after efforts in Congress dating back at least to 1920, a Commission was established to choose a distinctive flag. Largely guided by A. E. DuBois, the leading heraldic scholar who worked for the Quartermaster General's Staff designing flags, arms, medals, and other insignia, the Commission announced its choice on 15 October 1938. This flag (XIX-b) has flown since then as the official District of Columbia flag.

The basis for the flag design is the shield from the coat of arms (XIX-a) used by the Washington family. This had been confirmed to Laurence Washington of Sulgrave Manor (Northamptonshire, England) in 1592 by one of the heralds. In heraldic language it is described as "Argent, two bars gules in chief three mullets of the Second; Crest, out of a ducal coronet or a raven, wings endorsed, proper." The illustration makes these terms clear. The motto which George Washington used frequently, "Exitus Acta Probat" ("The Test of Actions is in Their Outcome"), was not made part of the arms. The shield has sometimes falsely been associated with the origin of the United States flag (see p. 62).

The specifications issued with the flag in 1938 are interesting in a number of ways. They provided rules of etiquette for the District flag which read almost word for word like the law adopted by Congress four years later covering the use of the national flag. While setting out carefully the widths of the stars and stripes in the District flag, the specifications stated that the length of the flag might vary. (The proportions of 10:19 shown here are correct when the flag is flown with the national flag.) Also red fringe was made an optional accessory for the flag.

FLORIDA

The Spanish possession of the territories of East and West Florida was a source of irritation to many Americans in the early nineteenth century. Negotiations and a filibuster republic sponsored by President Monroe in 1812 having failed to secure United States rule, certain private citizens sponsored an expedition by Gregor MacGregor—who had been active in several Latin American revolutions—designed to seize the area. On 29 June 1817 he captured the island of Amelia off Florida and hoisted a white flag with a green cross. Four months later he was forced to flee and his flag was forgotten, although American efforts to obtain Florida continued until they were successful.

When William D. Moseley was being inaugurated on 25 June 1845 as the first Governor of the newly admitted State of Florida, a special flag (XIX-c) was hoisted. The meaning of its colors is not clear, but the motto "Let Us Alone" was strongly objected to by the Whigs, who viewed it as a partisan slogan of the ruling Democratic Party. Despite debate on the motto, a resolution was presented to the Legislature to legalize this as the State flag. There is some question whether the flag was actually made official, since the House approved a joint resolution while the Senate gave its consent on 27 December 1845 in the form of a Senate resolution. In any event the flag seems never to have been employed.

The next action on the flag question came on 30 November 1860, when, in anticipation of Florida's leaving the Union, a motion was made to create a new national flag. No action was taken immediately, but on 11 January 1861 when the State passed the Ordinance of Secession an unofficial flag made by the "Ladies of Broward's Neck" was hoisted over the Capitol. It included red and blue stripes, a circle with stars, and the motto "The Rights of the South at All Hazards." Other flags were flown elsewhere, including the provisional flag prescribed by the commander of the Florida armed forces on 13 January 1861. This flag (L-c) was of the same design as the old Texan naval flag. On 8 February the Legislature delegated the power of creating a flag to the Governor. Since Florida soon joined the Confederacy, the flag selected by the Governor on 13 September 1861 represented only a State instead of an independent nation. The flag probably was little used, for no contemporary picture is available and the illustration given here (XX-a) is reconstructed from a written description. The seal shows an oak, the Gulf of Mexico, a stand of flags, and military equipment.

After the war the legislature called for a State flag of white with the seal in the center. Rejecting the seal design which had been selected in 1846, the legislature on 6 August 1868 completed the flag (XX-b) by

XXIX. FLAGS AND SEALS OF MARYLAND
a.   MARYLAND   Seal (obverse and reverse)   27 February 1879–present
b.   MARYLAND   Government   flag   (unofficial)   c1638–1652;   1658–
       1692; 1715–1776   (arms-banner of the Lords Baltimore)
c.   MARYLAND   Government flag   9 March 1904–present

a.

b.

c.

approving a new seal which is still in use. Late in the century Governor Francis P. Fleming suggested the addition of a red saltire behind the seal so that it would look less like a flag of truce when no breeze was blowing. Since the seal and flag had been incorporated in the State constitution, an amendment to this document was necessary. This was ratified on 6 November 1900. However, the proportions of three to four which were selected for the flag in 1900 did not correspond to those generally in use for other state flags. Thus on 8 November 1966 a further amendment was ratified, specifying a greater flexibility in the proportions of the flag (XX-c), the width of the seal, and the saltire.

GEORGIA
Seal (reverse)
8 February 1799–
present

GEORGIA

Like many other former members of the Confederate States of America, Georgia has borrowed the Confederate flag as the inspiration for its own State flag. The first step in this direction was taken on 17 October 1879 when the Governor signed into law a measure creating the first State flag (XXI-a). Except that the blue canton was extended into a vertical stripe and the stars were omitted, this flag was the same as the first national flag of the Confederacy (LXIV-b)—the famous Stars and Bars. The bill had been introduced by Colonel Herman H. Perry, a Confederate veteran.

On 22 August 1905 it was further provided that the State coat of arms should be "stamped, painted, or embroidered" on the blue stripe. A modification in the State seal on 17 August 1914, as described below, created the third version of this flag (XXI-b). This was reaffirmed in a legislative act of 1916. The coat of arms—actually the State seal—has never been given any official colors and generally it has been shown on the flag in blue outline on a white circle. Occasionally, however, the encircling band and pillared arch have been shown in yellow on a white circle, the ribbon and soldier being in blue.

The present flag of Georgia (XXI-c) was the idea of John Sammons Bell, Chairman of the Democratic Party in the State. Wishing more clearly to commemorate the association of Georgia with the Confederacy, Bell substituted the Battle Flag of that nation (minus its white border; see LXV-a) for the scarlet and white stripes of the Georgia flag. The General Assembly approved this design and it became effective on 1 July 1956. The Secretary of State was designated as the custodian of the flag. The official salute to this flag, adopted in 1935, reads: "I pledge allegiance to the Georgia Flag and to the principles for which it stands, Wisdom, Justice and Moderation."

These words are inscribed on the ribbons which drape the structure in the State seal; the pillars stand for the three branches of government (legislative, judicial, and executive) which support the arch marked "Constitution." The soldier represents the military forces of Georgia, ready to defend these principles; 1776 is the date of independence both for Georgia and the United States. Georgia is one of the few States with a distinctive design for the reverse of its seal (opposite). The figures on this side are illustrative of its motto, "Agriculture and Commerce." There have been minor changes in the seal since it was first created in 1799. The only one affecting the flag was the alteration in 1914 of the date at the bottom of the seal from 1799, the year the Constitution of Georgia was approved, to 1776.

A number of flags were flown in Georgia during the Civil War era, but none apparently received legislative sanction. During the period when Georgia was independent, between 19 January 1861 when it seceded from the Union and 8 February of the same year when it joined the Confederacy, a white flag bearing the State seal in the center flew over the Capitol. Another flag flown at that time was white with a red star. Georgian troops carried the Stars and Bars with the State seal within the circle of stars.

GUAM

From the time of its discovery in 1521 until the Spanish-American War of 1898, this Pacific island, being a colony of Spain, was under the flags which are described on pp. 14-15. As a Territory under United States administration, Guam has flown the flag of the United States except for the period between December 1941 and August 1944 when Guam was occupied by Japan and lived under the rising-sun ensign of the Japanese naval forces (XLIV-c). This flag, a variation of the centuries-old Japanese national flag, was apparently adopted in imitation of the many European naval ensigns bearing crosses on a white field.

In 1917 Mrs. Carrol Paul designed the territorial flag (XXII-a) which is flown locally on Guam. It was officially adopted on 4 July 1917 and confirmed on 12 May 1931 and 9 February 1948. The flag has the unusual proportions of 21:40. The Government Code provides that this flag "shall be displayed in the open only from sunrise until sunset and during such hours shall be displayed only on buildings, flagstaffs or halyards. . . . No pledge of allegiance shall be required to be given by anyone to the territorial flag of Guam."

The coat of arms of Guam which appears in the center of the flag is usually, but unofficially, shown with a red border to separate it from the blue field. The seal in use also varies from the official description: it should have the encircling inscription "Great Seal of the Government of Guam, Guam, Mariana Islands, United States of America" whereas in fact it reads "Great Seal of the Territory of Guam, United States of America." The design in the center of the seal (and coat of arms) is characteristic of the island as seen from the mouth of the Agaña River. The flying proa, a type of canoe employed by the native Chamorros,

XXX. FLAGS OF MASSACHUSETTS

a. **MASSACHUSETTS Ensign 29 April 1776–31 October 1971 UNITED STATES Naval ensign 1775–1776 (unofficial, variant)**

b. **MASSACHUSETTS (obverse) 6 March 1915–present**

c. **MASSACHUSETTS (reverse of flag b through 31 October 1971)**

a.

b.

c.

appears in the foreground. This coat of arms was employed before 1917 and was confirmed in 1930 by an Executive Order issued by the Governor, Captain Willis W. Bradley, Jr., U. S. N.

In 1950 the administration of Guam was transferred from the Navy to the Department of the Interior. The official flag of the Naval Governors when embarked in a boat on official business had been the United States Union Jack displayed in the bow. However, unofficially these Governors long used a standard consisting of the territorial flag fringed in gold and bearing in a semicircle over the coat of arms the word "Governor" embroidered in gold. This flag is still in use today by the civil Governor.

HAWAII (KINGDOM) Flag of the Kuhina Nui 1850's

HAWAII

King Kamehameha I, who succeeded in uniting the Hawaiian islands into a single kingdom, received a British Union Jack from the explorer, Captain George Vancouver, in 1793. On 25 February of the following year the King accepted an informal British protectorate over his islands and, although this act was never ratified by the British government, the Union Jack in both its pre- and post-1801 forms (IV-c and IV-e) flew as the unofficial Hawaiian flag until 1816. By this time, Hawaiians realized that there were disadvantages as well as advantages to the use of another nation's flag. In 1816 when the *Kaahumanu* sailed for China as the first

HAWAII (KINGDOM) Coat of arms 18?–189?

Hawaiian ship to travel abroad, it flew a distinctive Hawaiian flag which added red, white, and blue stripes to the Union Jack. The flag was designed by the King with the assistance of Alexander Adams, Isaac Davis, and John Young, although Captain George Beckley later claimed credit for the design. There was no standard pattern for the Hawaiian flag in its early years. The form illustrated in XXII-b was the usual version, but contemporary pictures and accounts indicate variations (seven stripes instead of nine, no stripes of blue, etc.).

Throughout the nineteenth century the Kingdom of Hawaii fought to preserve its independence against threats of annexation posed by the United States, Britain, France, and other countries. From 25 February until 31 July of 1843 British troops occupied Hawaii and all Hawaiian flags were destroyed. On the restoration of freedom, King Kamehameha III watched while a Hawaiian flag which included a dove and olive branch was hoisted. Then he gave a prayer of thanksgiving containing the phrase which thereafter became a national (now State) motto: "Ua mau ke ea o ka 'aini i ka pono" ("The life of the land is perpetuated by righteousness").

On 20 May 1845 a slightly modified version of the national flag (XXII-c) was introduced in which the number of stripes was set at eight, to represent the principal islands of Hawaii (Hawaii, Oahu, Molokai, Maui, Lanai, Niihau, Kauai, and Kahoolawe). The French did not lower the Hawaiian flag during their brief occupation in 1849. In order to forestall another French occupation in 1851, the King and Council approved a measure establishing a temporary American protectorate. The new flag was to have been sewn with the Hawaiian flag on one side

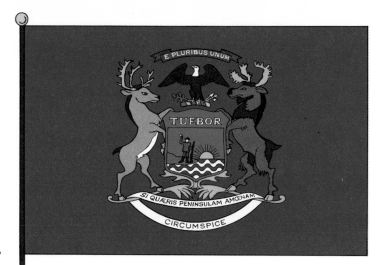

a.

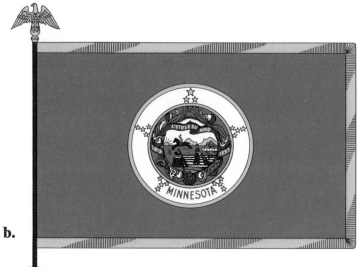

b.

c.

and the United States flag on the reverse, but the plan never went into effect. In 1887 Hawaii adopted a jack and ensign.

In the 1850's the flag (see p. 130) of the *Kuhina Nui,* who was next in authority to the King, bore the royal crown and the initials of her title in red on white. Another royal emblem, the coat of arms of Hawaii (see p. 131). was originally designed by High Chief Haalilio. The shield and crown of these arms appeared in the center of the royal standard (XXIII-a). The background of the standard and the first and fourth quarters of the arms display the stripes of the national flag. The supporters are the brothers Kamanawa and Kameeiamoku, who aided Kamehameha I in uniting Hawaii; their royalty is shown by the feather cloaks and helmets they wear. Kamanawa holds a spear, symbolic of state power, while his brother has a *kahili* or feather-covered staff, which indicates royal prerogatives. The second and third quarters of the shield each show a *puloulou,* the emblem of protection and refuge, which was set up near the King's palace door. In the center are the *alia* (crossed spears) and *puela* (triangular standard) which appeared near the palace door as religious symbols. The *puela* was also raised by the ancient Hawaiian chiefs as a kind of flag on their boats.

In the last decade of the nineteenth century American settler and commercial interests increased their agitation for annexation of Hawaii to the United States. Finally, in January 1893 the Reform Party which represented these groups staged a *coup d'état* and deposed Queen Liliuokalani. While their Provisional Government waited for news of American annexation, the flag of the United States flew over Hawaii from 1 February until 1 April. When annexation was rejected, plans were made for a Republic of Hawaii. This regime was inaugurated in 1894 and lasted until 12 August 1898 when Hawaii became a territory of the United States. Under the Provisional Government and then as a

XXXI. FLAGS OF MICHIGAN AND MINNESOTA

a.   **MICHIGAN   1 August 1911–present**

b.   **MINNESOTA   Government flag   19 March 1957–present   Proportions 3 x 5**

c.   **MINNESOTA   4 April 1893–19 March 1957   (obverse)**

HAWAII (STATE)
Seal
1959–present
(basic design
authorized 1894)

Republic, Territory, and State (since 1959) Hawaii has kept its former national flag, as legally confirmed in 1894, 1903, and 1959.

Using the royal arms as a basic pattern, Viggo Jacobsen created a new Hawaiian coat of arms which the Republic accepted in 1896. The supporters are now King Kamehameha I and the Goddess of Liberty holding a Hawaiian flag; a rising sun replaces the royal crown; and a phoenix appears at the bottom, framed with taro leaves, maidenhair fern, and banana foliage. In the center the *alia* and *puela* were replaced by a star, indicating the desire to be admitted to Statehood. In 1901 and 1959 the coat of arms was appropriately modified to serve as a seal, first for the Territory and then (above) the State of Hawaii.

In 1925 Governor Wallace R. Farrington asked Colonel P. M. Smoot, the Adjutant General, to report on the Governor's flag which his predecessor had designed. Finding no legal basis for it, Colonel Smoot proposed a flag of blue over red stripes with eight white stars surrounding the initials TH (for the Territory of Hawaii) in white in the center. This was approved on 14 March 1925. In 1959 the flag (XXIII-b) was modified for use by the Governor of the new State when the word "Hawaii" was substituted for the initials.

IDAHO

As a Territory Idaho employed for government business a seal adopted on 5 March 1866. The central shield showed a steamer on the Shoshone River, a view of mountains, and the new moon above them. The crest was an elk's head and the motto below was "Salve," the Latin word for welcome. Figures representing Liberty and Peace served as supporters of the arms. This seal was replaced on 14 March 1891, following the admission of Idaho to Statehood. The new design, closely patterned after the old, was designed by Miss Emma Edwards. In 1957 the State legislature approved the original drawing and colors done by Miss Edwards as a model for all uses.

This seal eliminates from the 1866 version the steamer and moon from the shield, but adds a man plowing, a stamp mill, and a pine tree to represent agriculture, mining, and forestry. These themes are repeated in the wheat (both growing and in a sheaf) and cornucopias of produce, the miner with his pick and shovel, and the elk head which surround the outside of the shield. The single female figure, combining the scales and liberty cap emblematic of Justice and Liberty, stands for women's rights, which was a heated political question at the time the seal was chosen. The motto "Esto Perpetua" means "May She Last Forever" and the star indicates Idaho's place in the Union.

The first State flag of Idaho, approved on 12 March 1907 by the legislature, was supposed to be "blue charged with the name of the state, in such colors and of such size and dimensions as shall be prescribed by the adjutant general of the State." Brigadier General C. A. Elmer subsequently issued specifications for a flag which, while conforming to the general pattern used by State military forces, did not correspond to the legal description. In addition to the words State of Idaho "embroidered in with block letters [of unspecified color, but usually gold], 2 inches in height, on a red band 3 inches in width by 29 inches in length, the band being embroidered [i.e., bordered] in gold and placed about 8½ inches from the lower border of fringe and parallel with the same" the order called for the State seal, twenty-one inches in diameter, to be placed above the motto. The flag itself was to be four feet four inches by five feet six inches with a two and one-half inch gold fringe. The model prepared by General Elmer was used despite its inconsistency with the law and finally on 15 March 1927 the legislature altered the law to conform to the flag design actually in use. After the new law regarding the seal was passed on 1 March 1957, the present form of the State flag (XXIII-c) became official.

ILLINOIS

When the legislature approved a measure on 6 July 1915 creating a State flag (XXIV-a), it established two alternative designs. Officially, the emblem from the State seal which forms the central design of this flag may appear either in black or in "the national colors," although in practice the former is never seen. In 1970 new specifications were established for the rendition and a new law required the name of the State to appear in blue below the seal (not illustrated in this book).

The Illinois flag was created in a contest sponsored by the Daughters of the American Revolution. The prize of $25 was won by its Rockford Chapter, and Senator Raymond D. Meeker introduced the motion which made the flag official. Two years earlier Wallace Rice had created an Illinois flag in anticipation of the centennial of Illinois Statehood, but it had failed to gain legislative approval. Rice's design showed horizontal stripes of white, blue, and white with ten blue stars on each white stripe to symbolize the equal number of slave and free States at the time Illinois joined the Union. There was also a large white star on the blue stripe for Illinois itself.

The State seal which appears on the present flag dates back to 1810, the year after the Illinois Territory was created, when a crude version was made of the eagle and shield from the United States arms. In 1818 Illinois became a State and the legislature authorized the Governor to use his personal seal on public papers until such time as a State seal might be ready for use. Although no instructions for its design are to be found, papers from 1820 testify that the Governor had the new seal made on the basis of the territorial seal. The only changes were the rewording of the encircling band to read "Seal of the State of Illinois— August 26 1818" and the addition of a scroll in the eagle's mouth. This

XXXII. FLAGS AND ARMS OF MISSISSIPPI

a.   **MISSISSIPPI**   26 January 1861–? (reconstructed)
b.   **MISSISSIPPI**   7 February 1894–present   Proportions 2 x 3
c.   **MISSISSIPPI**   Coat of arms   7 February 1894–present

a.

b.

c.

scroll bore the motto "State Sovereignty, National Union." Some time later a new cutting was made of the seal, but with only minor artistic changes.

After the Civil War the Secretary of State asked the legislature to pay for a new seal and to legalize the design then in use, but with the motto reversed to read "National Union, State Sovereignty." This proposal was resisted in the legislature and a new seal was approved only on the condition that the motto be unchanged. However, the seal cutter showed the ribbon in such a fashion that the words "National Union," while following "State Sovereignty," are at the top and appear more prominently. The seal maker was also the one responsible for adding the dates "1818" and "1868" to the rock and for eliminating the arrows which the eagle had previously held.

INDIANA
Seal
11 March 1963–present
(unofficial since 1816)

INDIANA

With Illinois, Kansas, and the Dakotas, Indiana shares the distinction of having two State flags. The first action concerning an Indiana flag was taken at the beginning of the century when the Legislature approved a bill resolving that the "flag of the United States, representing each State with a star in its blue field, be and is hereby adopted as the flag of the State of Indiana." Although the preamble erred in stating that "the flag of the United States is recognized as the flag of every State and Territory," the Governor signed the bill on 9 March 1901. Thus the first Indiana State flag (XXIV-b) was the forty-five-star United States flag in use from 1896 to 1908. This has been followed up to the present by the forty-six-, forty-eight-, forty-nine-, and fifty-star patterns, since the 1901 law is still in effect.

In 1917 the State created a "State banner" (renamed the State flag in 1955) which was required to be used by the military forces of the State, as well as the government and the general public. Indeed the dimensions of the flag—four feet, four inches, by five feet, six inches—have been standard for military colors, and are found in many State flags of military origin. Since it is distinctive of Indiana, this flag (XXIV-c), rather than the one provided for in 1901, is used to represent the State. In 1955 provision was made for the use of the State flag at schools, a practice followed in many other States as well.

The design may be either in gold or in buff, the gold in practice being preferred. The outer circle of thirteen stars is for the original members of the Union, while the inner six are for the subsequent States up to and including Indiana. The State itself is represented by the star at the top which is larger than the others. The torch symbolizes both enlightenment and liberty, while its rays stand for their spread throughout the land. Paul Hadley of Mooresville submitted this flag in a competition held in 1916, under the sponsorship of the Daughters of the American Revolution, at the time of the centennial of Indiana Statehood. His design won the competition and was adopted as the State banner on 31 May 1917 by the legislature.

Copies of a seal similar to the one now in use by the State (opposite) are to be found on papers of the Territory of Indiana as early as 1801. The design was first made in 1816, but was adopted only in 1963. It portrays a woodsman cutting down trees while a bison in the foreground flees. This scene, symbolic of the rolling back of the frontier, was retained long after Indiana ceased to be on that frontier. The Constitution of Indiana provides that the seal shall be in the custody of the Governor, although in other States it is more common for this to be a responsibility of the Secretary of State.

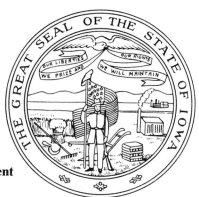

IOWA
Seal
25 February 1847–present

IOWA

Soon after the establishment of the Territory of Iowa its Secretary, William B. Conway, proposed a seal design bearing in the center simply an American eagle holding an Indian bow and arrow. This pattern was accepted officially on 4 January 1839 and used until 3 March 1847. By that time Iowa had become a State and felt the need for a revised seal. A committee of the legislature worked out a new design (above) which retained the eagle but added many other elements. In the foreground is a soldier with a United States flag on a pole which bears the liberty cap. The steamer *Iowa* sailing on the Mississippi River and scenes symbolizing agriculture and industry fill in the background. From the beak of the eagle floats a ribbon bearing the motto "Our Liberties We Prize and Our Rights We Will Maintain." Although this seal has undergone the usual minor artistic modifications, the basic design is still in official use.

Just prior to the First World War the Iowa section of the Daughters of the American Revolution became interested in the question of a State flag for Iowa. The first formal step taken was the creation by the Iowa General Assembly in 1913 of a special commission charged with consid-

XXXIII. FLAGS OF MISSOURI, MONTANA, AND NEBRASKA
a. **MISSOURI** Government flag 22 March 1913–present Proportions 7 x 12
b. **MONTANA** 27 February 1905–present
c. **NEBRASKA** Government and general usage flag 2 April 1925–present

a.

b.

c.

ering the advisibility of adopting such a flag and of suggesting a design. The commission soon found itself in the midst of a dispute between the D. A. R., which favored such a flag, and others, in particular certain members of the Grand Army of the Republic, who felt that the United States national flag was sufficient as a symbol. The latter group suggested that a distinctive State flag would be contrary to the ideal of national unity for which the Civil War had been fought.

The entrance of the United States into the European war in 1917 provided an opportunity to arouse public interest in a State flag. The D. A. R. submitted its choice for a design to the War Council of Iowa, which approved of it. Copies were then made and sent to troops from Iowa fighting in France; the same flag (XXV-a) greeted the troops on their return home. The eagle and ribbon of this flag were borrowed from the State seal. Opposition still existed, however, and it was not until 29 March 1921 that the legislature finally accepted an official State banner. (The term "banner" rather than "flag" was used in deference to the men of the G. A. R.)

The banner approved in 1921 (XXV-b) differed from the earlier flag in that the background consisted of three stripes instead of plain white. Mrs. Dixie C. Gebhardt, a D. A. R. member, had suggested this change. The blue, white, and red tricolor, she explained, was the French flag (see p. 18) at the time of the Louisiana Purchase and since Iowa was one of the States which evolved from this territory it would be appropriate to commemorate her former link to France. She also suggested, unsuccessfully, that a pole displaying the Iowa flag should be surmounted by an ear of corn. The Governor flies a State flag, eighteen inches by twenty-five inches and fringed in gold, on the front of his car.

KANSAS

The question of whether the Territory of Kansas should become a slave State or a free State long kept her from attaining Statehood at all. When admission to the Union was finally granted in 1861 the secretary of the

State Senate, John J. Ingalls, proposed as a seal for the new State "a single star rising from clouds at the base of a field, with the constellation (representing the number of states then in the Union) above." This emblem was to be completed by the motto "Ad Astra Per Aspera," "To the Stars through Difficulties." The symbolism would have been immediately evident, except that the Legislature in making the design official added a rising sun, oxcarts, and Indians chasing bison, all suggesting the advance of the frontier; a steamboat standing for commerce; and a man plowing the fields before a cabin, representing agriculture. These added emblems apparently were taken from *The Herald of Freedom,* a newspaper published in Kansas in 1855. This pattern has been used as the official seal of the State ever since 1861.

More immediately recognizable as a State emblem is the sunflower, selected as the official Kansas flower in 1903. This is used in many ways to symbolize the State. On a flag, it first appeared officially on 27 February 1925 when the original State banner (XXV-c) was created by the legislature. In the center of the flower was the State seal. Later Adjutant General Joe Nickell designed a new State banner (XXVI-a) in which the size of the flower was enlarged and the other elements were eliminated. This flag design corresponds to the shoulder patch worn by Kansas National Guard troops not serving in a separate infantry brigade. The legislature substituted the new banner for the old on 30 June 1953; it can be seen in the Governor's office, along with the State flag and a national flag. Otherwise, the banner is rarely used except by the Kansas National Guard, although the laws of the State make no distinction in usage between the banner and the flag.

The first State flag (XXVI-b) was approved on 23 March 1927. In addition to the State seal in color, it included the sunflower crest of the State. (When used by military units this crest frequently has its heraldic wreath in colors other than blue and yellow.) The present State flag (XXVI-c) dates from 30 June 1963; it differs from the old State flag only in the addition of the word "Kansas." Very similar to it in design is the flag of the Governor, as used at military reviews. The only difference between it and the State flag is the addition of a white star in each corner to symbolize the Governor's military rank.

a.

b.

c.

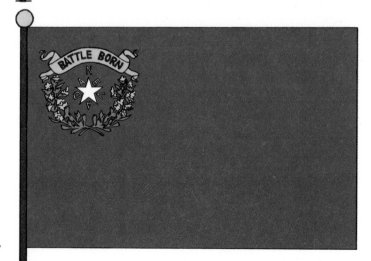

KENTUCKY

Immediately after its admission into the Union, Kentucky undertook to provide itself with a seal for official business. On 20 December 1792, the General Assembly of the Commonwealth passed an act empowering the Governor to have a seal made; and the following year we find a note that David Humphries received twelve pounds sterling for this work. The design, as specified by the law, was "two friends embracing with the name of the state over their heads; and around them, the following motto 'United We Stand, Divided We Fall'." A reenactment of this law in 1893 retained essentially the same wording.

Since no explanation was given at the time, we are forced to guess the meaning of the emblem. The words appear to be a paraphrase of the refrain in a popular song from the Revolutionary War period. John Dickinson had written in this "Liberty Song" of 1768, "Then join in hand, brave Americans all,/By uniting we stand, by dividing we fall." Similar sentiments were common in political cartoons, editorials and sermons, and on flags and other symbols. It is interesting that this unionist motto is also used by Missouri, which like Kentucky was one of the border States that remained loyal during the Civil War.

Taking the motto together with the figure of the two men embracing, further interpretations become possible. In 1866 the grandson of Senator John Brown, who supposedly was a member of the committee which designed the seal, claimed that the scene was supposed to be "two friends in hunter's garb, their right hands clasped, their left resting on each other's shoulders, their feet on the verge of a precipice." In other versions, including the one which in 1962 became official for use on the State flag, one man is dressed in frontier buckskins, the other in formal frock coat and striped pants. If these men represent the then frontier State of Kentucky and the older States of the East Coast, the motto then would be symbolic of the need of both parts of the country for one

XXXIV. FLAGS OF NEVADA

a. **NEVADA**   **25 February 1905–22 March 1915**
b. **NEVADA**   **22 March 1915–26 March 1929**
c. **NEVADA**   **Government flag   26 March 1929–present**

another. This would be especially appropriate, since Kentucky was the first "western" State admitted to the Union. However, many original documents and seal impressions have been lost by fire and it is unlikely that the true story will ever be known for certain.

The flags borne by Kentucky troops in the Civil War were blue with the seal in the center. In 1880 the Governor sanctioned a special flag for use by the Kentucky State Guard which was essentially the same as the earlier military colors. On 26 March 1918 the State flag was officially adopted, but no copy was made until ten years later. Gradually, the flag attained wider recognition and Senator James C. Ware introduced a bill, which was passed and became effective on 14 June 1962, standardizing the details of the flag. As it now exists, the flag (XXVII-a) bears the seal in the center with a wreath of the State flower, goldenrod, below. The pole is topped by the State bird, the Kentucky cardinal, "in an alert but restful pose, cast in bronze, brass, or other suitable material." The seal itself as stamped on official papers differs somewhat by placing the motto on a ribbon and by showing the men, both in formal dress, in an awkward right-to-left handshake.

LOUISIANA

While the date of the earliest use of the pelican as a local symbol for Louisiana is not known for certain, the seal of the territory under Governor William C. C. Claiborne (1804-1816) pictures this local bird. In 1812 the Legislature authorized the Governor to procure and employ a seal, but no description is given of its design. There are also references in the early nineteenth century to a "Pelican Flag" for the State. In any event it is certain that a flag bearing a pelican was displayed in the hall of the Convention on 26 January 1861 when Louisiana adopted its Ordinance of Secession. A Pelican Flag was also removed from the State House in Baton Rouge when Admiral Farragut captured the city the next year.

The first official action regarding the pelican emblem came in 1902 when the State seal was officially described, thus eliminating the variations that had existed at different periods. Ten years later the present State flag (XXVII-c) was legalized on 1 July 1912. It shows the pelican in its traditional heraldic form, known as "a pelican in her piety," or "a pelican vulning herself." That is, the pelican's beak is tearing at her breast to feed her own young, the bird being considered a symbol of self-sacrifice. In the seal the motto "Union–Justice–Confidence" appears in a ring around the bird and within a ring reading "State of Louisiana." The 1966 Legislature designated the brown pelican as the official State bird.

Despite its long service as an emblem of the State, the pelican was rejected in 1861 by the committee appointed to design a national flag for Louisiana. Instead the committee, consisting of Messrs. Elgee, Roman, and Briscoe, took as their inspiration the flag of the United States. As in Texas and Florida a single star, the symbol of sovereignty, was substituted for the constellation of stars in the national flag (XXVII-b). In this case, however, the committee or perhaps their artist, C. A. De-Armas, while retaining the familiar stripes of red and white added stripes of blue. The symbolism created refers to the history of Louisiana: red, white, and blue are the colors of the flags of the United States and France, while red and yellow are the colors of Spain, all of which had once flown in the area. This flag was adopted on 11 February 1861 and after 23 March, when Louisiana joined the Confederacy, it was transformed into a State flag. Even after Farragut captured New Orleans in 1862, the flag continued to fly in the northern part of the State.

Another, unofficial Louisiana flag was the one hoisted on the revenue cutter *Robert McClelland* in January 1861. It consisted of the French tricolor (see p. 18) of blue, white, and red vertical stripes, with a circle of seven white stars on the blue. Despite Secretary of the Treasury Dix's famous telegraph ordering that "if any one attempts to haul down the American flag, shoot him on the spot," the *McClelland* was successfully seized by Louisiana and, as the *McRae,* served in the Confederate Navy.

MAINE

Until 1820 Maine was a district of Massachusetts and had no distinctive symbols of its own. In that year a seal was adopted for the new State, the same design without modification serving as a coat of arms. As the northernmost State at that time, Maine chose as a symbol the North Star. The motto "Dirigo" ("I Direct") indicates that sailors used to steer their way by the North Star. The central feature of the shield is a pine tree, at the foot of which rests a moose. The white pine, which often grows as high as two hundred feet, was used for ship masts in the eighteenth and nineteenth centuries and provided the State's most important source of income. The pine may also have been chosen because it had long been used as a State symbol in Massachusetts. This tree is now the official Maine State tree; its cone and tassel are the official State flower; and the nickname for Maine is "The Pine Tree State."

The recumbent moose is said to stand for the large areas of forest which still remain in their undisturbed natural condition. The supporters of the shield are a farmer, representing agriculture, and a sailor to symbolize commerce and fishing. The original idea for the arms is credited to Benjamin Vaughan, while Colonel Isaac Reed and his stepdaughter Bertha Smouse are supposed to have made the first artistic rendition. The version of the arms in common use today varies from the official pattern (XXVIII-b) in a number of details.

Before and during the Civil War military colors used by Maine troops were of one or another of two patterns: one was the familiar coat of arms on blue, while the other was made by using the first design as a canton for the national flag. The former, described in the standard military fashion (a flag of four feet four inches by five feet six inches mounted on a brass spearheaded nine-foot staff and bearing fringe, cords, and tassels), was adopted as the State flag (XXVIII-b) on 24

XXXV. EMBLEMS OF NEW HAMPSHIRE AND NEW JERSEY

a. **NEW HAMPSHIRE** Seal c5 September 1775–c12 September 1776
b. **NEW HAMPSHIRE** Government flag 1 January 1932–present
c. **NEW JERSEY** Government and general usage flag 26 March 1896–
     present

a.

b.

c.

February 1909 and is still used in this capacity. The National Guard color approved on this date was the same, but with two red scrolls added for appropriate inscriptions. In 1954 one of these scrolls was omitted. Maine also has had two other flags approved by the Legislature. Previous to the selection of the present Maine flag in 1909, a State flag of buff (XXVIII-a) bearing the pine tree and North Star was adopted on 21 March 1901. On 21 July 1939 Maine became the second State—Massachusetts being the other—to adopt a special "merchant and marine" flag (XXVIII-c). This law is still in effect, although the flag itself is rarely seen.

MARYLAND

The present state flag of Maryland embodies a long history, since the basis of its design is found in the coats of arms of the Calvert and Crossland families. Sir George Calvert, the first Lord Baltimore, received as a grant of arms in 1622 "Paly of six pieces, Or and Sable, a Bend counterchanged"—that is, a shield bearing six vertical stripes of gold and black crossed by a diagonal stripe of the same colors reversed. Sir George's grandfather, Leonard, had married Alicia Crossland who was the heiress of the Crosslands of Yorkshire. Perhaps because the Crossland arms ("Quarterly, Argent and Gules, a Cross flory counterchanged," i.e., a cross terminating in fleurs-de-lys on a field of red and white) were more ancient, the Calverts sometimes used a combination of the two coats of arms as in XXIX-c.

In 1632 Sir George Calvert was made Lord Proprietor of an American colony which included what is now the State of Maryland. His son, Leonard, was the person actually responsible for leading an expedition to the new territory. In 1638 we find Leonard writing his brother Cecilius, the second Lord Baltimore, that he had flown the banner of the Proprietor in battle. Subsequent accounts in 1655, 1741, 1750, and 1755 made it clear that the personal arms of the Lords Baltimore, apparently without the addition of the Crossland arms, served as the flag of the colony. Thus the flag of Maryland from its establishment until the adoption of a republican constitution in 1776, except for two periods when a Royal Governor was in control, must have been as shown in XXIX-b.

The seal of Lord Baltimore (XXIX-a) continued to be used by the Maryland government until 1794, when a less aristocratic device was substituted. In 1854 an attempt was made to revive the colonial arms, but a faulty model was copied and it was not until 1876 that the true seal of the old proprietary colony was restored. This bears on the obverse a fanciful picture of Lord Baltimore as a medieval knight with the inscription (in Latin), "Cecilius, Absolute Lord of Maryland and Avalon, Baron of Baltimore." (Avalon was a short-lived colony in Newfoundland sponsored by the Calverts.) The reverse has the full family coat of arms, including the motto (in Italian) "Deeds are masculine, words feminine," and an adaptation from Psalm 5: "As with a Shield You Will Crown Us by Your Good Will."

During the nineteenth century the military flags of Maryland were mostly blue with the State seal in the center. The old symbols were not forgotten, however; the cross of the Crosslands, for example, served as a regimental badge for Marylanders during the Civil War. By this time the original cross flory had become what is known heraldically as a cross botonée—a cross whose arms end in three balls. This form is still in use in both the seal and the flag and, since 1945, as a special finial for staffs from which the State flag is flown. After the late 1880's the old Calvert flag, sometimes with the Crossland arms added, was seen in use during celebrations. In 1901 the Governor began to use this flag (XXIX-c), and on 9 March 1904 it became the official State flag.

MASSACHUSETTS

When the Massachusetts Bay Colony was chartered, it received a seal which was used on all official documents from 1629 until 1684 when the charter was annulled. This seal (see p. 153) shows an Indian between two pine trees—symbols which have been representative of Massachusetts ever since that time. The motto "Come Over and Help Us" is a

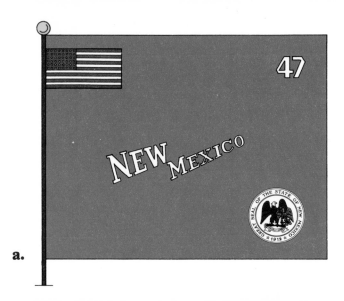

a.

b.

c.

MASSACHUSETTS BAY
Seal
4 March 1628/9–1684

paraphrase of Acts, 16:9. From 1684 until 1775 there were no official symbols distinctive of the colony, although the pine tree flag was a very popular unofficial emblem.

The seal (see p. 48) adopted by the government of 1775 indicated the sentiments of the citizens: an "Anglo-American" holds in one hand the Magna Carta, symbolic of the rights of Englishmen, and a sword in his other hand. The motto, including a part omitted, freely translates as "This Hand Opposed to Tyrants Searches, with a Sword, for Peaceful Conditions under Liberty" ("[Manus Haec, Inimica Tyrannis,] Ense Petit Placidam sub Libertate Quietem"). This line from a couplet written in the seventeenth century by Algernon Sidney was retained, with the arm and sword as a crest, in the arms chosen by the State in 1780. This new form, designed by Nathan Cushing, has been in use ever since; it was standardized in 1898 and in 1971. It appears on the State flag (XXX-b) and, with an encircling band reading "Sigillum Rei Publicae Massachusettensis" ("Seal of the Commonwealth of Massachusetts"), serves as the State seal. Its Indian derives from the seal of 1629, while the star indicates that Massachusetts is one of the United States.

XXXVI. FLAGS OF NEW MEXICO AND NEW YORK

a. **NEW MEXICO   19 March 1915–15 March 1925**

b. **NEW MEXICO   Government and general usage flag   15 March 1925–**
       present

c. **NEW YORK   8 April 1896–2 April 1901**

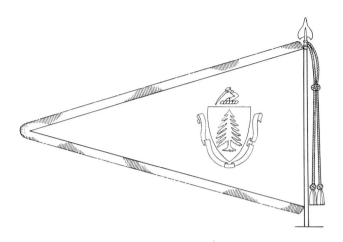

**MASSACHUSETTS Flag of the Governor (reverse) 18 June 1935–
31 October 1971 (unofficially in use earlier)**

Until 1971 the Commonwealth had the distinction of possessing the oldest official flag still used in the New World (XXX-a). This naval flag, adopted on 29 April 1776, was rarely flown after the Revolution until its use was revived in the 1960's. Its motto "Appeal to Heaven" (omitted since 1971) was a phrase frequently used by the rebellious colonists to indicate their conviction that God would vindicate their cause. It appears to have been borrowed from John Locke, a seventeenth-century philosopher who inspired much of the political propaganda of the American Revolution, including the Declaration of Independence. Earlier still, Massachusetts had an unofficial merchant flag (VI-a).

The military forces of the State have carried a white flag with the coat of arms on the obverse ever since ordered to do so in June 1787 by the Governor. The reverse of the flag usually bore the arm and sword crest, although sometimes other emblems were employed including the pine tree and liberty cap. On 18 March 1908 the General Court (legislature) transformed the military flag into a State flag for general usage. The obverse bore the arms, while the reverse was supposed to show a green pine tree on a blue shield (XXX-c). In practice a ribbon without any motto and the crest were usually added (as above). On 6 March 1915 the provisions were repealed which had required as accessories to the flag gold fringe, cords, and tassels and a gold spearhead on a pole "of white ash or of wood of a similar light color." Since the beginning of the twentieth century the Governor has made use, unofficially until 1971, of a personal standard (opposite). Its design is the same as that of the State flag, except that the field is triangular in shape.

MICHIGAN

On 29 April 1911 a law was passed by the State legislature fixing the design of the coat of arms and flag of Michigan. Following the example of many other States, Michigan approved a blue flag bearing its arms (XXXI-a) and defined the arms as being the seal of the State without its encircling inscriptions. Both of these emblems have a history stretching back into the first part of the nineteenth century.

The design of the seal is credited to General Lewis Cass, who was Territorial Governor of Michigan from 1813 to 1831. It was adopted on 2 June 1835 and has continued in use since then, with minor artistic modifications. The central figure on the shield raises his hand as a sign of peace, but carries a gun to show determination to protect the State, thus illustrating the motto above—"Tuebor" ("I Will Defend"). The motto at the bottom refers to the lower peninsula of Michigan (the upper peninsula was not added until 1837) on which the figure stands. This motto, "If You Seek a Pleasant Peninsula, Look Around You" ("Si Quæris Peninsulam Amœnam, Circumspice"), is obviously only a paraphrase of the tribute to architect Sir Christopher Wren inscribed on St. Paul's Cathedral, London, which he designed—"If You Seek His Monument, Look Around You." The elk and moose which serve as supporters of the shield are said to have been taken from the arms of the Hudson's Bay Company, which ruled vast areas of Canada at the time the arms were designed. The crest is a modified version of the coat of arms of the United States.

The first recorded Michigan flag is the regimental color which was presented to the Detroit military company known as the Brady Guards on 23 February 1837 by Michigan's first State Governor, Stevens T. Mason. The flag was blue with the State seal on the obverse supported by a Brady Guard and a woman. On the reverse was painted a portrait of

Mason, known as the "Boy Governor" because of his election to the office at the age of 23. Similar blue flags with the State seal were used by local troops until 1865 when the design was regularized. At the suggestion of Adjutant General John Robinson and with the approval of Governor Henry Crapo, the military color of Michigan was determined to be blue. The obverse was to display the coat of arms of the State and the reverse showed the coat of arms of the United States. The national arms were omitted in 1911 when the present law was adopted.

Michigan is one of several States whose flags are difficult to distinguish clearly because of the combination of a dark blue field and a coat of arms in dark colors. (This problem does not arise in the case of the flag which the Governor of Michigan uses in his office: this flag, adopted in 1915, displays the arms on a white field.) To correct this problem and give the State a more distinctive flag, Senator Harold M. Ryan introduced a bill in the legislature in 1962 which would have created a new design. The motion lost when it was discovered that the amended design incorporated the bow tie made famous as a campaign symbol by former Governor G. Mennen Williams. The proposer of the amendment had disguised his intentions by describing the tie in heraldic terms as "two vert lozenges conjoined, with roundlets argent."

MINNESOTA

The three States which have successively been the northernmost in the Union—Maine, Minnesota, and Alaska—have all used the North Star as a symbol. The top star in the first flag of Minnesota (XXXI-c) represented this North Star, which was also referred to in the French inscrip-

XXXVII. FLAGS OF NEW YORK AND NORTH CAROLINA

a. **NEW YORK** Government flag 2 April 1901–present Proportions 10 x 19

b. **NORTH CAROLINA** 22 June 1861–9 March 1885 Proportions 3 x 4

c. **NORTH CAROLINA** Government flag 9 March 1885–present Proportions 3 x 4

a.

b.

c.

tion ("L'Etoile du Nord") on the seal. The flag, adopted on 4 April 1893, bore eighteen other stars, the total number suggesting that Minnesota was the nineteenth State to join the Union after the original thirteen. This flag followed almost exactly the design of a military color that had been carried by State troops. The principal difference was that in the original standard the designation of the unit was inscribed in gold letters on the reverse, which was blue instead of white, while the State flag omitted this inscription and left the reverse plain blue. Mrs. Edward H. Center is credited with the design.

Over the years it was found that a flag with emblems spread across the field and with a distinctive reverse cost much more than most State flags. In order to make the State flag less expensive and therefore more available to citizens, a commission was created in 1955 by the legislature and given the responsibility of simplifying the design. Their recommendations were adopted on 19 March 1957. The front and back of the new flag (XXXI-b) are now the same, and the central emblem of the old flag is placed on a yellow-bordered white circle in the center of a blue field. The flag is decorated with gold fringe and its pole is surmounted by a spread eagle. The central emblem in both the old and new flags consists of the State seal surrounded by white moccasin flowers (*Cypripedium reginae*) on a blue border. The dates 1819, 1858, and 1893 refer respectively to the dates of the first settlement in Minnesota, its admission to the Union, and the adoption of the flag.

Minnesota has had three official seals. The first one was designed by a legislative committee in 1849 for the Territory of Minnesota, but was never engraved. Instead a pattern very similar to the present one, except that the figures faced the other way and the motto was different, came into use. After Minnesota became a State the Legislature adopted a new seal designed by Dr. R. O. Sweeny on 16 July 1858. When the cut was received from the engraver, however, it was discovered that the old pattern had been made—in mirror image—instead of the correct design. Later this pattern was officially adopted and continues to be employed today. The seal shows a farmer plowing, but with a musket and powder horn nearby. An Indian on horseback rides away from St. Anthony Falls and into the setting sun.

MISSISSIPPI
Seal
1817–present

MISSISSIPPI

When the United States concluded the Louisiana Purchase with France in 1803, it expected to receive the territory known as West Florida which included parts of the present States of Florida, Alabama, Mississippi, and Louisiana. Spain claimed, however, that she had never ceded this to France and refused to evacuate her troops. American settlers living in this area were prompted by this to revolt. In 1804 Reuben, Nathan, and Samuel Kemper and their faction hoisted a flag of rebellion consisting of seven blue and white stripes with two white stars on a red canton, a design probably inspired by the flag of the United States.

A more successful movement was that which broke out six years later. It was sponsored by a secret society which used a five-pointed star as a symbol of fellowship. When they succeeded in establishing the Republic of West Florida, a national flag (LXIV-a) was hoisted on 22 September 1810. Although it flew only until 4 December of that year when the United States occupied the territory, the flag itself appears to have made a lasting impression on the South. The same design, which came to be known as the Bonnie Blue Flag, was the basis for the first Texan national flag, and in the Civil War was frequently flown by Confederate Troops.

Mississippi was one of the States to recall this flag in its own. On 9 January 1861 when the State passed an Ordinance of Secession removing it from the Union, a large Bonnie Blue Flag (LXIV-a) was hoisted on the Capitol building. Then on the 26th of that month a national flag

a.

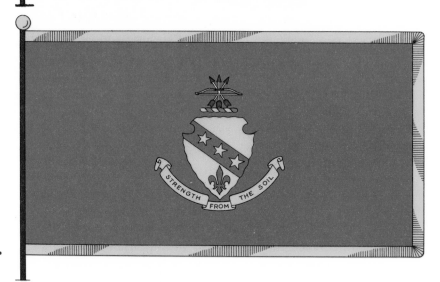

b.

c.

(XXXII-a) was adopted for the new republic, in which the white star on blue served as the canton. (The magnolia tree which appears in the center of the flag was selected in 1938 as the official State tree.) When Mississippi became one of the Confederate States the Magnolia Flag appears no longer to have been displayed.

On 7 February 1894 the Legislature approved the report of a committee which had been appointed to select an appropriate State flag for Mississippi. The design chosen (XXXII-b) by them is believed to be the idea of Senator E. N. Scudder. It combines the Stars and Bars of the Confederacy and its Battle Flag, although the committee report does not indicate this. The gilt staff and combined battle-axe and spear at the top were made part of the correct flag which became official when the committee report was accepted.

Mississippi has used as a seal a modified version of the arms of the United States ever since 1798 when it was a territory, except of course during the Civil War. The State coat of arms (XXXII-c) is based on the seal and was adopted at the same time as the State flag. Its motto means "By Virtue and Arms." The shield is wreathed with cotton, an important Mississippi crop, and the eagle holds a palm branch instead of the usual olive.

MISSOURI

When the first General Assembly of the new State convened in November 1821, Governor Alexander McNair brought to its attention the fact that Missouri would need a seal in order to carry on State business. The Assembly therefore appointed Representatives Chauncey Smith, James Alcorn, and Elias Elston as members of a committee which prepared a

XXXVIII. FLAGS OF NORTH DAKOTA AND OHIO

a. **NORTH DAKOTA** **General usage flag** **3 March 1911–present** **Proportions 26 x 33**

b. **NORTH DAKOTA** **Government flag** **15 March 1957–present** **Proportions 10 x 19**

c. **OHIO** **Government flag** **9 May 1902–present** **Proportions 8 x 13**

design the following month. On 11 January 1822 their recommendation received final approval and has remained the seal of Missouri ever since. During the Civil War period this emblem was painted on the flags carried by State troops.

The design of the seal consists of the coat of arms of Missouri surrounded by the name of the State. The law of 1822 described these arms in detail, although frequently the artistic renditions actually in use have varied from this legal requirement. The central part of the arms is a shield parted per pale, i.e., divided in half vertically. On the heraldic left* appear the arms of the United States on a white field; on the right are symbols which represent the State itself. The silvertip or grizzly bear which formerly lived in the area symbolizes strength and courage, while the two upright grizzlies supporting the arms suggest the loyalty of the people to both the State and Federal Governments. On the chief of the shield is a crescent, the heraldic sign indicating the second son, which Missouri displays as an indication that it was the second State carved from the Louisiana Purchase. The crest of the shield is a helmet of sovereignty below a cloud-framed blue sky bearing twenty-three stars. Another star, representative of Missouri joining the Union, ascends from a smaller cloud. At the bottom the design is completed by the date of the State constitution and the motto (in Latin), "Let the Welfare of the People Be the Supreme Law."

In the State flag (XXXIII-a) the twenty-four stars are repeated on a ring around the arms. Loyalty to the Union is suggested by the stripes of red, white, and blue. The arms in the center of the flag recall the central location of Missouri in the United States. This flag was designed by Mrs. Robert B. Oliver, a member of the Daughters of the American Revolution, and submitted in 1909 to the State legislature by her husband's cousin, Senator Arthur L. Oliver. A proposal submitted at the same time by Dr. G. H. Holcomb substituted the abbreviation "MO." and a ring of twenty-four stars for the stars in the national flag. Both these ideas were rejected by the legislature that year and again in 1911. Resubmitted, the Oliver proposal became the official State flag of Missouri on 22 March 1913.

* Left and right in heraldry are determined from the standpoint of the imaginary shield-bearer, not the viewer.

MONTANA

It has long been a tradition in the United States that local military groups, even ones serving in a major war far from home, be provided with locally made colors. Many examples of such flags still exist, one of them being the regimental flag of the First Montana Infantry, United States Volunteers, which is preserved in the Historical Society of Montana at Helena.

Originally the flag was a dark blue but it has now faded to a lighter shade. Embroidered in the center in generous proportions is a colored version of the State seal, minus the encircling inscription "The Great Seal of the State of Montana." Above the emblem is the designation in white lettering "1st Montana Infty U.S.V." The flag is attached to a jointed pole bearing a golden spread eagle at the top. Attached below is a long cord of silver with tassels of blue and white at each end. The top and bottom of the flag are decorated with gold fringe: if the fly end once bore fringe, it is now completely gone. The measurements of the flag are forty-seven and a half inches by fifty-eight and a half inches.

The colors were made in 1898 and carried by the Montana Volunteers in the Philippines during the Spanish-American War. Several years after its return to Montana, Representative Jacob M. Kennedy proposed to the Legislative Assembly that this flag be made the official flag of the State. His bill received final approval on 27 February 1905 and the flag (XXXIII-b), without the military inscription above the seal, has flown since that time.

The seal in the center was created by Representative Francis McGee Thompson, who presented it to the Legislative Assembly convoked in Bannack City in 1864. The then Territory accepted his pattern in early 1865, after correcting his faulty Spanish from "Oro el Plata" to "Oro y Plata" ("Gold and Silver," products of the State mining industry). Four years after Montana achieved Statehood, the word "Territory" in the encircling inscription was changed to "State."

The scene in the seal includes mountains suggestive of the State name, with a setting sun behind them; also the Great Falls of the Missouri River; and symbols of agriculture and mining—a plow, pick, and shovel. As in a number of other States, no consideration was given at the time of adoption of the State flag to the question of proper colors for the seal. In the absence of better indications, the colors employed in the original First Montana Infantry colors (reproduced here) would seem best.

NEBRASKA

When Nebraska became a State in 1867 its legislature made provision for a seal to be used on official documents. As was customary at that time, emblems were included to suggest the geographical position of the State and the livelihood of its citizens. The official description of the seal is as follows: "The eastern part of the circle to be represented by a steamboat ascending the Missouri river; the mechanic arts to be represented by a smith with hammer and anvil; in the foreground, agriculture to be represented by a settler's cabin, sheaves of wheat and stalks of growing corn; in the background a train of cars heading towards the Rocky Mountains, and on the extreme west, the Rocky Mountains to be plainly in view . . ." Despite occasional attempts to alter the design, this has been the State seal since that time. The motto "Equality Before the Law" may refer to the struggle for civil rights which was being carried on at the time of the adoption of the seal. Isaac Wiles, the designer of the seal, insisted however that the motto related to the right of each individual to a portion of public land in the frontier territory.

During the First World War various women's groups sewed flags which were presented to Nebraska troops, many of which were yellow with the State seal in the center. This flag had no official standing, although it was published in a widely read flag book of the era. After the war the local Daughters of the American Revolution organization encouraged the adoption of an official flag. Representative George A. Wil-

XXXIX. FLAGS OF OHIO AND OKLAHOMA
a. **OHIO   Governor's flag (de facto pattern)   3 October 1945–15 December 1967 (unofficial from 1905)   Proportions 40 x 63**
b. **OKLAHOMA   Governor's flag   1 December 1957–present (unofficial)**
c. **CHOCTAW INDIANS   c1861–c1864   (unofficial; reconstructed)**

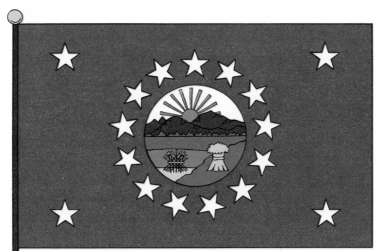

a.

b.

c.

liams introduced a bill into the legislature which provided for a new State seal. The "emblem and motto" of this seal were to appear in gold and silver on a field of national blue, as a State flag. In the upper field was to appear a representation of goldenrod, the State flower. The Legislature did not approve this bill.

Several years later Mrs. B. G. Miller of Crete, Nebraska, led another movement for the creation of a State flag. Her design was similar to the one first proposed to the legislature, but omitted the goldenrod and did not call for a new seal. This campaign was successfully terminated with the approval of the flag (XXXIII-c) on 2 April 1925. Six years later Mrs. Miller wrote "The Flag Song of Nebraska," with music by George H. Aller. In 1963 the flag was readopted and a provision made for its display over the Capitol at all times, as well as "on such occasions, at such times, and under such conditions as the flag of the United States."

NEVADA

During the Civil War the Union government was concerned to protect its territory in the Far West and to replenish its low reserves of gold and silver. These factors were influential in the admission of Nevada to statehood in 1864. Since that time the State symbols have recalled its wartime role in a number of ways. Almost forgotten is the first official Nevada flag (XXXIV-a), drawn by Governor John Sparks and Colonel Harry Day and sanctioned by the legislature on 25 February 1905. Here the gold and silver produced by the mining industry of the State are very explicitly symbolized by the inscriptions and coloring of the flag.

The first emblem of Nevada was the seal adopted on 24 February 1866. In addition to the usual emblems of agriculture and industry, the seal bears the motto "All for Our Country" and thirty-six stars, indicating Nevada's rank as the thirty-sixth State to join the Union. This seal, modified artistically better to fit a rectangular background, was the principal emblem in the second State flag (XXXIV-b), adopted on 22 March 1915. Miss Clara Crisler, a historian, was the designer of this flag. As has been the case in a number of States, it was found that a flag with a seal is too complicated to manufacture inexpensively and very few copies were ever made. Consequently, except in the office of the Governor or on the battleship *Nevada,* the flag was rarely seen.

In 1926 Lieutenant Governor Maurice J. Sullivan offered a prize of $25 for the best design for a new flag. Louis (Don) Shellback III submitted the winning pattern (XXXIV-c). It included the State flower—in the form of a wreath of sagebrush—a star of silver, and a motto referring to Nevada's admission to statehood during the Civil War. C. C. Doak suggested the addition of the name of the State, and the modified flag was adopted on 26 March 1929. The word "Nevada" is usually shown in golden yellow, although the law does not specify the correct color.

In 1953 a new flag was approved by the legislature, but vetoed by the Governor, whose veto was confirmed in 1955 by the legislature itself. The flag consisted of three equal vertical stripes with the State silhouetted on the center stripe in red. It also bore the name of the State and the words "Battle Born." The stripes were dark blue, white, and silver-gray, a color almost unknown in flags.

NEW HAMPSHIRE
State emblem
3 May 1945–present

NEW HAMPSHIRE

As in other royal colonies, New Hampshire sealed its documents before the Revolution with an emblem consisting of the coat of arms of the reigning British monarch, surrounded by a special inscription in Latin. The inscription in this case read (in English) "The Seal of Our Province of New Hampshire in America." A new seal became necessary when the royal government was overthrown, and New Hampshire was one of the first States to create its own seal. Although no legislative enactment can be found for it, this seal (XXXV-a) was used as early as September 1775. A year later another seal was cut, which differed only in the change in inscription from "Colony" to "Commonwealth." The motto included in the margin is "Vis Unita Fortior"—"Strength United is Stronger"—a concept emphasized by the bundle of arrows in the center of the design. On either side are the principal products of the State at the time, a codfish and the New England pine tree.

In 1784 a new seal design was created which, with minor artistic modifications, has been in use ever since. The principal changes were made in 1931 when an official pattern, including a scale drawing, was adopted by the General Court (the State legislature). At this time the date "1784" which had been included in the seal without authorization was amended to "1776." Although the law is silent about the name of the boat shown in the stocks, it is commonly assumed to be the *Raleigh,* built in Portsmouth, New Hampshire, in 1776. If this is true the flag she flies is incorrect, since it is of the pattern adopted by Congress a year later, in June of 1777. In addition to a seal, New Hampshire has a "State emblem" (see p. 167) bearing the Old Man of the Mountains, a natural granite formation made famous by Nathaniel Hawthorne's short story.

The first provision for a New Hampshire flag was made on 28 December 1792 when it was required by the General Court that each regiment should have the national flag and a State color displaying the arms of the State. Similar laws were made in the nineteenth century, although the flags were used solely for military purposes. It was not until 24 February 1909 that a State flag for general usage was approved. It was of blue with the State seal "in suitable proportion and colors" in the center, surrounded by a wreath of laurel with nine stars interspersed. The date 1784 was officially incorporated into the design. The present flag (XXXV-b) became official on 1 January 1932 when the seal was modified.

XL. FLAGS OF OKLAHOMA
a. **OKLAHOMA** Government flag 2 March 1911–2 April 1925
b. **OKLAHOMA** Government flag 2 April 1925–9 May 1941
c. **OKLAHOMA** Government flag 9 May 1941–present

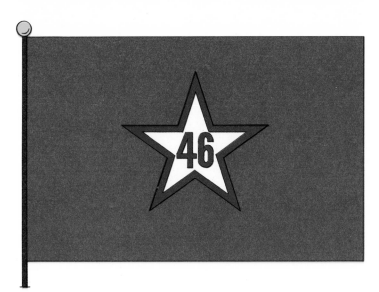

a.

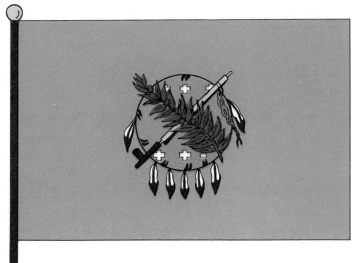

b.

c.

In 1944 a study was made by the Adjutant General of New Hampshire, as the result of which certain proposals were made the following year to the General Court. Since the State flag was legally restricted to use by the Governor, the General Court, and military units, it was suggested that a simpler flag might be created for general purposes. This was to be blue with the gold ship shown in the seal. A Governor's flag was also proposed, but the measure was never adopted and thus New Hampshire continues with a single flag. By an Executive Order dated 7 August 1956, however, the right to fly the State flag was, by implication, extended to private citizens.

It should be mentioned that a semi-independent Indian Stream Republic existed along the border between New Hampshire and Quebec from 1832 to 1836. Unfortunately, nothing is known at present about the flag or seal, if any, used by this state.

NEW JERSEY

Before the American Revolution New Jersey had many seals, both royal and proprietary. In 1776 the new government ordered that the seal of William Livingston be the State seal until a new design could be cut. It placed the responsibility for this work in the hands of Francis Hopkinson, who in turn called Eugène Du Simitière. Du Simitière was an artist who worked on the seals of the United States and of a number of individual States. Despite a legislative description of the seal, Du Simitière added a number of details. No objection was raised, however, and the seal began to be used in 1777.

The horse's head in the crest appeared on the early coins of New Jersey. The three plows in the shield symbolize agriculture while Ceres, the Goddess of Agriculture, serves as one of the supporters. The other supporter is the figure of Liberty, who bears a pole surmounted by a liberty cap. This symbol was frequently shown in engravings, seals, medals, flags, and other items during the American and French Revolutions. It derives from the ancient Phrygians, who gave such a cap to freed slaves so that they might be readily identified. The earl's helmet beneath the crest—one of Du Simitière's innovations—is used in coats of arms as a symbol of sovereignty. In 1928 the exact details of the seal, including its colors, were specified by law to guarantee a standard form.

The earliest State flag of which there seems to be reference was in use, perhaps unofficially, after the Civil War. Preble's classic book on American flags described it in this fashion: "The State flag has thirteen horizontal stripes, alternating red and white, in the centre a blue square or shield, on which is the coat of arms of the State." This may have been a military color, as it was common in that era to substitute the State or national coat of arms for the stars in the United States flag. The present State flag (XXXV-c) bears the coat of arms, i.e., the seal without its encircling inscriptions, on a field of buff. Since the law of 26 March 1896 which created the New Jersey flag designated it as the "headquarters flag for the governor as commander in chief," there was some doubt about the possibility of using it elsewhere. A law passed in 1938 made it clear that display of the flag was not limited to the Governor.

Representative Hopkins in offering the original bill creating the flag gave some historical background. The buff, he explained, was the proper color for the State military flag according to the order of 28 February 1780, which specified that the field of a regimental color should correspond to the color of the uniform facings worn in the State. And General Washington himself had decided that the New Jersey uniform should be blue, faced with buff, in his directive of 2 October 1779. While it is true that Washington designated the colors blue and buff for New Jersey and New York and that both these States were settled by the Dutch, there is no proof that Hopkins was correct in assuming that the choice was made because blue and buff were derived from the Dutch colors. In fact the Dutch flag did not contain buff: it was *orange,* white, and blue (see p. 19). Blue and white also appear in the New Jersey Public Service pennant.

a.

b.

c.

NEW MEXICO
Seal
15 March 1913–
present

NEW MEXICO

As a general rule it is true that the flags of provinces and states of a nation are more distinctive when the states have real powers and are more uniform in design when the central government has great political authority. Thus the flags of the Länder of Germany or of the states of Malaysia are very different from one another, each expressing the history of the area and its local autonomy. In the Soviet Union the differences between the flags of different states are slight. Because state power has always been very strong in the United States, the flags have reflected State rather than national symbols. It is not surprising, therefore, to find that the first flag of New Mexico (XXXVI-a) is one of the very few State flags ever adopted which incorporates the Stars and Stripes in its design. The United States flag included here is the one with forty-eight stars, the correct number at the time New Mexico adopted the pattern on 19 March 1915. Three years earlier New Mexico and Arizona had become

XLI. FLAGS OF OREGON AND PENNSYLVANIA

a.   **OREGON (obverse)**   **Government and general usage flag**   **26 February 1925–present (specifications from 20 January 1966)**   **Proportions 500 x 833**

b.   **OREGON (reverse of flag a)**   **Proportions 500 x 833**

c.   **PENNSYLVANIA**   **Government flag**   **13 June 1907–present**   **Proportions 27 x 37**

the forty-seventh and forty-eighth States, as the figures in the upper right-hand corner of the New Mexican flag indicate.

In the lower right-hand corner of this flag, which was designed by Colonel Ralph E. Twitchell, appeared the seal of the State (see p. 173). Although it had been used as early as 1860, the seal was not made official until 1 February 1887. After New Mexico ceased to be a Territory the seal was readopted on 15 March 1913 with an appropriate change in the inscription. The seal bears two eagles: the larger one is an American bald eagle with the arrows of war, while the smaller one is the Mexican eagle with its snake and cactus (see p. 25). The two together symbolize the transition of sovereignty over New Mexico which occurred in 1846. The motto "Crescit Eundo" means "It Grows as It Goes."

On 15 March 1925 a new State flag, sponsored by the Daughters of the American Revolution, was adopted. The designer was Dr. Harry Mera, a physician and archeologist. The central feature of this flag (XXXVI-b) is the ancient Sun symbol of the Zia Indian Pueblo. The Capitol of the State is built in the shape of this Sun and it is used elsewhere as an emblem of New Mexico. The colors of gold and red are derived from the banners of Spain (see p. 15) which flew in the area from the early 1500's until 1821. In 1963 the Legislature adopted the following official pledge to the flag: "I salute the flag of the state of New Mexico, the Zia symbol of perfect friendship among united cultures."

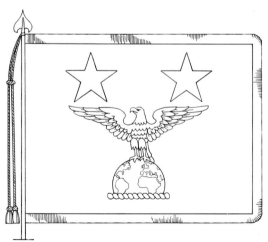

NEW YORK Color of the Chief of Staff (Adjutant-General of New York) 1954–present Proportions 26 x 33

NEW YORK

During the Revolutionary War the Third New York Regiment had a blue flag with the arms of the State in the center. This flag, flown at Yorktown according to tradition, is one of the few colors from the Revolution still in existence. It dates from 1778 or 1779, i.e., just after the creation of the State arms in 1777. Since then the same flag, often with inscriptions, has been used by the armed forces of the State. New York is unlike most States, however, in that it very early adopted a State flag for general use in addition to its military banners. The first reference we have to such a flag dates from 1858, although this flag appears to have been in use before then. It was specified by the *General regulations for the military forces of the State of New York* to be "of white bunting, twelve feet fly by ten feet hoist, bearing in the center the arms of the State." No legislative sanction for this flag is known.

Major Asa B. Gardiner was instrumental in obtaining approval for a new flag on 8 April 1896. This flag (XXXVI-c) differed from the old one in having a field of buff, the color of the facings on New York uniforms during the Revolution. The buff field was contrary to the custom of the time, however, and on 2 April 1901 the present flag with its field of blue (XXXVII-a) was approved. The Governor has flown the same design since about 1900, but adds a white star in each corner to symbolize his rank as Commander in Chief of the State military forces. His Chief of Staff, the Adjutant General, has a color (opposite) bearing the crest from the New York coat of arms and two stars to designate his rank as a Major General. When the Chief of Staff is in the Army the field of this flag is red; if he is a Navy or Air Force man, the color is dark or light blue, respectively.

The crest which appears on this flag and in the arms of the State shows the New World on a globe surmounted by an American eagle. The arms themselves varied frequently in artistic interpretation from 1777 until given an official pattern in 1882. Two explanations, possibly both correct, are given for the rising-sun emblem. One tradition suggests that it derives from the arms of Jonas Bronck, seventeenth-century Danish settler. (His farm, "the Bronck's land," is now called simply the Bronx.) Another tradition asserts that the sun is employed because it was the badge of the Dukes of York who were given control of the area now known as New York in 1664. The motto "Excelsior" means "Higher" or "Loftier." The supporters are Liberty, who holds a liberty cap and brushes aside a royal crown with her foot, and Justice with her customary sword and scales.

When the Dutch were in possession of New York, their colony of New Netherland had a seal bearing a beaver and a ring of wampum. The beaver as a symbol of the natural riches of the area also was part of the coats of arms adopted later by the cities of New York (LXI-b) and Albany. There is no conclusive evidence, however, that the State of New York ever used a white flag with a black beaver, as has been asserted in some books.

NORTH CAROLINA
Seal
21 February 1893–present

NORTH CAROLINA

In the seventeenth century when it was a proprietary colony, Carolina had a seal bearing a coat of arms. In addition to the Indians which were common elsewhere as supporters in colonial arms, and a stag for a crest, the arms bore two crossed cornucopias—presumably as a sign of the great wealth that was expected from the territory. When North Carolina became a royal colony the obverse of its seal took on the traditional

XLII. FLAGS AND ARMS OF PUERTO RICO

a. **PUERTO RICO** Coat of arms 8 November 1511–25 December 1901; 1 July 1905–present (reconstruction in use since 1958)

b. **PUERTO RICO** Government and general usage flag 24 July 1952–present (unofficial from 22 December 1895)

c. **PUERTO RICO** Grito de Lares flag 23 September 1868 (unofficial) Proportions 9 x 13

a.

b.

c.

form, the royal arms surrounded by a motto referring to the colony. The reverse, however, again included the cornucopia; this time it was a single one being presented to a seated King George by the allegorical figure of Plenty. Liberty, with a liberty cap on her staff, stands behind the royal throne and the whole scene is set against a map of the area showing a ship in the Atlantic.

The royal seals just described were in use from 1730 until 1776, but the figures have continued in all the seals used by the State since that time. The first republican seal, for example, shows Liberty on the obverse holding the Constitution, and Plenty on the reverse with an ear of corn. In 1794 the next seal again placed both women on the obverse of the seal and restored Plenty's cornucopia, although the Constitution held by Liberty is retained. The present seal (see p. 176) was adopted in 1893 and revised in 1971. It adds the State motto "Esse Quam Videri" ("To Be Rather Than Seem to Be") and the date of the Mecklenburg Declaration of Independence, 20 May 1775.

The same date has also appeared on both official State flags (XXXVII-b and XXXVII-c). The significance of the date is that it represents what is reputed to be the first outright affirmation by American colonists that they wished to reject the authority of Britain completely. It has not yet been conclusively proven, however, that the citizens of the town of Mecklenburg did in fact assert their independence in 1775 as claimed. The other dates on the two flags are also related to proclamations of independence. The date 12 April 1776 refers to the Halifax Resolves, adopted by the Provincial Congress assembled at Halifax, which provided that representatives from the State "be empowered to concur with the delegates of the other Colonies in declaring Independency." The date 20 May 1861 marks the secession of North Carolina from the Union.

During the brief period in which North Carolina was independent before joining the Confederacy, it did not fly an official flag although a legislative committee was working on a design. Their choice (XXXVII-b), prepared by William G. Browne, was adopted on 22 June 1861. It was used during and after the Civil War, although probably after 1865 the lower date was omitted. In 1885 General Johnstone Jones introduced a measure into the General Assembly of the State which was ratified on 9 March. It provided for a new flag (XXXVII-c) which differed from the old only in certain details. This has been flown ever since. There are also unsure references to pre-Civil War flags in North Carolina, including the usual blue military flag bearing the State seal.

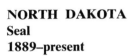

NORTH DAKOTA
Seal
1889–present

NORTH DAKOTA

The regimental color for United States infantry forces has been altered slightly a number of times. One pattern, which was official from 1890 until 1904 forms the basis for the present State flag of North Dakota (XXXVIII-a). The first display of this flag as a regimental color for the Dakota Territorial Guard is uncertain, but it is recorded as early as 1887. After North Dakota joined the Union in 1889, its National Guard continued to use a similar design with the inscription "First North Dakota Infantry" below the eagle. As such it was carried by State troops in the Philippines during the campaign there in 1898-1899. The battalion commander of this group, Major (later Colonel) John H. Fraine, was the individual who promoted adoption of the colors as an official State flag. As a Representative in the legislature, he secured the adoption of House Bill No. 152 which went into effect on 3 March 1911. Later it was discovered that there were two errors in the wording of the law: instead of a border of fringe around the flag the law allowed a border *or* fringe; and the eagle was said to have the arrows in his right foot instead of the olive branch. These points contradicted the legal requirement that "the flag shall conform in all respects as to color, form, size, and device with the regimental flag carried by the First North Dakota Infantry . . .

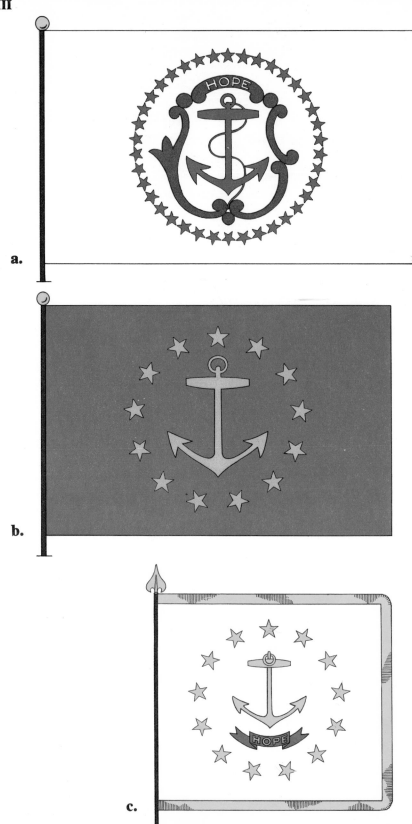

a.

b.

c.

except in the words shown on the scroll below the eagle," so in 1943 the law was corrected.

In the late 1950's the National Guard of North Dakota became concerned about the propriety of displaying as a State flag a design so similar to a regulation Army color. Therefore a design for a State coat of arms was proposed and accepted on 15 March 1957 by the legislature with provision for its use on a flag (XXXVIII-b). The arms are composed of distinctive North Dakota symbols. The colors green and yellow and the motto are indicative of the State's agriculture and livestock. The shield is in the shape of a Sioux arrowhead: the original inhabitants of the area are represented as well by the bow and arrows in the crest. On the shield are three stars denoting the executive, legislative, and judicial branches of the government, and the three nations which have ruled the area. Three stars also were found in the coats of arms of two early explorers of the area, Lord Selkirk and Meriwether Lewis. The first known European to visit what is now North Dakota was Pierre Gaultier de Varennes, Sieur de la Vérendrye, who came in 1738. The fleur-de-lys alludes to him.

The coat of arms has not replaced the State seal (see p. 179), which was adopted in 1889 on the basis of the old Dakota Territory seal. This seal, used on official documents, includes the bow and arrows later found in the coat of arms. The new coat of arms, displayed on a flag of green, is employed by the government of North Dakota, including its schools and National Guard, and by veterans' and patriotic organizations. The Governor uses the same flag with a white star in each corner.

XLIII. FLAGS OF RHODE ISLAND

a. **RHODE ISLAND   30 March 1877–1 February 1882**
b. **RHODE ISLAND   1 February 1882–19 May 1897**
c. **RHODE ISLAND   19 May 1897–present   Proportions 29 x 33**

OHIO

From 1862 until 1885 the cavalry guidon used by the United States Army (X-c) followed the national flag as its basic design, but with a deep triangle cut into the fly and the stars made of gilt rather than white. This banner saw extensive service during the Civil War and the subsequent battles with Indians in the West. (General Custer, for example, flew this guidon at his famous "last stand.") It is not surprising, therefore, that the design should be familiar to many people.

From his description, it seems apparent that the flag of Ohio (XXXVIII-c) designed by John Eisenmann was inspired by this cavalry guidon, although the guidon had been out of use for sixteen years at the time. There are notable differences in the two flags, however, and probably Eisenmann only wished to suggest the loyalty of Ohio to the Union. He patented his design in 1901; the General Assembly (State legislature) adopted the flag officially on 9 May 1902. At that time Eisenmann signed over his patent on the design.

The originator explained the inspiration of his flag as follows: "The triangles formed by the main lines of the flag represent the hills and valleys as typified in the State Seal, and the stripes [represent] the roads and waterways. The stars, indicating the thirteen original states of the Union, are grouped about the circle which represents the Northwest Territory; and that Ohio was the seventeenth state admitted into the Union is shown by adding four more stars. The white circle with its red center, not only represents the initial letter of Ohio, but is suggestive of its being 'the Buckeye State.' " (The buckeye was made the official State tree in 1953.) The flag of Ohio first received public attention when it flew over the Ohio Building at the Pan-American Exposition in 1901 at Buffalo, New York. President McKinley saw it there just before his assassination at that Exposition. The bill to legalize the design was submitted by the Speaker of the Ohio House, William S. McKinnon, who had been a member of the commission which organized the Pan-American Exposition.

The State seal was adopted in 1803, abolished in 1805, readopted in 1868, and modified to its present form in 1967. Between 1805 and 1866 there was no official seal. The current design represents the sun rising over Mount Logan and the Scioto River. The order of admission of Ohio into the Union is suggested by the seventeen arrows in the foreground and the seventeen rays of the sun. The same design without the encircling inscription "The Great Seal of the State of Ohio" serves as the coat of arms of the State.

In 1905 Adjutant General A. B. Critchfield created a flag for the Governor. This was used unofficially until 1945 when it was formally established by the then Adjutant General, D. F. Pancoast. The General Assembly in 1963 ordered four flags of different proportions and dimensions for use by the Governor in his office, on military review, on his automobile, and on a boat. The design shown here (XXXIX-a) is the one displayed in the Governor's office. In practice the Governor's flag usually bears the coat of arms instead of the seal, as required by law.

OKLAHOMA

In 1905 the leaders of the five Indian republics existing in what is now eastern Oklahoma called a convention at Muskogee. A constitution was drawn up and ratified in an election, and a petition was sent to Congress asking that the Indian Territory be admitted to the Union. The name of the new State was to be Sequoyah, in honor of the Cherokee scholar who had invented the syllabary which allowed his people to put their language into written form for the first time. Dr. A. Grant Evans proposed as a seal for the State a circle bearing forty-five small stars arranged around one large one. The large star was divided into five parts, each bearing one of the seals used by the Indian governments then existing (see pp. 254-263). Sequoyah himself appeared as the crest.

The federal government rejected Sequoyah's application for Statehood, however, forcing it to merge with Oklahoma Territory. The proposed seal then became the basis for the design of the Oklahoma State seal adopted in 1907. Added in the center was the old Oklahoma Territory seal, with the following devices: the Latin motto "Labor Conquers All"; a pioneer farmer and Indian shaking hands beneath scales held by the figure of Liberty dressed in stars and stripes; and scenes on either side depicting, in the words of the law which legalized the seal in 1893, "the peaceful conquests of the Anglo-Saxon and the decadence of the red race." Sequoyah was omitted from the design.

This seal is still in use. It appears in the flag of the Governor (XXXIX-b) which was designed by Ralph Hudson, the State Librarian. This flag was first used in 1957, the year of the State's semicentennial, but has not yet been officially adopted. Since none of the older seals had colors, the seal pattern shown in the Governor's flag is unofficial in this respect. The dark green and white, on the other hand, were made the State colors by a legislative enactment in 1915. The five stars stand for the former Indian nations and for the military rank of the Governor— improperly, since he is only entitled to four stars.

The first flag of Oklahoma (XL-a) was proposed by Senator Tom F. McMechan and Representative John H. Wright and approved by the legislature on 2 March 1911. The number "46" corresponds to the order of Oklahoma's admission to Statehood. After World War I objections were made to the red field and star because of their association with Communism, and in 1924 the Daughters of the American Revolution sponsored a contest to create a new flag. Mrs. Louise Funk Fluke sub- mitted the design (XL-b) which received legislative approval on 2 April 1925. She had based her idea on suggestions made by Dr. Joseph Thoburn of the Oklahoma Historical Society in Oklahoma City. The blue field came from an old Choctaw flag (see XXXIX-c and p. 256) and the shield was patterned after an Osage bison-hide shield, both of these artifacts being preserved in the Museum of the Society. Dr. Tho- burn gave this explanation of the symbolism: "The blue field signifies loyalty and devotion; the shield implies defensive or protective warfare when justifiable; the small crosses on the shield are the Indians' graphic sign for stars and may indicate lofty ideals or a purpose for high en- deavor; the shield thus surmounted by, but always subservient to, the

XLIV. FLAGS OF RHODE ISLAND AND THE RYUKYU ISLANDS

a. **RHODE ISLAND   Governor's flag   21 March 1931–present**

b. **LIUCHIU (KINGDOM)   (arms-banner of the Sho dynasty)   ?–1879**

c. **JAPAN   Ensign   1879–1945 (in the Ryukyus)   Proportions 2 x 3**

a.

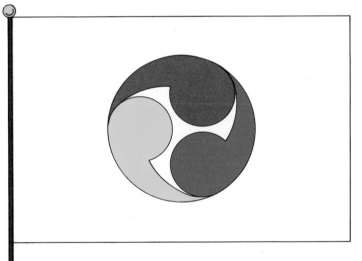

b.

c.

calumet and the olive branch, betoken[s] a predominant love of peace by a united people." The present flag (XL-c) was adopted on 9 May 1941.

OREGON

The military regulations of the State at the turn of the century specified that "the regimental or state flag shall be blue silk, with the arms of the state embroidered or painted in the center with the number and arm of service of the regiment in a scroll underneath." In accordance with traditional practices, the flag was four feet four inches wide by five feet six inches long. It was mounted on a pole ten feet long with a spearhead at its top. The flag was fringed with yellow and had cords and tassels of blue and white.

Such a flag was not suitable for general, nonmilitary usage. By 1925 the number of occasions for such display prompted various organizations to urge the adoption of a State flag. As in Alaska, a flag was needed in particular to complete the display of State flags in the Post Office Building in Washington, D. C. A measure to create an Oregon flag introduced by Senators Milton R. Klepper and J. O. Bailey in the Legislature became law on 26 February 1925. Two flags were made up, one being sent to the Post Office, the other presented to the Governor. The latter copy was loaned out to the sesquicentennial celebrations held in Lexington (Mass.) to honor the first battle in the Revolutionary War. Ten years later this flag and the old military colors of the State were lost when the Capitol building burned. Gradually, greater interest developed in the Oregon flag and many more flags were made. In 1953 a law was passed requiring it to be flown over schools and other public buildings.

The law adopted in 1925 had described the State flag as being navy blue with "the state escutcheon in gold, supported by thirty-three stars and bearing above said escutcheon the words 'State of Oregon' in gold and below such escutcheon the figures '1859' in gold." In order to give greater clarity to this design, specifications were issued in 1962, and in 1966 in amended form, by the Procurement Section of the State Department of Finance and Administration. The patterns shown in XLI-a and XLI-b correspond to the 1966 specifications. Since 1971 Oregon has had the distinction of being the only State to have a different design on the reverse of its State flag. The beaver, important in the early commerce of the Oregon Territory, appears in the official State colors of blue and gold.

The seal of Oregon, adopted in 1859 and reaffirmed in 1903, shows characteristics of the area—an elk, trees, mountains, and the Pacific Ocean—as well as emblems of agriculture (a sheaf and plow), mining (a pickaxe), and the frontier (a covered wagon). On the ocean an American steamer arrives as a British man-of-war leaves. The State motto, "The Union," is emblazoned across the center and the American eagle appears as a crest. The thirty-three stars recall that Oregon was the thirty-third State.

PENNSYLVANIA
Seal (reverse)
1 July 1809–present
(authorized 1776)

PENNSYLVANIA

Under the proprietorship of William Penn, the State that bears his name employed a double-faced seal. The obverse had Penn's shield (three white balls on a black horizontal stripe across a white shield), while the reverse had ears of corn and grape vines with the motto "Truth, Peace, Love and Plenty." In 1776 the independence of the State from Britain led the Constitutional Convention to establish a committee empowered to create a new seal. From examples of various documents and local currency, it is evident that their design was ready by early 1777, although it did not receive legislative sanction until 1791. A full description of the arms was still further delayed until 1809 when one was enacted into law by the General Assembly. Subsequently, different artistic interpretations were current until 1875 when the present form was standardized.

The full arms as they appear on the State flag (XLI-c) include draft horses standing on gold scrollwork and the motto "Virtue, Liberty and Independence." These accessories are omitted in the seal, which has only the shield, crest, and wreath of corn and olive, all within a band carrying the name of the State. The reverse of the seal (see p. 187) has a lion, the symbol of tyranny, being subdued by the figure of Liberty who holds a liberty cap. Such devices with allegorical motifs were common in the seals adopted by the States at the time of the Revolution. In contrast the arms on the front of the seal correspond to traditional heraldic forms. The ship and wheat sheaves probably derive from the 1701 seal of Philadelphia, and the plow served as the crest for the Chester County coat of arms under Penn's administration.

The legislature of the Commonwealth first established flags in its enactment of 9 April 1799. This provided that two colors should be provided to every regiment of the Commonwealth's militia. One of these showed the shield of Pennsylvania on the breast of an American eagle, the unit designation being given within a circle of stars in the upper canton. The other color was composed of thirteen horizontal stripes of red and white with the design of the first color serving as a canton. Such flags were in use until the time of the Civil War.

A State flag (XLI-c) for nonmilitary purposes was approved by the legislature on 13 June 1907. In specifications issued in 1964 by the Bureau of Standards, State Department of Property and Supplies, the precise colors and manufacturing procedures for the flag were carefully

XLV. FLAGS OF THE RYUKYU ISLANDS

a.   **RYUKYU ISLANDS   "Maritime ensign"   Merchant flag   June 1950–1 July 1967   Proportions 76 x 91**

b.   **RYUKYU ISLANDS   "Maritime ensign"   Merchant flag   1 July 1967–15 May 1972   Proportions 7 x 20; 7 x 10**

c.   **RYUKYU ISLANDS   High Commissioner's color   14 April 1959–15 May 1972   Proportions 26 x 33**

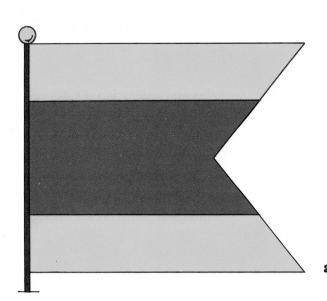

a.

RYUKYUS

b.

c.

defined. However, nothing has been done to correct the problem of visibility which arises from the positioning of the black horses on a dark blue field. No legal description exists at all for the standard of the Governor, which is like the State flag except that the field is white instead of blue.

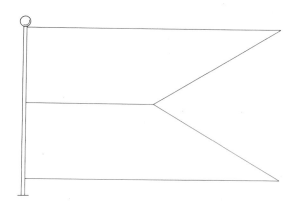

SAN JUAN (P.R.) Port of registry distinguishing flag (unofficial Puerto Rican general usage flag on land) ?–1898   Proportions 160 x 267

PUERTO RICO

Act No. 1, adopted on 24 July 1952—the day Puerto Rico gained a limited degree of autonomy as a "Commonwealth" associated with the United States—made official the traditional flag of that island (XLII-b). So important is this symbol to the people, the Constitution of Puerto Rico provides that no change in the flag's design shall go into effect until one year after its adoption. Yet only twenty years' before, the same flag had provoked riots when flown by Puerto Rican nationalists protesting American rule. The first time the flag was displayed in public, on 22 December 1895 in New York, it represented only the Puerto Rican Section of the Revolutionary Party of Cuba. Since the two islands were working closely to overthrow Spanish rule, it is not surprising that the Puerto Rican flag had the same form as the Cuban flag except that the colors were reversed. The flag of Puerto Rico was probably designed by Manuel de Besosa and sewn by his daughter Mima. It has also been

PUERTO RICO
Coat of arms
25 December 1901–1 July 1905

claimed, however, that Antonio Vélez Alvarado created the pattern and that Micaela Dalmau de Carreras made the first flag.

There is no dispute, however, about the origin of an earlier Puerto Rican flag. This revolutionary banner (XLII-c) was sewn by Mariana Braceti after a design by Ramón Emeterio Betances. It was flown on 23 September 1868 during the *Grito de Lares,* an unsuccessful revolt

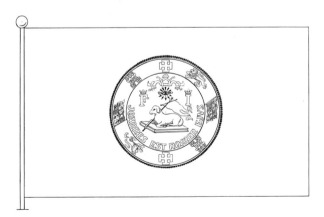

PUERTO RICO Governor's flag ?–c1948

a.

b.

c.

against Spanish rule. The original flag is preserved in the University of Puerto Rico museum at Rio Piedras and shows a pale yellow star, even though most history books speak of it as being white. This flag was inspired by the flag of the Dominican Republic, the base of operations for the Puerto Rican revolutionaries at the time.

Although there was no recognized Puerto Rican flag in the period 1506-1898 while the island was under Spanish rule, the flag of the port of San Juan (see p. 190) became an unofficial local symbol. Its stripes of red over white were the inspiration for certain Puerto Rican political party flags and, possibly, for the flag of the island itself. The signal flag was established in the nineteenth century.

Two other flags are associated with Puerto Rico. A flag of green and red with a gold border, granted to Diego Ramos in 1546 as part of his coat of arms, may possibly have been used in the island at that time. Although the United States flag alone was official for Puerto Rico as a whole, from 1898 until 1952, the Governor for several decades displayed a white flag bearing the seal of the island (see p. 191).* This seal is one of many artistic interpretations that have been given to the coat of arms granted by the King of Spain to San Juan, as Puerto Rico was first called. The arms have been in continuous use since 8 November 1511, except when replaced in 1901-1905 by the arms shown on p. 191. They are the oldest arms in the Western Hemisphere still in use.

The center of the shield bears the lamb representing the patron saint of Puerto Rico, John the Baptist. (In the seal the motto "Joannes Est Nomen Ejus" means "John is His Name.") Around the border are

---

* After 1948, when the Governors became elected officials instead of Presidential appointees, the flag ceased to be used.

XLVI. FLAGS OF SOUTH CAROLINA

a.   **SOUTH CAROLINA**   **Ensign**   **20 December 1860–c1865 (unofficial; variant)**   **Proportions 3 x 4**

b.   **SOUTH CAROLINA**   **December 1860?–1 January 1861? (unofficial; reconstructed)**

c.   **SOUTH CAROLINA**   **26 January 1861–28 January 1861   (reconstructed)**

the castle of Castile, the lion of Leon, the crosses of Jerusalem, and the banner of Aragon and Sicily. The circular form has the crowned initials F and I for King Ferdinand and Queen Isabella, as well as their symbols—the arrows and yoke. The form shown in XLII-a, which has been used since 1958, probably corresponds most nearly to the original shield of 1511.

RHODE ISLAND
Seal
24 February 1875–
present
(basic design
authorized 21 May 1647)

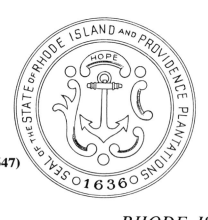

RHODE ISLAND AND PROVIDENCE PLANTATIONS

In 1647 the first Rhode Island General Assembly ordered that the provincial seal should display an anchor. In 1664 the word "Hope" and the official name of the State, Rhode Island and Providence Plantations, were included and the engraver of the seal, apparently on his own initiative, added a cable to the anchor. Except for the usual minor artistic changes, this design has been used as the State seal (above) ever since. No formal law concerning a coat of arms was passed by Rhode Island until 1881, but the seal without its encircling inscriptions in practice served as a coat of arms. In 1881 it was voted by the General Assembly that the arms of the State after 1 February 1882 should be "a golden anchor on a blue field" with the motto "Hope." With four stars and a ribbon bearing part of the State's name, these arms now appear on the flag (XLIV-a) and pennant of the Governor which were established on 21 March 1931. The anchor has in fact been one of the most widely used of any of the State symbols in the country: it has appeared in Rhode Island architecture, currency, signposts, watermarks, monuments, clothing, cartoons, personal as well as public seals, maces, commercial advertising, flags, and documents of all kinds.

The earliest Rhode Island flags of which we have any record are the company colors mentioned, but not described, in a law of 1640. In a campaign in 1746 in Canada, Rhode Island troops were designated by a blue signal flag with a white ball. During the Revolutionary War the First and Second Rhode Island Regiments flew white flags with blue cantons. The First Regiment had its unit designation on a blue ribbon in the field and thirteen white stars in the canton. The Second Regiment color (VII-b) had gold stars and a blue anchor and ribbon in the center. The stars in the flag of the Second Regiment are often incorrectly shown as white.

The State military colors during the Civil War had the usual blue field with the coat of arms, but the influence of the older white flags prevailed when the first State flag (XLIII-a) became official on 30 March 1877. On 1 February 1882 the flag was simplified (XLIII-b); except for the ring of stars, the new flag corresponded in design to the coat of arms. In 1892 the Governor became convinced that the cable which had been shown on the anchor since 1664 was in fact unauthorized and he ordered it removed from the seal, arms, and flag. On 19 May 1897 the present flag (XLIII-c) was created.

RYUKYU ISLANDS

For many centuries a small nation existed in the islands off the coast of China, in the Pacific between Formosa and Japan. It was called the Kingdom of Liuchiu or, as the Japanese pronounced it, Ryu-kyu. Its rulers were warlords of the Sho dynasty which held power from 1469 until 1879 when Japan seized the islands. After World War II the United States occupied the Ryukyus and neighboring Volcano and Bonin Islands and made arrangements to establish military bases there. In 1951 the Peace Treaty recognized Japanese sovereignty, but allowed the American administration of the Ryukyus to continue. The end to American occupation came in 1972 when the islands were reestablished as the Japanese prefecture of Okinawa. From that time on its symbols were no longer subject to American influence.

Because of their unusual political situation, the Ryukyus have had a complicated flag history. The earliest flag of which we have record is the personal dynastic banner of the Sho kings. This flag (XLIV-b) was white with the *mon* of the family in the center. Such *mon* are the Japanese equivalent of the coats of arms formerly used in Europe by members of the clergy, nobility, and military. Occasionally, this flag is still seen in the Ryukyus but it has no official standing.

The Japanese national flag (a red circle on white) and naval ensign (XLIV-c) were the most commonly flown flags during the period of Japanese rule. In 1945, of course, they gave way to the United States flag. In June 1950 it was decided that a distinctive flag was needed to identify locally registered ships, mostly fishing vessels, and a "Ryuyku Islands Maritime Ensign" was therefore created. Following a pattern used in occupied Germany and Japan, American authorities took one of the flags from the International Code of Signals—in this case the D or Delta flag—as the basis for the design. A triangle was cut from the fly, leaving the flag shown in XLV-a.

On land the local population made increasing use of the national flag of Japan and on 16 March 1955 an official ordinance recognized this custom. It was provided that on certain popular holidays the Japanese flag might even be flown on government buildings. Eventually continued expressions of loyalty to the flag of Japan by the islanders brought about a change in the maritime ensign. On 1 July 1967 the blue and yellow flag was discontinued and in its place boats were allowed to fly the Japanese flag surmounted by a pennant (XLV-b). This pennant bore the word "Ryukyus" in both Roman and Kanji script. The only other Ryukyuan flag recognized by law was the standard of the High Commissioner. This flag (XLV-c) came into existence on 14 April 1959. Okinawa now uses a prefectural flag and the flag of Japan.

XLVII. FLAGS OF SOUTH CAROLINA AND SOUTH DAKOTA

a.   **SOUTH CAROLINA   28 January 1861–present**

b.   **SOUTH DAKOTA (obverse)   1 July 1909–11 March 1963   Proportions 3 x 5**

c.   **SOUTH DAKOTA   Government and general usage flag   11 March 1963–present   Proportions 3 x 5**

a.

b.

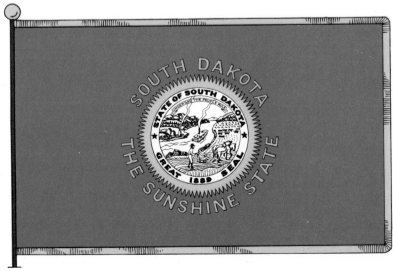

c.

SOUTH CAROLINA September 1775–?

SOUTH CAROLINA

When the American Revolution broke out two regiments were formed in South Carolina, their uniforms being blue and their cap badges silver crescents inscribed "Liberty or Death." On 13 September 1775 Fort Johnson was taken by these troops and Colonel William Moultrie made a flag for the fort which bore a white crescent in the corner of a blue field. The next spring this flag, possibly with the inscription "Liberty" added (above), was displayed over the unnamed fort on Sullivan's Island in Charleston Harbor. During the British attack on this fort on 28 June 1776, according to tradition, Sergeant William Jasper saved the flag when it fell and, braving the fire from British ships, attached the flag to a sponge staff and planted it where it could again be seen. The successful defense of the fort, named Fort Moultrie for its commander, and the rescue of the flag both served to establish this design as the unofficial South Carolina flag. Since the fort had been built with palmetto tree logs (which absorbed the cannon balls fired at them) a palmetto was subsequently placed in the center of the flag.

Shortly after the battle a legislative commission reported its design for a State seal. It bore a scene emblematic of the battle: an oak (for the British ships) is fallen before a palmetto, to which the Latin motto "He

Has Planted One Better Than the Fallen" refers. To the tree are attached shields bearing the dates of independence of South Carolina and the United States. The other States are represented by the twelve crossed spears, bound with the motto "Quis Seperabit?"—"Who Will Separate [Them]?" On the reverse a new day dawns on the figure of Hope, whose name in Latin ("Spes") appears below, as she crosses a shore covered with weapons. The Latin motto at the top reads (in English) "While I Breathe, I Hope." This seal has been used ever since, with modifications.

Early in November of 1860 when the news of Lincoln's election to the Presidency became known, palmetto flags of various designs were hoisted throughout South Carolina. On the thirteenth of the month a palmetto flag was hoisted on the State House itself. Three days later a ninety-foot pole was erected, from the top of which flew a white flag with a green palmetto and a motto from the seal, "Animis Opibusque Parati" ("Ready in Spirit and Resources"). On 20 December 1860, the day South Carolina declared herself an independent republic, some Charleston women presented a flag of red, six by eight, with a white star in the center and a white crescent in the upper hoist (XLVI-a). This and similar red flags were flown by South Carolina ships until the end of the Civil War.

Various unconfirmed reports indicate that the first flag to be flown by the new republic, probably unofficially, was red with the white crescent and palmetto in the upper hoist (XLVI-b). Across the flag was a cross of blue with fifteen white stars to represent the slaveholding States, the central star for South Carolina being the largest. A similar flag was presented by a South Carolina delegate to the Montgomery (Ala.) convention held in February 1861 which considered, among other matters, a design for a Confederate flag. The first official action on a South Carolina flag of which we have record is the adoption on 26 January 1861 of a national flag (XLVI-c), after a long debate over various alternatives. This flag lasted only one full day, however, because on the twenty-eighth the General Assembly changed its mind and modified the design (XLVII-a). This flag served as South Carolina's national flag until it acceded to the Confederate States; since then it has been used as the State flag under both the Confederacy and the United States.

a.

b.

c.

SOUTH DAKOTA

Captain Seth Bullock, a Spanish-American War veteran, first raised the question of a State flag for South Dakota in 1908. Senator Ernest May became interested in the subject and talked about it with Doane Robinson, Secretary of the State Historical Society. They finally worked out a design which was painted by Miss Ida Anding, Dr. Robinson's secretary. It showed a blazing sun on a blue field, surrounded by the name South Dakota and the motto "The Sunshine State." The motto and sun were based on the song "South Dakota Is the Sunshine State," written by Willis Johnson. This design (XLVII-b) won favor in the Legislature, but it was proposed that the seal of the State be added on the reverse. This suggestion was accepted and the flag became official on 1 July 1909.

Certain problems arose with regard to the flag after its adoption. Flag manufacturers, used to making dark-blue State flags with the seals on the obverse and in color, disregarded the law describing the flag. Therefore in 1939 the Legislature specified that the flag should be sky blue and reaffirmed that the seal should be in dark-blue outline on the reverse side. Lack of publicity and the great expense of a double-sided flag still strictly limited the number of flags displayed. This problem became acute when various local organizations requested the donation of flags from the State. Finally, Will G. Robinson, who had succeeded his father as Secretary of the State Historical Society, decided to revise the flag so that the same design would appear on both sides. This greatly reduced its cost.

Robinson's pattern was made up by a manufacturer in two sample versions to be presented to the State legislature. In one copy the seal was on a circle of white, while in the other the background circle within the sun's rays was the same shade of blue as the field of the flag. The motion before the Legislature was worded to allow either the white or light blue,

XLVIII. FLAGS OF TENNESSEE

a. **TENNESSEE**   **1 May 1897–17 April 1905**   **Proportions 2 x 3**
b. **TENNESSEE**   **17 April 1905–present**   **Proportions 3 x 5**
c. **TENNESSEE**   **Governor's flag**   **1939–present (unofficial)**

so that the Senators and Representatives might choose between them. Instead they passed the measure without striking out either phrase; and thus on 11 March 1963 South Dakota changed from having one double-sided flag to having two official single-sided flags. (In practice the version illustrated in XLVII-c is preferred.) It was specified that flags for indoor and display purposes should have a gold fringe.

The seal which has appeared on all the State flags was made part of the Constitution of South Dakota adopted in 1889. It includes a scene from nature which represents the commerce, agriculture, industry, stock raising, and geography of the State. In 1961 an official colored version of the seal was approved by the Legislature.

TENNESSEE
Seal (de facto design)
14 November 1801–
present
(authorized 1796)

TENNESSEE

Both the original and the present official State flags of Tennessee have taken as their basic inspiration the geographic regions which cut the State into three vertical parts. In the center of the State lie the Nashville Basin and Highland Rim, framed to the west by the Gulf Coastal Plain and to the east by the Appalachian and Blue Ridge areas. Corresponding to these are the diagonal stripes on the first flag (XLVIII-a), adopted on 30 April 1897 by the legislature. The stripe in the fly bears the number 16, referring to the fact that Tennessee was the third State to join the Union after the original thirteen. "The Volunteer State" is a nickname which has been gained by the reputation of the State in supplying troops to the nation's armed forces. These words were written in either yellow or gold letters.

This first State flag, apparently created especially for the Tennessee Centennial Exposition of 1897, was little used. The new flag (XLVIII-b), whose pattern was conceived by Captain LeRoy Reeves of the Tennessee National Guard, obtained official approval on 17 April 1905. In addition to the regional symbolism mentioned above, it has been suggested that the stars stand for the three Presidents who lived in Tennessee—Andrew Jackson, James Polk, and Andrew Johnson. Whether or not this is correct, it is true that President Jackson inspired the emblem which has served as a military crest for the Tennessee National Guard since 1923. This consists of a hickory tree, in reference to Jackson's nickname "Old Hickory." On the tree are the three stars of the State flag and below is a heraldic wreath of the colors of England, the ancestral home of most of the early settlers. The crest forms the central feature of the flag of the Governor of Tennessee (XLVIII-c); its four stars indicate the rank of the Governor as Commander in Chief of State military forces.

Records indicate that in the nineteenth century a blue flag with the State seal surrounded by an oak wreath was employed, presumably by the local military. The official seal, described by law in 1801, differs from the seal actually in use (opposite), which adds the words "of the State" and omits "Feb. 6th" from the inscription. Prior to 1801 the official papers of the State were stamped with the personal seal of the Governor.

TEXAS

The theme "six flags over Texas" has received considerable attention in that State, and in 1961 it was permanently honored in the coat of arms (XLIX-a) adopted as a design for the reverse of the Texas seal. The flags shown behind the shield represent the six nations which have held sovereignty over Texas—France, Spain, Mexico, the Republic of Texas, the Confederate States, and the United States. The shield itself includes the Alamo mission, the cannon at Gonzales, and Vince's Bridge, all of which are associated with the Texan war of independence. The arms were designed by Mrs. Sarah R. Farnsworth and sponsored by the Daughters of the Republic of Texas.

TEXAS   Flag of the independence movement led by the filibuster, Dr. James Long   1819–1820

While six flags are popularly credited to Texas history, in fact there have been many more. Texas was part of the Spanish dominions in April 1813 when José Gutiérrez and Lieutenant William Magee organized a Republic of Texas around Béxar. Their venture was crushed in August of the same years and the green flag they had flown disappeared. The weakness of Spanish control continued, however; in the early nineteenth century privateers operating out of Texan ports flew the flags of those governments from which they held letters of marque, allowing them to prey on Spanish ships. Thus in addition to the privateers' own flags, the recognized ensigns of Venezuela, Anáhuac, Argentina, and Cartagena were to be seen. In 1819-1820 another filibuster from the United States, Dr. James Long, tried unsuccessfully to establish a Texan Republic. His red-and-white-striped flag (above) was obviously patterned after the

XLIX. FLAGS AND ARMS OF TEXAS

a.   **TEXAS (STATE)   Seal (reverse)   26 August 1961–present**

b.   **TEXAS (REPUBLIC)   Privateer ensign   November 1835–9 April 1836   Conservative party flag   1835–36**

c.   **TEXAS (REPUBLIC)   Color of the Harrisburg Volunteer Company flown at Washington-on-the-Brazos 2 March 1836   Proportions 1 x 3**

a.

b.

c.

United States flag, but substituted a single star on red for the usual constellation of stars on blue. Since Long organized his movement in Louisiana, which only nine years earlier had known the single-starred flag of the West Florida Republic (see p. 159), it is possible that this influenced his design. In any event his flag seems to have been the first in what became a long series of one-starred flags and other symbols that have given Texas the name of "The Lone Star State."

Except for the brief display of a white and red flag by the ephemeral "Republic of Fredonia" in 1826, Mexican flags flew undisputed in Texas until 1835. By that time the preponderance of settlers in Texas were Americans who were opposed to the policies of Mexican President Antonio de Santa Anna. One group, the Conservatives, were willing to have Texas continue as a Mexican state as long as the liberal constitution of 1824 was lived up to. Therefore they displayed the flag of Mexico with the date of the constitution replacing the usual coat of arms (XLIX-b). The autonomous General Council which established itself on 3 November 1835 at Austin designated this as the correct flag for Texan vessels possessing letters of marque and it was also carried on land for several months during that winter. Like the Continental Colors of the United States, the 1824 flag disappeared when those favoring complete independence became predominant. The flag of the group favoring independence was blue with a white star (LXIV-a) which symbolized their desire both for independence from Mexico and for adhesion to the United States.

While exact influences in design can only be guessed at, many Texan flags seem clearly related to the Bonnie Blue Flag (see p. 265). Existing records list a number of flags which included a single star, including those of Captains Baker, Burroughs, and Scott, the Gonzales garrison, and Johanna Troutman. The flag created by Sarah Dodson (XLIX-c) is supposed to have floated in the capital city (Washington-on-the-Brazos) on 2 March 1836, the day that the independence of Texas was proclaimed. This tricolor more closely resembled the present Texas flag (LI-a) than did any of the other local flags.

The first national flag of Texas (L-a) was designed by Lorenzo de Zavala, a high Mexican government official who had joined the Texans. This pattern was official, although apparently unused, between 11

March and 10 December of 1836, when a new flag (L-b) was adopted at the suggestion of President David G. Burnet. During the first three years of its existence Texas sought to be annexed to the United States. This is evident in the design of the naval ensign (L-c) provisionally approved by President Burnet on 9 April 1836 and confirmed by Congress on 10 December of the same year. The naval ensign was of almost the same design as the flag which Dr. Long attempted to establish in 1819–1820; it also looked like the 1861 naval flag of Florida (see p. 124). Since domestic American political problems made annexation impossible, the third and permanent national flag (LI-a) was approved on 25 January 1839.

The new design, the idea of Dr. Charles B. Stewart, served as the basis for the merchant flag (LI-b), revenue service ensign, and pilot signal which the Republic of Texas adopted in 1839. This national flag has also been hoisted as the State flag of Texas under both the United States (1845-1861 and 1870 to the present) and the Confederate States (1861–1865). Another flag, flown in 1861 immediately before Texas seceded from the Union, was the old white-star-on-blue-field, with the motto (in Latin) "Let Justice Be Done Though the Heavens Fall."

Soon after declaring its independence, Texas adopted the five-pointed star as its national emblem. The seal used by the provisional government under Henry Smith was simply an old pearl button with a design resembling a daisy, but this was soon replaced with a regular seal. In 1839 the wreath of laurel and oak was added and in 1846 the inscription was changed from "Republic of Texas" to "State of Texas"; since then the seal has been unchanged. The coat of arms, i.e., the seal in color and without its inscription, appears on the flag (LI-c) used by the Governor of Texas as the Commander in Chief of its National Guard.

TRUST TERRITORY OF THE PACIFIC ISLANDS

Traditionally, international law has recognized the right of a conqueror to keep any colonial territories gained in a war. After the two World Wars, however, a new policy developed which placed such conquerors under an obligation to help local peoples in creating self-supporting independent nations. Such areas were called "Mandated Territories" under

L

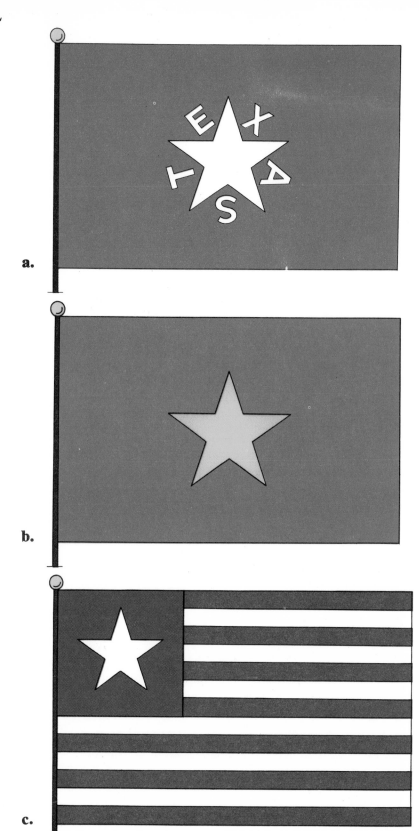

a.

b.

c.

**TRUST TERRITORY
OF THE
PACIFIC ISLANDS**
Seal
?–present

the League of Nations and "Trust Territories" under the United Nations. One such territory is a collection of Pacific islands under American administration, known unofficially as Micronesia. From the time of their capture in 1944 from Japanese rule, these islands have officially flown the United States flag. Since 18 July 1947 the United Nations has been an overseer of the American administration in Micronesia. Therefore the flag of the United Nations (LII-a) is frequently flown in the islands alongside that of the United States. The standard of this organization bears a world map in polar projection, surrounded by an olive wreath symbolizing its peaceful mission. In 1975 a separate Commonwealth of the Northern Marianas was formed.

On 24 October (United Nations Day) 1962 a third flag was hoisted (LII-b). This represents the Trust Territory itself, although the colors and stars suggest an origin in the flags of the United States and United

L. FLAGS OF THE TEXAS REPUBLIC

a. **TEXAS (REPUBLIC)   National flag   11 March–10 December 1836** (reconstructed)

b. **TEXAS (REPUBLIC)   "National standard"   National flag   10 December 1836–25 January 1839**

c. **TEXAS (REPUBLIC)   "National Flag for the Naval Service"   Ensign 9 April 1836–29 December 1845?**

FLORIDA   Government flag   13 January–13 September 1861

Nations. The stars represent peace and the districts of Palau, Yap, Truk, Ponape, the Marshall Islands, and the Mariana Islands. The blue field stands for freedom and loyalty. The design was created by Gonzalo Santos, a Government clerk from Yap, who won a prize of $250 for his idea. The flag approved on 3 October 1962 by the Council of Micronesia, an advisory body, was made official in 1965 by the Congress of Micronesia. Another flag is that of the High Commissioner of the Trust Territory, which shows his seal in dark blue on a white field. The seal (see p. 209) features a palm tree and a flying proa similar to those pictured in the arms of Guam.

The islands have seen many flags in the past. From 1668 until 1899 the Caroline Islands (including Truk, Ponape, and Yap) and the Mariana (or Ladrone) and Palau Islands were under Spanish flags (I-b and I-c)—except for Guam, which was ceded to the United States in 1898. The following year Germany bought the rest of the Spanish colony and ruled it until World War I when the islands were seized by Japan. Then these islands plus the Marshalls became a Mandated Territory, but because the League of Nations had no flag of its own only Japanese flags (XLIV-c and the bottom half of XLV-b) were flown.

The Marshall Islands became a German colony on 1 April 1906. Previously these had been administered since 1885 by the Jaluit-Gesellschaft, a German chartered company. At that time the German national flag had horizontal stripes of black, white, and red; these colors were repeated in the flags of the Jaluit Company and the Ralik Islands (LII-c and LIII-a). The Ralik Islands, part of the Marshalls, had first hoisted its flag on 20 November 1878; German influence is clear in its design, which differs from the German flag itself only in the addition of the two bottom stripes. The Ralik flag was lowered when a German protectorate was established on 15 October 1885.

UTAH

The first settlements in what later became the State of Utah were made by the Mormons in 1847 around Salt Lake City. This date and the date of Utah's admission to Statehood forty-nine years later are both inscribed on the seal adopted in 1896. The State motto, "Industry," is exemplified in the beehive, which is surrounded by the State flower, the sego lily. Both of these are significant in Utah history. The lily was eaten by the early inhabitants in years when food was scarce, and the original name for the area, Deseret, is a word meaning "honeybee" found in the *Book of Mormon.* The seal of the Territory of Utah, adopted in 1850, had had only that part of the device appearing on the central shield. Harry Edwards designed the great seal* of the State by adding an American eagle and arrows to symbolize protection and crossed United States flags to indicate loyalty to the nation.

The first step towards the creation of a Utah flag was taken in 1903 when the local chapter of the Daughters of the American Revolution presented an embroidered flag to Governor Heber M. Wells. On 9 March 1911 this design (LIII-b) was officially adopted as the State flag. The following year the Sons and Daughters of Utah Pioneers decided to present such a flag to the battleship *Utah* and ordered a copy from a firm in the East. When the flag was received it was discovered to have the design in full color rather than white, the whole surrounded by a gold ring. These modifications were highly regarded and the next year the legislature rewrote the law, making the new pattern (LIII-c) official on 11 March 1913. The law requires that the design be in "natural colors," but these are not specified.

Although the Daughters of Utah Pioneers continued to work to make the State flag better known, for many years few copies were used. The first flag in the hall of the Utah legislature, for example, was hung twenty years after its adoption. As in a number of other States, most of the flags made before World War II were either hand-painted or embroidered and thus reflected the individual style of the maker. The flags were usually made to order for use in special flag displays outside the State or for schools, associations, and similar groups. Many Utah flags were made "banner style," that is with fringe at the fly only, a horizontal staff, and the emblem turned so that it would appear correct when the flag hung vertically. Since the War the use of the flag has been expanded and standardized.

---

* The term "great seal" is frequently used by the States, but has no meaning except in the case of Virginia, which alone of the States has a lesser seal. The name originated centuries ago in Europe when seals of different sizes were used.

VERMONT
Seal
20 February 1779–present
(authorized 1777)

VERMONT

Vermont was not one of the thirteen original States, because its territory was claimed by New York and New Hampshire, so on 15 January 1777 a convention proclaimed the independence of New Connecticut.* Nevertheless men from the Green Mountain State fought against the British in the Revolution and some of them carried the first known example of the Stars and Stripes (IX-b). Since 1963 this "Bennington Battle Flag" has been officially hoisted at the State House on the fifteenth through the seventeenth of August each year in commemoration of this important victory of 1777. Vermont continued to be an independent republic until 4 March 1791, but we have no record of what flag, if any, it flew.

    Twelve years after its admission to Statehood Vermont adopted a State flag (LIV-a) which became official on 1 May 1804. Today there exists only a written description of this flag, but it is apparent that the intention of the legislators was simply to adopt the United States flag with the name of the State added at the top. Since the thirteen-star flag

    * The name was changed to Vermont on 4 June of the same year.

LI. FLAGS OF TEXAS

a.   **TEXAS (REPUBLIC AND STATE)**   General usage flag on land   25 January 1839–present   Proportions 2 x 3

b.   **TEXAS (REPUBLIC)**   National flag at sea   1839–1845

c.   **TEXAS (STATE)**   Governor's flag   ?–present   Proportions 4 x 5

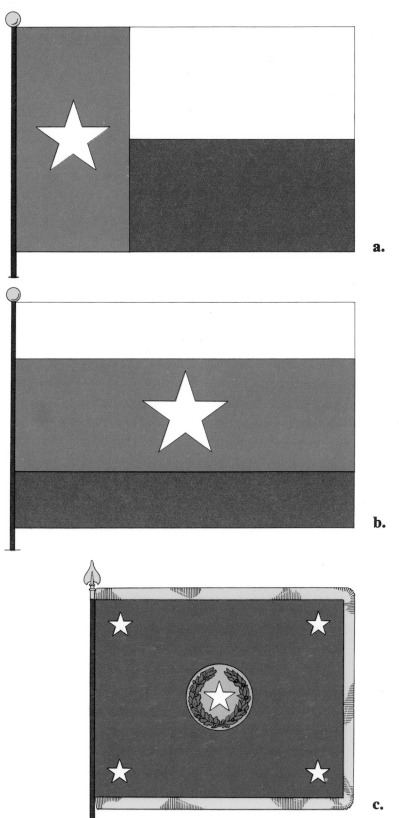

a.

b.

c.

had been changed when Vermont and Kentucky became States, it was assumed that the new States of Tennessee and Ohio would soon be represented by two new stars and stripes. In fact the country kept its flag of fifteen stars and fifteen stripes until 1818, when it adopted one of twenty stars and thirteen stripes, and thus the Vermont flag of seventeen stars and stripes became anomalous.

A second flag (LIV-b) was adopted by the State on 20 October 1837. While it, too, was based on the United States flag, it included as a distinctive emblem the State coat of arms on a star. Both five- and eight-pointed stars were used, since the law did not clarify this detail. The State seal was often shown instead of the arms, as required by law. During the various wars in which Vermont troops participated, the regimental colors were of the usual design—the State coat of arms on a blue field. Because the official flag was rarely used, it was decided to create a new State flag (LIV-c) based on the military standards. This design went into effect on 1 June 1923. The same pattern had been used since the turn of the century as a Governor's flag.

The history of the Vermont seal begins in 1777 when provision for such a seal was included in the Constitution. Two years later Ira Allen produced a seal which was used until it wore out in 1821. The seals subsequently cut were of the same general design, but varied in certain details. In 1937 when the sixth seal was being cut, Allen's original model was followed exactly and this design (see p. 212) is the one in use today. The cow, wheat sheaves, and forest are characteristic of the State; the emblem resembling a fleur-de-lys is probably only decoration. The central pine tree is of interest because it bears fourteen branches, suggesting that even in 1779 there was strong sentiment in Vermont favoring State-hood. The actual tree after which the seal is reputed to have been modeled still stands in southern Vermont.

The coat of arms of the State, also subject to varying artistic interpretations, first came into unofficial use in 1821 as an adaptation of the seal. In 1862 official legislation defined the arms and they have remained the same ever since. The branches of pine at the bottom of the shield are referred to as "the Vermonter's badge" because such branches were worn by troops from the State in the Battle of Plattsburgh in 1814. The mountains in the arms are said to be those first seen by Champlain when he came down the lake that now bears his name.

VIRGIN ISLANDS

Although Columbus discovered the Virgin Islands in 1493, they were not settled by the Spanish; the British and Danish each established a colony in the islands in 1625. Later Spanish and French attempts to acquire certain islands failed. The British still have a Virgin Islands colony, but in 1917 the Danes decided to sell their islands to the United States. Thus the flag of the United States was first officially hoisted there on 31 March of that year.

As a Territory administered first by the Navy and later by the Department of the Interior, the Virgin Islands have flown the flag of the United States. However, on 17 May 1921 Governor Sumner E. W. Kittelle established a local flag by Executive Order (LV-a). This bears the initials of the Territory on either side of a stylized and simplified version of the United States coat of arms. Following the practice of many State Governors, the Governor of the Virgin Islands flies the territorial flag and the flag of the United States on his automobile. Before the transfer of administration to civil government, the Naval Governors flew the United States Union Jack at the bow of any boat in which they embarked on official business within territorial waters. There is no special Governor's flag at the present time.

Under Danish administration public buildings had flown the state flag of Denmark while private individuals used the national flag of that country. Both were similar in appearance, consisting essentially of a white cross on a red field. The national flag, however, was rectangular (with proportions of 28:37) while the state flag had a section cut out of the fly, a common Scandinavian practice (see III-b). The Danish flag, known as the *Dannebrog,* is one of the oldest national flags in the world, having been used at least as early as the thirteenth century. There were two other flags, flown from c1798 to c1842 in the Danish West Indies, about which very little is known. One was dark blue, the other white, both having the *Dannebrog* as a canton.

Like other chartered companies having governmental functions in colonial territories, the Danish West India Company, which administered the Virgin Islands, had its own flag (LV-b) based on the state flag. The emblem added in the center bore two lions and two royal crowns together with the cipher of the reigning monarch and the initials DOP. The cipher shown here is that used by Frederick VII (1848-1863). Towards the end of the Danish rule, after the company had relinquished its authority to the Danish Government, a coat of arms was proposed for the Danish West Indies. It showed, in stylized heraldic form, three islands in the sea; on each island was a palm tree and a Danish flag. Since 1917 the seal of the United States, with an appropriate encircling inscription, has been used by the Territorial Government.

VIRGINIA

In 1584 Sir Walter Raleigh received permission from Queen Elizabeth I to establish English colonies in North America. Although his expeditions did not lead to permanent settlements, Raleigh's name for the territory, Virginia in honor of Elizabeth "the Virgin Queen," remained in use. In 1606 King James I of England granted privileges to the Virginia Company to encourage colonization. Their charter was revoked in 1624, but the coat of arms of the Company (LV-c) continued to be used by the royal Colony of Virginia until the American Revolution. Queen Elizabeth was honored by the virgin queen which served as a crest for these arms. The cross of St. George was the principal charge on the shield and

LII. FLAGS OF THE TRUST TERRITORY OF THE PACIFIC ISLANDS

a.   **UNITED NATIONS**   Government flag (jointly with U.S. flag) of the Trust Territory on land   20 October 1947–present   Proportions 2 x 3 or 3 x 5

b.   **TRUST TERRITORY OF THE PACIFIC ISLANDS**   General usage flag on land   19 August 1965–present Proportions 10 x 19

c.   **MARSHALL ISLANDS**   Flag of the Jaluit Company   ?1885–1 April 1896

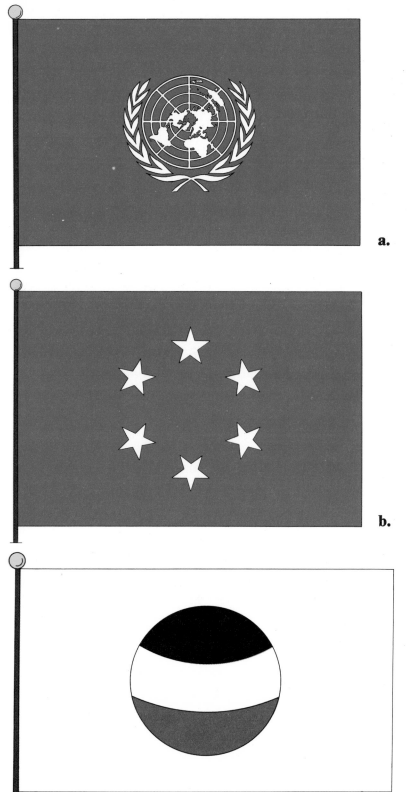

a.

b.

c.

VIRGINIA
Seal (reverse)
2 December 1931–present
(basic design authorized 5 July 1776)

was repeated on the breastplates of the supporters. The smaller shields bore the arms of the territories claimed by the successive queens and kings of Great Britain. The version shown here, used from 1619 to 1707, has the quartered arms of France and England in the first and fourth quarters and the arms of Scotland and Ireland in the second and third quarters. Combined in a single shield, these were the royal arms of the Stuarts. The Latin motto, which translates as "Behold, Virginia Gives the Fifth," suggested that the territory was to be the fifth kingdom under the British crown. The shields and motto were modified as necessary after 1707 to reflect the changing British political structure.

When Virginia established a republican government in 1776 it wanted to show that it had rejected all royal and aristocratic symbols. Its new seal, therefore, was composed of classical Roman figures rather than heraldic forms. The obverse of the great and lesser seals, which differ only in size, bears the figure of "Virtus, the genius of the commonwealth, dressed like an Amazon." Underfoot she treads on Tyranny, who holds a scourge and chain. Although the crown nearby implies that the tyrant is a king, the Latin motto "Thus Ever to Tyrants" rather suggests that Virginia is opposed to all forms of oppression, whether or not they are associated with monarchy. The reverse of the seal (above) shows Liberty holding a wand and liberty cap; Eternity with a globe and phoenix; and Ceres, the goddess of agriculture, with a cornucopia in her left hand and an ear of wheat in her right. The design is credited to

George Wythe, who probably took his information and illustrations from Joseph Spence's book on Roman antiquities.

On 30 April 1861, soon after the Commonwealth of Virginia had seceded from the Union, it adopted a State flag. Unlike most of the southern State flags of the Civil War era, this design (LVI-a) survived the war and has been used ever since. It received more precise form in 1931 and 1949 when first a drawing of the seal and then its colors were made official. Although the Governor is authorized to issue specifications for the correct dimensions of the flag as used for various purposes, no such action appears ever to have been taken. Perhaps the most unusual aspect of the flag is its white fringe, shown only at the fly end.

WASHINGTON

In 1914 the national headquarters of the Daughters of the American Revolution wrote to the State chapter in Washington, asking for a flag to be displayed in Continental Hall in the District of Columbia. Since there was no State flag at that time, a committee headed by Mrs. S. J. Chadwick was established for the purpose of creating such a standard. The flag they made in 1915 bore a bust of President Washington, for whom the State was named, on a field of green to symbolize the "Evergreen State." Independently of this work, Grover C. Gaier, the Secretary-Treasurer of the Washington State Nautical School, created in 1920 a design which was almost exactly the same. This flag flew briefly over the training ship owned by the School. Prior to either of these flags there had been military colors used by State troops; these, however, had a field of blue instead of green.

Through the efforts of the D. A. R. the State legislature was induced to adopt the green flag, which became official on 7 June 1923. The proportions were variable and the option was given to users of the flag to add a green fringe if they wished. On 7 June 1925 the law was slightly modified to alter the fringe color to gold. In practice many variations of the design existed, so in 1955 the Secretary of State issued exact specifications in order to assure a uniformity of design. Manufacturers were required to submit a sample flag to him for approval before making large quantities. The flag was again slightly modified on 19 April 1967

a.

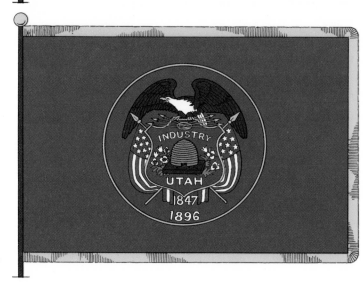

b.

c.

when a law went into effect which gave the State seal a precise artistic form. The flag now in use is shown in LVI-b; when the seal is used separately in black and white the area behind the bust is crosshatched (as in the one-dollar bill) rather than filled in solid.

The seal of Washington as a Territory bore a steamer and sailing vessel, a pioneer wagon and cabin, forest, and in the foreground the goddess of Hope with an anchor. Above appeared the State motto, "Al-Ki," which is Chinook for "By-and-By." When the State was organized in 1889 a new design, created by a legislative committee, showed Mount Rainier, wheat fields, grazing sheep, and the port of Tacoma. The committee took its emblem to the Talcott brothers, who ran a jewelry store in Olympia, to obtain an engraving. Charles Talcott suggested that the design was too complicated. With an ink bottle and a silver dollar he drew two concentric circles in which he wrote "The Seal of the State of Washington—1889" and inside he stuck a postage stamp bearing a vignette of George Washington. This was accepted as the basis for the seal adopted on 4 July 1889. In the original drawing of the bust, copied from an advertisement for Dr. Jane's Expectorant, Washington faced to the left.

WEST VIRGINIA

When the Louisiana Purchase Exposition was held in St. Louis in 1904, the commissioners of the West Virginia Building on their own initiative created a State flag for display. This flag was double-sided, having the coat of arms on the reverse and the State flower on the obverse (LVI-c), both within a border. The flower was the big laurel (*Rhododendron maximum*) which had received official recognition from the Legislature in 1903. The Legislature adopted this flag on 24 February 1905, but changed its mind two years later. On 25 February 1907 the rhododen-

LIII. FLAGS OF THE RALIK ISLANDS AND UTAH

a.   **RALIK ISLANDS** National flag   20 November 1878–15 October
    1885

b.   **UTAH**   9 March 1911–11 March 1913

c.   **UTAH**   11 March 1913–present

WEST VIRGINIA
Seal (reverse)
26 September 1863–present

dron was placed on the reverse side of the flag and the coat of arms on the obverse. Instead of the motto, the words "State of West Virginia" appeared on a scroll below the arms and the fringe was changed from red to gold. This flag was flown at the Jamestown Exposition in 1907 and a copy of it was presented to each school in the State by Henry G. Davis on the occasion of West Virginia's semicentennial in 1913.

At the time of this celebration numerous flags were made showing the rhododendron and coat of arms together on both sides of the flag, since this greatly reduced the cost and eliminated manufacturing problems. This led to the creation of the present form of the flag (LVII-a), approved by the Legislature on 7 March 1929. The law reads in part "the flag of the State of West Virginia when used for parade purposes shall be trimmed with gold-colored fringe on three sides and when used on ceremonial occasions with the United States ensign, shall be trimmed and mounted in similar fashion to the United States flag as regards fringe, cord, tassels and mounting."

The coat of arms, whose colors were standardized in 1905, forms part of the obverse of the Great Seal which has a ring reading "State of West Virginia—Montani Semper Liberi." This Latin motto translates as "Mountaineers Are Always Free"—referring to the formation of West Virginia in 1861 from those mountainous counties of Virginia which refused to secede from the Union. The date of the State's admission into the Union is graven on a rock; the liberty cap and guns stand for a willingness to fight for freedom. The seal was designed by Joseph H. D.

Debar and adopted in 1863. On its reverse (opposite), which is rarely used, appear a wreath of oak, laurel, fruits, and cereals. The scene from nature includes an oil derrick, a log cabin, sheep and cattle, and "the viaduct of the Baltimore and Ohio Railroad in Preston County." The motto "Liberty Out of Loyalty" (in Latin) is taken to mean that the freedom of West Virginia is the result of fidelity to the United States Constitution. Four months after its adoption the obverse of the seal and certain battle inscriptions were placed on the State's first flag, a blue color presented to the Fourth Regiment of the West Virginia Volunteer Infantry.

WISCONSIN

During the Civil War a joint select committee was established by the Wisconsin legislature to consider the question of flags for the state. Its report, as approved on 25 March 1863, created a State flag and a regimental color for Wisconsin troops. The latter flag was the same as the former, except that it added the name of the regiment on a scroll to the obverse. The State flag was described as having the Wisconsin coat of arms painted or embroidered on the obverse and the United States arms, as prescribed by Army regulations, on the reverse. Contemporary evidence indicates that in fact the State arms were placed on a gold-ringed gray circle, rather than directly on the blue field as required by law.

In 1887 the Legislature inadvertently abolished the State flag when the legal code in which it was incorporated was repealed. Twenty-six years later a new flag (LVII-b) was created by a law which became effective on 29 April 1913. It differed from the previous Wisconsin flag only in that the State arms appeared on both sides and the arms of the United States were removed. This is the flag presently in use, although in 1955 an entirely different design came close to being adopted by the Legislature. This flag, proposed by Assemblyman William Belter, had a blue field with thirteen red and white stripes in the canton. In the fly one large white star was surrounded by two rings of smaller stars, twelve in the inner ring and seventeen in the outer. These stars represented the States of the Union up to and including Wisconsin itself.

After having used two nonheraldic seals as a territory, in 1851 Wisconsin adopted its present coat of arms which appears on both its seal and flag. The supporters are a sailor and a miner, representing labor on sea and land. At their feet are a cornucopia and pile of pig-lead ingots, for the State's agricultural and industrial products; the shield likewise includes symbols of labor. Loyalty to the Union is symbolized by the central escutcheon bearing the shield and motto from the arms of the United States. (Usually the chief of the shield is incorrectly shown with thirteen stars.) The crest refers to the fact that Wisconsin is known as The Badger State because the burrowlike huts in which the early miners lived resembled badger holes.

In 1881 a new seal was required because the old one had worn out. In cutting this seal, Henry Mitchell of Boston made some artistic alterations within the scope of the legal description. The shield had previously been of another shape; the motto "E Pluribus Unum" had been on a scroll; the supporters rested their arms on top of the shield; the shield of the United States was wreathed with laurel; and the four emblems on the shield were arranged in a different pattern. When the recut seal became official it caused revisions in the State flag as well. The coloring of the arms has also varied from time to time because no standard colors have ever been established.

WYOMING

Finding that the State was without a flag, in 1916 the Wyoming section of the Daughters of the American Revolution sponsored a contest to select an appropriate design. From the thirty-seven entries received, that submitted by Miss Verna Keays of Buffalo, Wyoming, was chosen. This design (LVII-c) was submitted to the legislature, where it was officially

LIV. FLAGS OF VERMONT

a.   **VERMONT   1 May 1804–20 October 1837 (authorized 31 October 1803; reconstructed)**

b.   **VERMONT   20 October 1837–1 June 1923**

c.   **VERMONT   1 June 1923–present (authorized 26 March 1923)**

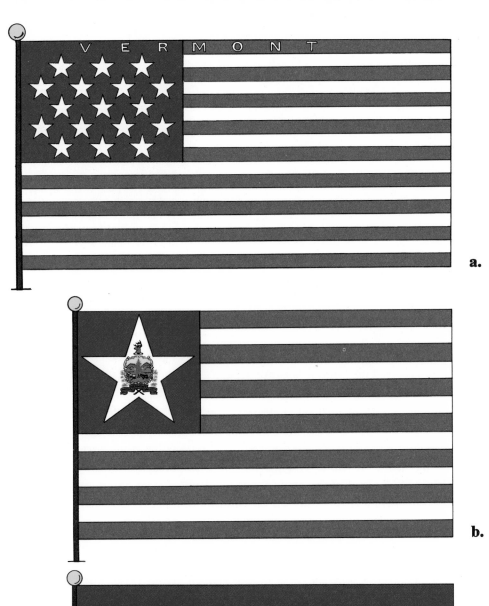

a.

b.

c.

WYOMING
Seal
1 April 1921–present
(basic design authorized 1890)

adopted on 31 January 1917. In its original form the bison which appears in silhouette faced towards the fly of the flag, but this was later reversed. (The law does not specify in which direction the bison should face.) This animal is stamped with the State seal which, according to the designer, suggests the Western tradition of branding.

The seal itself (above) dates back to 1890, the year of Wyoming's admission to the Union. The figures on either side are a cowboy and a miner, symbolizing the principal occupations current in nineteenth-century Wyoming. The dates of the creation of Wyoming Territory (1869) and of the State (1890), together with the number 44 indicating the order of the State's admission to Statehood, appear in the design. The pillars bear lamps of learning and a ribbon listing the products of the State. Between the pillars is a pedestal on which stands a woman with a banner proclaiming "Equal Rights." This is symbolic of the fact that Wyoming was the first major government in the world to provide for unrestricted women's suffrage. The first woman Governor in the United States, Nellie T. Ross, was elected in 1924 by Wyoming voters.

According to the law creating the seal, the woman holding the banner was to be a draped figure modeled after the statue the "Victory of the Louvre," i.e., the Winged Victory of Samothrace. This pattern had been proposed by Representative H. E. Buechner, a member of the committee selected to prepare the seal. However, when the act approved by the Legislature was taken to the Governor for his signature, Buechner's model was replaced by one proposed by Senator Fennimore Chat-

terton, who had also been on the committee. This seal differed principally in that a nude figure was substituted for the Victory of the Louvre.
This pattern was used for several months until it was discovered that it
did not conform to the law, at which time the correct design was established.

The flag, of which the seal constitutes the heart, is bordered in red.
This color stands both for the original Indian population and for the
blood shed by early pioneers. The inner white border represents purity
and uprightness. The blue field symbolizes the color of the sky and of
distant mountains as well as virility, justice, and fidelity. The law specifies that the shades of red and blue shall be exactly the same as for the
flag of the United States. It also gives exact proportions for all the parts
forming the flag and requires that gold cord and tassels be employed with
the flag.

LV

a.

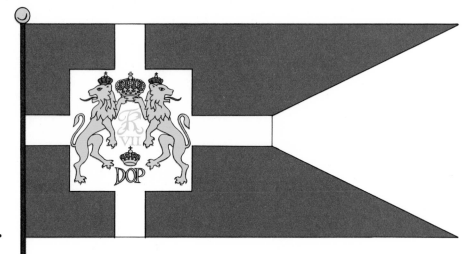

b.

c.

EN DAT VIRGINIA QVINTAM

Chapter VI

OTHER AMERICAN FLAGS

From its earliest beginnings the United States has been characterized by a rich diversity in the cultural inheritance, race, religion, livelihood, politics, and interests of its peoples. While a unified culture has evolved from the hundreds of traditional ways of life brought to the New World, America is still very much a pluralistic society. This is evident in the wide variety of symbols which are used, both in official and unofficial circumstances. The contrast with certain other countries is striking. In some nations flags of any kind are very rarely seen, especially on private homes and businesses. In still other countries flags are extensively used, but only by the civil government and military authorities or at the direction of an authoritarian political party. Even where flags are fairly common, they may have a general uniformity of design so that in a parade, for example, such flags appear as a sea of one or two colors.

LV. EMBLEMS OF THE VIRGIN ISLANDS AND VIRGINIA
a. **VIRGIN ISLANDS   17 May 1921–present**
b. **(DANISH) WEST INDIA COMPANY   1848–1863   Proportions 56 x 107 (reconstructed)**
c. **VIRGINIA   Coat of arms   1619–1707**

One important factor favoring the multiplicity of flags and other symbols in the United States is its federal system, which gives considerable autonomy to different parts of the country and to different parts of each government. In many countries the same flag is used by all levels and divisions in the political system; even the seals of office differ only in their encircling inscriptions. Of course, this is not true of all nations; but it seems likely that no country has so many different symbols as the United States. Ignoring those used by private persons and groups, there are still hundreds of distinctive flags and tens of thousands of seals. The number of coats of arms, while much smaller, is continually increasing.

This chapter cannot begin to encompass all these symbols. Its purpose is rather to outline the types of symbols that may be found and to deal with the most important examples among them. Within the federal government there are civil and military ranks and institutions which have recognized flags, arms, and seals of their own. Below the State level America is divided into counties (parishes in Louisiana, boroughs in Alaska), cities, towns, and Indian nations. In the past there have been other governments operating in the area now included in the United States, including the republics of Hawaii, Texas, and Vermont and small short-lived "independent" states like Amelia, the California Republic, Fredonia, the Indian Stream Republic, and West Florida. These have already been discussed under the States of which they became parts, but the most important government in this category—the Confederate States of America—encompassed many States and deserves more detailed consideration. And, finally, an overview will be presented of the flags flown by private citizens and their associations.

GOVERNMENT FLAGS

Until modern times the government of most countries was in the hands of a small, closed circle. Since aides and advisers to the king or other rulers were usually chosen on the basis of family connections or wealth or influence, they had no flag except possibly a personal banner. Only gradually did political attention shift from the individual holding power within a certain sphere to the office itself. When this change did occur,

UNITED STATES
Supreme Court seal
1905–present
(basic design authorized
3 February 1790)

symbols of rank became important means of guaranteeing the dignity of an official position and respect for it. In many countries today, including the United States, there are dozens of flags and pennants for government officials which serve to enhance their prestige and to distinguish them in the proper administrative hierarchy. At the same time separate institutions within the framework of government have become more distinct. They, too, have need for flags to be used in offices and on buildings and ships. Because the structure of American government has been frequently modified, it would be difficult to list and describe every flag that has been used in this way, but the most important flags, presented here, will give the reader a general idea of their forms and functions.

The legislature and judiciary do not have flags of their own, although the Supreme Court, Senate, and House of Representatives do have seals of office (above, p. 234, and p. 235). The executive branch of government is headed by the President who has had a distinctive signal for over a century. The first need for a Presidential flag arose in the Navy, which had long been accustomed to hoisting a flag for the senior officer on board a given ship. The President, as Commander in Chief, could hardly be ignored when lesser officers were honored, yet the idea of a special standard at first seemed to Americans contrary to their cherished principles of republicanism. Therefore on 18 April 1865 it was prescribed that the presence of the Chief Executive should be denoted by the flying of the national flag on the mainmast or in the bow of a small boat. The next year the Union Jack with its star for each State substituted, but on 31 December 1869 the national flag was restored. Only on 9 August 1882 was a special Presidential flag created; it bore the arms of the United States on a blue field, a design unofficially dating back several decades. In 1916 President Wilson added a white star in each corner of the flag. This continued as the flag of the President for naval usage until 1945 when the general pattern now in use was made official.

In early 1945 President Roosevelt noted that the four stars of his flag were no longer appropriate, since the newly established ranks of Fleet Admiral and General of the Army were each entitled to five stars. The chief herald of the Quartermaster Corps also pointed out that the eagle traditionally used on the Presidential flag was incorrect in several details. A new flag was therefore created which corrected the coat of arms and replaced the four stars with a circle of forty-eight. In 1959 and 1960 when new States were added, the stars in the circle were increased and the present flag (LVIII-a) has fifty stars. In addition to the naval flag, it should be mentioned that the President also had distinctive colors for Army use from 1898 until 1916. One of these designs had the United States coat of arms on a white-bordered blue star surrounded by smaller white stars, one for each State, all on a red field with a white star in each corner. The White House flies the United States flag.

Until the mid-twentieth century the Vice President, with rare exceptions, was not charged with major responsibilities, and the need for a Vice Presidential flag was never as pressing as for a Presidential flag. The naval regulations of 1865 specified that the national ensign should be flown at the fore when the Vice President was on board an American

LVI. FLAGS OF VIRGINIA, WASHINGTON, AND WEST VIRGINIA

a.   **VIRGINIA   Government and general usage flag   30 April 1861– present**

b.   **WASHINGTON   Government and general usage flag   19 April 1967– present (basic design authorized 7 June 1923)   Proportions variable or 2 x 3**

c.   **WEST VIRGINIA   (obverse)   24 February 1905–25 February 1907 (reconstructed)   Proportions 9 x 13**

a.

b.

c.

UNITED STATES
Seal of the House of
Representatives
1912–29 July 1964
(basic design first used 1830)

ship in a foreign port. But within the United States the first known instance of display for a Vice Presidential flag dates from 1915. This flag was the same as the President's except that its colors were reversed, i.e., it had the arms of the United States (with a blue eagle) on a white field. On 7 February 1936 this design was made official and a blue star was added in each corner of the flag. On 10 November 1948 a new design, unlike the Presidential flag, was created as the Vice Presidential standard (LVIII-b).

Over the years most of the heads of the Executive Departments, including the members of the President's Cabinet, have acquired personal rank flags. The oldest such flag, a white anchor and four white stars on dark blue, is that of the Secretary of the Navy which dates from 1866. This probably set the precedent for putting four stars in the rank flags of civilian officials. In 1897 the Army prescribed colors for its Secretary, namely a red flag with a white star in each corner and the arms of the United States in color in the center. The Secretary of the Air Force is the most recent addition to this group: his present flag bears the Air Force coat of arms and four white stars. The field of the flag is ultramarine blue, not the lighter shade known as air-force blue. The Secretaries of the Army, Navy, and Air Force are not Cabinet members, although the Secretary of Defense is. His blue flag also has four white stars and a modified version of the United States eagle with three arrows in its claws in the center.

UNITED STATES
Seal of the Senate
20 January 1886–present

The Department of State conducts the foreign affairs of the country through the Foreign Service. Officers in this Service are entitled to fly one of four flags on their automobiles. A Chief of Mission displays the arms of the United States in color on a white disc set in the center of a dark blue flag and surrounded by thirteen white stars. The Chief of a State Department Mission has the same design, but the blue and white are reversed. A Consular Officer has a dark blue flag with a circle of thirteen white stars within which is a large white C. Other accredited Officers use this flag without the C. The Secretary of State uses the same flag as a Chief of Mission, except that the thirteen stars are replaced by four white stars, one in each corner of the flag. The United States Union Jack (LVIII-c shows the present design) was formerly flown in the bow of a boat bearing a diplomatic representative "of or above the rank of chargé d'affaires, within the waters of the country to which he is accredited." Embassies, consulates, and Foreign Service vehicles abroad fly the United States flag in accordance with the international rules of flag etiquette.

The Secretaries of Agriculture, Commerce, the Interior, Transportation, and the Treasury as well as the Attorney General are entitled to display blue flags bearing the symbols of the respective Departments. Except for the flags of the Interior and Treasury Secretaries, these each have four white stars in the corners. The Treasury seal is surrounded by thirteen stars, and the seven stars of the Interior Secretary's flag suggest

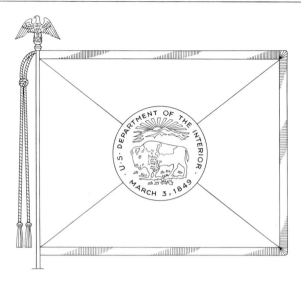

UNITED STATES Flag of the Department of the Interior 1962–present   Proportions 26 x 33

the seven principal activities of the Department at the time the flag was created. The Secretary of Health, Education, and Welfare has a flag of sanguine or maroon with the usual four white stars and the Departmental coat of arms in the center. A number of Departments have special Departmental flags in addition to the personal flags of their officers. The Labor Department flag, designed by Arthur Goldberg, is blue with twelve white stars around the shield of the Department, which is surmounted by an eagle. The flag of the Interior Department (above) is divided diagonally with light blue at the top and bottom and white at the hoist and fly. As is usual in such flags, there is a fringe (gold in this case) on the flag and cords and tassels on the pole,

LVII. FLAGS OF WEST VIRGINIA, WISCONSIN, AND WYOMING

a. **WEST VIRGINIA   7 March 1929–present   Proportions 10 x 19**
b. **WISCONSIN   29 April 1913–present   Proportions 26 x 33**
c. **WYOMING   Government and general usage flag   31 January 1917-present   Proportions 7 x 10**

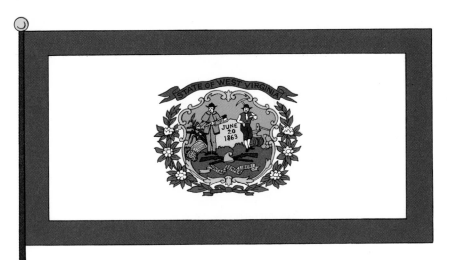

a.

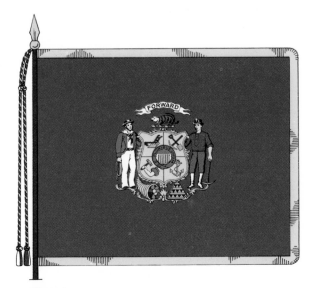

b.

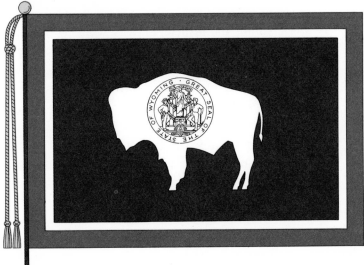

c.

which has a spread eagle at the top. The Secretaries of Transportation and of Housing and Urban Development have white flags bearing the respective Departmental emblems.

In a number of cases the Under Secretaries and Assistant Secretaries of certain Departments have flags which consist of their Secretaries' flags with colors reverse or altered. Thus the Assistant Secretary of the Navy flies a white flag with four stars and an anchor in blue. The following institutions and individuals also have or used to have flags of their own: the Coast and Geodetic Survey and its Director, the Public Health Service and the Surgeon General, the Immigration Service, the Customs Service, the Commissioner and the Superintendent of Lighthouses and the Lighthouse Service, the Bureau of Marine Inspection and its Director, the Bureau of Fisheries and its Commissioner, the Maritime Commission, the Smithsonian Institution and all fifteen of its branches, various programs in the Office of Economic Opportunity (such as Head Start), the Fish and Wildlife Service and its Director, the Geological Survey, and the National Aeronautics and Space Administration. A special mail pennant and an airmail flag were once used. The Commerce Department awards a white pennant with a blue E to firms having made significant contributions to export trade. The Treasury Department grants an award flag of red bearing an emblem in white to offices of the Government which have a one-hundred-percent enrollment in the U.S. Savings Bond plan.

MILITARY FLAGS

To the civilian, the armed services seem to have an endless number of flags of all shapes, sizes, and uses. In fact these flags can be reduced to a few basic types, each of which has numerous variations. Since there are many parallels between the flags of the different branches of the armed forces, they will be dealt with here together. It should be remembered, however, that each branch has a long and distinctive heritage of flags and other symbols of which it is justly proud.

All the military services display the national flag of the United States. It is flown on the stern of warships and Coast Guard vessels, on transport ships and airports, over forts and other Army installations. The same flag, fringed in gold and having cords and tassels, is used as the national color of military units, together with their own regimental or organizational colors. As a color the national flag is usually four feet four inches by five feet six inches. The Army hoists at camps, arsenals, and other installations one of three flag sizes. The Garrison Flag is twenty by thirty-eight feet; the Post Flag for everyday use is ten by nineteen feet; and the Storm Flag is five feet by nine feet six inches.

Each service also has a flag of its own which represents it in official ceremonies. These flags and the idea behind them date from the 1950's; very few countries have comparable flags. The Army flag (LIX-a) bears the central part of the seal which has been used since December 1777 by the Department of the Army (formerly called the War Department). The design includes a cap of liberty, various weapons and flags, and a rattlesnake with the motto "This We'll Defend." The date of the Army's creation appears below this emblem. The flag staff often bears streamers corresponding to the campaigns in which the Army has participated. A flag of the same design, but of differing colors and without battle streamers, is used by offices and installations not entitled to the Army Flag. This Army Field Flag created in 1962 has a field of ultramarine blue with the emblem all in white, except for the inscription which is in scarlet.

In the past the Marines have carried colors of white and of dark blue, but since 1939 Marine Corps Standards (LIX-b shows the present form) have had a field of scarlet, and gold and scarlet have been designated as the official Corps colors. The Western Hemisphere appears on the globe and the motto "Ever Faithful" is written in Latin ("Semper Fidelis") on the ribbon held by the eagle. The anchor also appears in the seal of the Navy Department on the Navy flag (LIX-c). This seal came into use sometime after the creation of the Department in 1798. The flag, dating from 1959, is not hoisted at sea, but is carried "at official ceremonies, in parades, during official Navy display occasions, at public gatherings when the Navy is an official participant, [and] on such occasions as may be specifically authorized by the Secretary of the Navy." Formerly, the flag generally used for such purposes was the Naval Infantry Battalion flag (see p. 241), a white diamond with dark-blue

LVIII

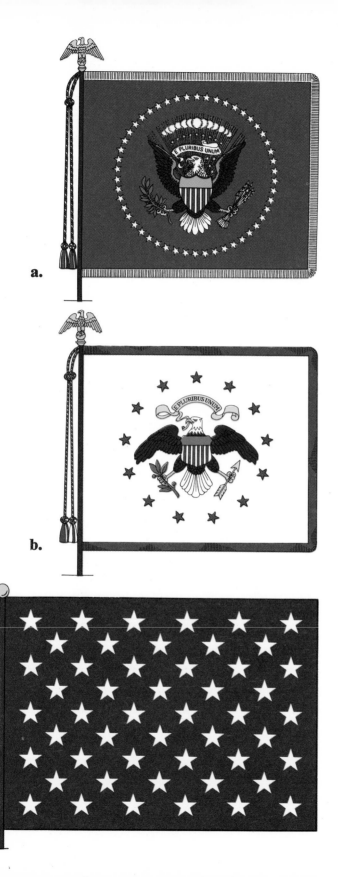

a.

b.

c.

UNITED STATES NAVY Infantry battalion flag ?-present
Proportions 41 x 52

anchor and background. The Naval Militia used the same flag, but with
a yellow diamond. The Merchant Marine Naval Reserve has a dark-blue
pennant with a special emblem, and yachts owned by certain Naval
Reserve officers may fly one of two other special pennants.

The Ceremonial Departmental U. S. Air Force Flag (LX-a) is the
basis for all the organizational colors used in that branch of the armed
services. The Air Force coat of arms in the center has a shield bearing a
winged thunderbolt and a white section suggesting clouds. The division
between the white and blue sections of the shield is of the type known in

**LVIII. FLAGS OF THE PRESIDENT AND VICE PRESIDENT;
JACK**

a. **PRESIDENT OF THE UNITED STATES** 4 July 1960–present
(basic design authorized 25 October 1945) Proportions 26 x 33

b. **VICE PRESIDENT OF THE UNITED STATES** 10 November 1948–
present Proportions 26 x 33

c. **UNITED STATES NAVY** Jack 4 July 1960–present (basic design
authorized c1785) Proportions 1077 x 1520

heraldry as nebulé or cloudlike. The Air Force flag is decorated with fifty-nine battle streamers.

The Coast Guard, run by the Department of Transportation in peace and the Navy during wartime, uses its Standard (LX-b) for ceremonial purposes on shore. This color includes the national arms, thirteen stars, the name and date of founding of the Coast Guard, and its motto "Semper Paratus" ("Always Ready"). The standard is a modified form of the canton in the Coast Guard ensign (LX-c). Actually this "ensign" is a distinguishing flag flown at the foremast only, since the United States national flag is the proper ensign for all American ships. The Coast Guard ensign was established on 1 August 1799, and its sixteen stripes correspond to the number of States in the Union at that time. In 1910 the badge of the service was added in the fly, except on the flag to be flown over customs houses. This badge appears in white on the dark-blue flag of the Coast Guard Auxiliary.

Aside from their service flags, the Army, Marines, Navy, Air Force, and Coast Guard—which is their official order of precedence for ceremonial purposes—all have other types of flags. Personal flags and pennants distinguish the rank of an officer present in the field, on board ship, or at an office. Organizational colors are carried by military units; institutions also have flags for display in offices and when two or more different units are participating in a ceremonial activity. Guidons are small flags generally reserved for distinguishing company-sized units when marching. Automobile and aircraft plates are metal facsimiles of flags and are employed where a cloth flag would obviously be unserviceable. Each branch of the military has a number of miscellaneous flags as well.

The personal rank flags begin with the civilian authorities and work down to the lower grades of military officers. For example the order of flag rank in the Navy would be President of the United States, Vice President, Secretary of Defense, Deputy Secretary of Defense, Assistant Secretaries of Defense, Secretary of the Navy, Under Secretary of the Navy, Assistant Secretaries of the Navy, Chairman of the Joint Chiefs of Staff, Chief of Naval Operations, Fleet Admiral, Admiral, Vice Admiral, Rear Admiral, and Commodore. The Navy also has flags or pennants for flag officers not eligible for command at sea, convoy commodores, and the Naval Aide to the President. There are broad and burgee command pennants and, formerly, a Senior Officer Present pennant. The Army and Air Force flags include those of the Chief of Staff and Vice Chief of Staff of the Army (or Air Force) and of a General of the Army (or Air Force), Generals, Lieutenant Generals, Major Generals, Brigadier Generals, and chaplains. The director of Defense Research and Engineering also has a flag.

For each of its military officers' flags the Army recognizes eight possible forms with similar types existing in the other services. A *field flag*, of bunting, is six feet eight inches by twelve feet. A *color* is silk, four feet four inches by five feet six inches, with fringe, cords and tassels. A *distinguishing flag* is silk, three feet by four feet, and fringed; a *boat flag* is the same size, but of bunting and without fringe. *Automobile flags* may be of silk (one foot six inches by two feet two inches), bunting (the same size), or felt (six inches by nine inches). Automobiles and aircraft have flags of metal. Modern "silk" flags are actually made of synthetic fibers.

The Chairman of the Joint Chiefs of Staff has a flag diagonally divided from upper hoist to lower fly, medium blue over white, with the eagle of the Secretary of Defense's flag in the center. In a line running from the lower hoist to the upper fly are two blue and two white stars. The Chiefs of Staff of the Air Force and Army and the Chief of Naval Operations also have four-starred flags with eagles and diagonally divided backgrounds of two colors.

The five levels of rank in each of the three services are represented in descending order by flags bearing five stars (for a Fleet Admiral, General of the Army, or General of the Air Force), four stars, three stars, two stars, and one star. The usual background colors are scarlet (Army), dark blue (Navy), and ultramarine blue (Air Force); the stars are white. In the Army a General in the Army Medical Service replaces the scarlet field with maroon, while for Chaplains the color is purple. Admirals not eligible for command at sea reverse the colors of the stars and background in their flags. Distinctions were formerly made between the flags of senior and junior Admirals and between staff and line Generals. The five-star flag (see p. 246) in each case has a pentagonal pattern. The Army and Air Force flags of four, three, and two stars shows the stars in rows; the Navy has four stars in a diamond shape, three in a triangle, and one over the other in the two-star flag. The one-star naval flag (Commodore's pennant) is swallow-tailed, unlike the Brigadier General's flag in the other two services. When a General or Admiral is the Adjutant General of a State he is entitled to include in his flag the National Guard crest of that State, but only a very few Adjutants General use such a flag. On p. 174 is the flag of the Adjutant General of New York, Chief of Staff to the Governor.

Organizational colors correspond to the traditional regimental colors of the past as shown in XVIII-a and XXXVIII-a. In the Army they display the American eagle, bearing on his breast the regimental coat of arms with a scroll below indicating the name of the unit. The field of the flag is scarlet in the artillery, dark blue in the infantry, and other colors in such branches as armor, signal corps, and military police. The flags of Air Force units such as air commands, air divisions, wings, and groups are ultramarine blue. Their central emblem is similar to that in the Air Force flag (LX-a), but the shield and inscription correspond to the unit represented. Except in landing-party battalions and other special cases where the Navy Infantry Battalion flag (see p. 241) is used, there is no comparable naval color. However, naval institutions such as the Bureau of Ordnance and Medical Department have had special flags. Special colors are also carried by the United States Military Academies at West Point (Army), Annapolis (Navy), New London (Coast Guard), and Colorado Springs (Air Force) and the United States Merchant Marine Academy at Kings Point.

The guidons in use in the different services vary, but are as a rule swallow-tailed. They bear a simple device and unit designation on a field of solid color, usually red or dark blue. In the past the Cavalry has

LIX. FLAGS OF THE ARMY, MARINES, AND NAVY

a.   **UNITED STATES   Flag of the U.S. Army   12 June 1956–present Proportions 26 x 33**

b.   **UNITED STATES   Flag of the U.S. Marine Corps   ?–present   (basic design authorized January 1939)   Proportions 26 x 33**

c.   **UNITED STATES   Flag of the U.S. Navy   24 April 1959–present Proportions 26 x 33**

a.

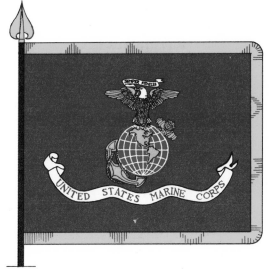

b.

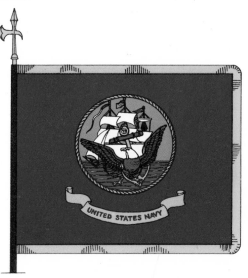

c.

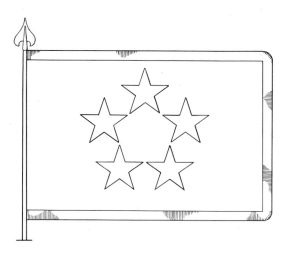

UNITED STATES Color of a Fleet Admiral, General of the Army, or General of the Air Force ?–present Proportions 26 x 33

carried two guidons: one (X-c) was patterned after the national flag and one (similar to the one on p. 190) was of red over white stripes. Both are well known from films about the Civil War and late nineteenth century. The miscellaneous flags used upon occasion by the armed services include the United Nations flag (LII-a), recruiting-service flags, award pennants, marking and signal pennants, trumpet tabards, chapel flags, the church pennant (see p. 278), and the Jack, Commission Pennant, Service Flag, and Geneva Convention flag.

The Jack, like the national flag of the United States, changes to reflect the addition of new States. The present form (LVIII-c) with its fifty stars and proportions exactly corresponding to the canton of the national flag (Frontispiece) became official on 4 July 1960. The tradition of having the "Union Jack" based on the naval flag goes back to the similar custom in British usage discussed in Chapter II. The earliest record of such a flag flown on an American ship dates from 1785: this jack shows three rows of four, five, and four stars. Under the Continental Colors (VIII-a) the jack would have been the same as that of Great Britain and thus was probably not used. There is evidence to suggest that a flag of stripes alone (VIII-b) or of stripes with a snake (VIII-c) was the jack at this time. The Jack flies from the jackstaff at the prow of a ship when it is in the harbor and on certain other occasions. In the United States the Jack has also been used as a rank flag for certain officials, e.g., Naval Governors of Territories and diplomatic personnel (see p. 235).

The Commission Pennant is a flag five units wide by one hundred forty-four units long. The hoist is blue with seven white stars and the fly, which is split in two points for part of its length, has a white stripe under a red one. This pennant is flown by all naval ships which are in commission but which do not have a flag officer or other commander on board and are not hospital ships. It is normally flown from the after truck of the ship or, in mastless ships, "at the loftiest and the most conspicuous point of hoist." In recent decades ship-flag etiquette has had to be modified by such rules to conform to changing naval architecture.

The Service Flag (LXVII-a) was first used unofficially during World War I by private citizens. It is white with a red border and one or more blue stars in the center; it has most often been hung vertically. The flag symbolizes the fact that the family using it has as many of its members in the armed forces as there are stars in the flag. In 1918 Massachusetts issued specifications for ten different kinds of stars to indicate "lost in action" and other conditions, but the only one which has ever found much favor is the use of a blue-bordered gold star to indicate "died in service." In 1942 and 1968 the Government prescribed regulations for use of similar service flags by businesses and other groups whose members were in the service. The flag has not been extensively used since the Second World War.

The Geneva Convention provides for the use by military medical services of a red cross on a white background as a flag, armband, and general symbol for hospitals, ships, vehicles, and elsewhere to indicate that they are protected during wartime. The Red Cross Societies of the United States also display this famous flag. The veterinary services in the American army employ a similar flag in which the cross is green.

CITIES AND COUNTIES

In Europe many cities have symbols that can be traced back for almost a thousand years. Many were first adopted from practical necessity: a seal was needed to authenticate documents, a badge was necessary for municipal property or troops, and ships registered in ports had to be properly identified when they sailed outside of local waters. Of course before the rise of the nation-state in the sixteenth and subsequent centuries, these cities were frequently semi-independent states and in almost all cases had much more local autonomy than modern cities. Even after the central authorities began to assert their claims to overlordship more effectively, the cities jealously guarded their ancient prerogatives, including the use of distinctive emblems. The rise of heraldry greatly expanded the number, variety, and ways of display of such flags, seals, and other symbols, and today the study of civic heraldry is an important part of European symbolism.

The situation developed somewhat differently in the United States. The oldest cities are only three hundred years old and many of large size are barely a century old; none of them has had an independent political existence of its own. Moreover, the traditions of European heraldry find little to sustain them in America where almost from the start there have been great changes in population composition, high social mobility, emphasis on industry, and economic interdependence with other areas. Traditional crafts, guilds, even buildings and neighborhoods have been subject to constant change, while the democratic forms of government, religious pluralism, the absence of established families and classes, and the direct involvement of Americans in events of national importance

LX. FLAGS OF THE AIR FORCE AND COAST GUARD

a.   **UNITED STATES   Flag of the U.S. Air Force   ?–present   Proportions 26 x 33**

b.   **UNITED STATES   Flag of the U.S. Coast Guard   28 January 1964–present   Proportions 26 x 33**

c.   **UNITED STATES COAST GUARD   "ensign" Distinguishing flag at sea   9 August 1966–present · (basic design authorized 1 August 1799)   Proportions 5 x 8**

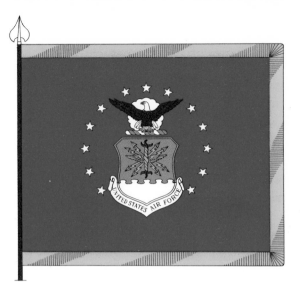

a.

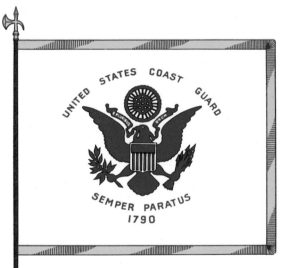

b.

c.

such as elections, wars, and the conquest of the frontier all have tended to minimize interest in purely local concerns.

In general, trends in the symbols of cities and towns have followed the same pattern found in State symbolism, as discussed in the previous chapter. The founders of the political systems in both cases were concerned and knowledgeable about symbols only in rare cases and the only immediate need they saw was for a seal of public office. In the eighteenth

ATTLEBORO (MASS.) City seal c1940–present

century and before the designs were usually simple, so that they might be easily engraved: as in Europe some of these were heraldic, while others bore ships or local trees or animals. One example, the Town Council seal of Portsmouth, Rhode Island, used in the late seventeenth century, suggests the influence of the arms of its namesake, Portsmouth, England (see p. 63).

In the nineteenth century and well into the twentieth seals continued to grow more and more elaborate, often encompassing pictures of the city or of factories, bridges, harbors, railroads, and the principal industrial products of which the inhabitants were proud. The twentieth century has seen the development of more vigorous and sophisticated designs which make use of only a few symbols to convey their message. The Massachusetts cities of Attleboro and Cambridge provide good examples. The former seal includes a lion from the arms of the Albini family of Attleborough, England, a watch chain to symbolize the local jewelry industry, and the three marks used by Chief Wamsutta on the deed by which he transferred to the first settlers an area now part of the town. Cambridge celebrates its leading place in American history and education by displaying the Washington Elm and old Gore Hall of Harvard University.

Comparatively few of America's 90,000 local governments have flags and most of those flags which do exist date from the twentieth century. Even fewer of the 3,000 counties have flags of their own, although there has been a slow increase in the number of both municipal and county flags since World War II. Generally, such flags have been adopted as part of a centennial or other municipal celebration, and very often they are the result of a contest run among school children to select the best design. The American preference for seals and inscriptions evident in the State flags is even more pronounced here. The problem of expensive manufacture is not so great, however, as city and county flags are seen almost exclusively in the chambers of the mayor or the governing council. Generally it is only in a few of the largest cities that city flags can be seen flying on buildings, except on special occasions.

**CAMBRIDGE
(MASS.)
City seal
1964–present
(basic design dates from 1864)**

The city flag of Chicago (LXI-a) was adopted in its present form on 21 December 1939. An earlier version with two stars had been designed by Wallace Rice and approved by the city on 4 April 1917. The colors and the points on the stars have elaborate historical symbolisms attributed to them. The blue stripes are for the Chicago River, Lake Michigan, and other waters surrounding the city. The four stars signify events famous in the history of Chicago—the Fort Dearborn Massacre

a.

b.

c.

of 1812, the Great Chicago Fire of 1871, the World's Columbian Exposition of 1893, and the "Century of Progress" World's Fair of 1933.

New York has a large number of flags. The city itself, four of its five boroughs, the transit authority, the police, the Port of New York Authority, and a number of other institutions fly their own flags. Most of these include the colors blue, white, and orange which derive from the Dutch flags flown in the area over three hundred years ago (see p. 19). In the flag of the city and in the Mayor's flag (LXI-b) the seal of New York is included. The date 1625 in this seal commemorates the founding of the city by the Dutch, and the American eagle is also found in the crest of the New York State arms; the supporters are an English sailor and a Manhattan Indian. The emblems on the shield, referring to the period of Dutch rule, consist of beavers and barrels between the arms of a windmill. Five stars representing the five boroughs appear on the Mayor's flag but are omitted on the flag of the city. Both flags became official on 1 May 1915 and were modified in 1975.

Pittsburgh has chosen black and gold for its flags, perhaps because it is an industrial city. The "city ensign" (LXI-c), which is for use on the merchant ships of the city, has the crest from the municipal arms on the center stripe within a circle of stars. The "civic flag" for use on land displays the entire arms, which are an adaptation of the coat of arms of William Pitt, First Lord Chatham, for whom the city was named. Pittsburgh also has a city pennant and a city streamer.

The City and County of San Francisco are coterminous and therefore share a seal and flag. The flag (LXII-a) was made official on 16 December 1940. The phoenix is the crest in the municipal arms and stands for the rise of the city after its disastrous fire of 1906. The mining of the area and the fact that San Francisco was a troop depot in the Spanish-American War are recalled in the motto which reads (in Spanish) "Gold in Peace, Iron in War."

LXI. CITY FLAGS

a. **CHICAGO**   **Government and general usage flag**   **21 December 1939–present**   **Proportions 2 x 3 but variable**

b. **NEW YORK**   **Mayor's flag**   **8 January 1975–present**   **Proportions 3 x 4**

c. **PITTSBURGH**   **"City ensign"**   **General usage flag on water**   **15 March 1899–present**   **Proportions 3 x 4**

INDIAN NATIONS

The original Indian and Eskimo inhabitants of the North American continent, as was pointed out in the second chapter, did not carry flags of the type known in Europe. While there are cases of Indian nations living peacefully under the flags of the United States (see p. 55), the general history of these peoples during the eighteenth and nineteenth centuries was marked by military defeat, loss of their traditional homelands, and decreasing population caused in part by famine and disease for which the white man was responsible. By the end of the nineteenth century most American Indians had been forced into reservations and deprived of civil rights. Although formerly the United States had made treaties with Indian nations, in 1871 Congress decided that these tribes had no standing as separate governments. The reversal of these policies has begun slowly in this century, but few Indians at present have the same access to the fruits of citizenship and economic well-being enjoyed by the majority of Americans.

In light of their history it is not surprising that few Indian nations (the Cherokee, Crow, Miccosukee, Navajo, Northern Cheyenne, Oglala Sioux, and Seminole*) have flags of their own. These flags are all of recent date and are so little used that information on them has never been published before. In designing both seals and flags the Indian nations of the United States are fortunate in having a rich fund of symbols on which to draw. These are evident both in the new flags and in the seals of the so-called "Five Civilized Tribes"—the Cherokee, Chickasaw, Choctaw, Muscogee, and Seminole Nations—who from 1820 until 1907 had recognized territorial governments in what is now Oklahoma. These seals appear today in the Oklahoma State seal.

In the 1700's the Cherokees lived in the southern Appalachian Mountains, but in the next century they were forced to move to their present home in Oklahoma. They were one of the first of the Indian tribes to create their own formal government, which dates from 1820. On 6 September 1839, as noted on their seal (opposite), the Cherokee Nation adopted a new constitution to serve them in their new territory.

* There may possibly be a few other tribal flags which the author's research did not uncover. Many tribes have seals, since these are necessary for the conduct of public business.

CHEROKEE NATION
Seal
11 December 1869–1907

The seal itself, created in 1869 and used until 1907, encompassed a number of symbolic meanings of importance to the nation. The seven-pointed star, for example, recalled the seven legendary clans from whom the Cherokee descended. The wreath of oak leaves stood for the sacred fire of oak logs which had always been kept burning in the Town House at the center of the nation. The emblem may also have been suggested by missionaries living in the Cherokee Nation, as a symbol of the rebirth of this nation following their sufferings in the Civil War. In the Cherokee seal the name of the Nation appears in English and in the native language as written in the syllabary invented by Sequoyah. The Cherokee flag is white and features seven red seven-pointed stars in the form of the Big Bear constellation.

The two principal tribal divisions of the Chickasaws were the Koi (panther) and Ishpani (Spanish) phratries. The former provided the war chiefs of the tribe and the latter provided its civil rulers, originally called kings and later governors. The war chiefs were important in tribal affairs because the tribe was frequently involved in battle. Therefore when the seal of the Chickasaw Nation was created in 1867 (see p. 256), its principal device was a warrior—probably intended to be Chief Tishomingo. He was the last war chief of the tribe and died in 1838 at the age of 104 while he and his people were on route to their new home in Oklahoma. The capital city of the Chickasaw Nation was also named after him. The bow and shield were emblematic of the war chief's de-

**CHICKASAW
NATION
Seal
16 August 1867–1907
(authorized 1856)**

scent from the Panther Phratry and the two arrows represented his guardianship over that clan and the Ishpani Phratry.

The Choctaws were the first tribe to sign a treaty with the United States government arranging for their establishment in what is today the State of Oklahoma. The three leaders who signed this treaty in 1820, Mosholatubbee, Apuckshenubbee, and Pushamataha, were each in charge of a subdivision of the Choctaw Nation. The three political districts in the new territory were named after these chiefs and they are also represented by the three arrows which lie across the bow in the Choctaw seal. The unstrung bow itself suggests that the people were at peace, but ready at any time to defend themselves; the same idea was implicit in the combined peace pipe and tomahawk which completes the seal design. Peace pipes were a European invention, although the Indians eventually came to use them. The original Indian calumet or council pipe was a ceremonial object without any blade on it, which was passed around and smoked by participants at meetings called to discuss important tribal affairs. In time of peace such calumets were decorated with white feathers, in time of war with red.

LXII. COUNTY AND INDIAN NATION FLAGS
a.   SAN FRANCISCO   City and county flag   16 December 1940–present
b.   CROW TRIBE   18 August 1967–present
c.   MICCOSUKEE TRIBE   ?–present

a.

b.

c.

Although the Choctaw government had been in operation for many years by 1860, it was not until then, when a new constitution was adopted, that the seal became official. The occasion was the centralization of the three formerly autonomous tribal divisions into a united nation; the seal, symbolic of that union, was necessary for government business. It continued to be used on official papers until 1907. Its design also appears in the flag (XXXIX-c) traditionally associated with the troop of Choctaw soldiers who fought with the Confederate Army in the Civil War. The original flag is lost, but a replica is displayed in the Oklahoma Historical Society Museum in Oklahoma City. It was this flag, together with an Osage shield, which inspired the design of the present Oklahoma State flag.

The seal of the Crow Tribe, which appears on the tribal flag (LXII-b) designed by Lawrence Big Hair, combines many traditional symbols. The thirteen original clans of the Crows and their chieftains are represented by the rising sun and war bonnets. The sun rises over the Wolf, Big Horn, and Pryor Mountains which are within the present homeland of the tribe. The teepee is the symbol of home to the Crow and its four poles stand for the corners of the territory which the tribe occupied after it made peace with the United States in 1868. Below the teepee appear a medicine bag which is associated with the Tobacco Society, an important part of Crow religion; the sweat lodge which is used in purification ceremonies; a peace pipe; and the Big Dipper constellation. These and the other elements present a summary of the cultural and religious values of tribal life. The flag was first formally hoisted at the annual Crow Rodeo on 18 August 1967.

MICCOSUKEE TRIBE
Seal
?–present

The Miccosukees were one of the leading groups in the Seminole Wars (see p. 262) and afterwards remained in Florida rather than move West as the United States government wished. In 1962 the tribe reorganized its administration and adopted a constitution. The tribal seal (opposite) shows the chickee, or palm-thatched open house, in which the people have traditionally lived. A flag (LXII-c) has also been adopted; it is flown outside chickees and on the boats in which tribesmen frequently travel in the swampy country they inhabit. The colors are said to constitute a strong medicine, favorable to Miccosukee advancement. They symbolize the points of the compass—white for the south, black for north, red for west, and yellow for east.

MUSCOGEE NATION
Seal
c1867–1907

After their immigration to Oklahoma the Creek Indians, who called themselves Muscogee, became proficient in agriculture and suggested this in their government seal (above) by showing a plow and sheaf of wheat. Similar emblems appear in the seals of twenty-two States. The Muscogee seal was adopted after the Civil War and used from about 1885 until 1907.

The Navajo nation, originally nomadic, was collected and settled in northern New Mexico by the United States Army in 1863. After five years of military occupation a treaty was signed between the Navajos and the United States, releasing the former from Army control. To celebrate the centennial of this event, in 1968 a Navajo flag was adopted and hoisted for the first time on 30 June. A white field bears symbols derived from the seal which had been designed some years earlier. Four sacred mountains mark the points of the compass and surround the outline of the tribal reservation. The Navajo symbol of life and figures representing agriculture and livestock were also included by Jay DeGroat, the student who designed the flag. The Navajos are the largest existing Indian nation within the United States; their sovereignty is symbolized by the rainbow in the flag.

The morning star, brighter than the other stars in the early sky, became an important symbol to the Cheyenne. The graphic figure which represents the morning star, called *wohehiv* in the Cheyenne language, has been used by the tribe for a long time: it was, for example, painted on dancers in the religious ceremony known as the Sun Dance. Its significance has been reenforced by the fact that Morning Star (or Dull Knife) was one of the principal Cheyenne leaders in the late nineteenth century. After the Cheyenne had been dispossessed of their original homes by white settlers and defeated in the Indian Wars by the Army, Morning Star helped lead them to their present home in Montana. Thus the *wohehiv* has come to stand for hope and guidance. Its use on the flag of the Northern Cheyenne (LXIII-a) dates from 1964 and was suggested the year before by the tribal President, John Woodenlegs.

The red field of the Oglala Sioux tribal flag (LXIII-b) refers both to the name "red men" and to the blood shed by the Sioux in the defense of their land in the wars of the past century. The rectangular shape of the flag suggests the outline of the Pine Ridge Reservation in South Dakota where the Oglala Sioux now live. The blue fringe has two meanings. It stands for the blue sky and thus reminds the tribe of the worship of the Great Spirit and of the Happy Hunting Grounds of departed relatives. In modern times the blue has come to represent tribal loyalty to the United States, whose national colors are incorporated in the Oglala Sioux flag. In the center of the flag are eight tepees, one for each of the political subdivisions of the tribe—the Wakpamni, Porcupine, Wounded Knee,

LXIII. INDIAN NATION FLAGS
a. **NORTHERN CHEYENNE TRIBE   c1964–present**
b. **OGLALA SIOUX TRIBE   9 March 1962–present**
c. **SEMINOLE TRIBE (FLORIDA)   August 1966–present   Proportions
    3 x 5**

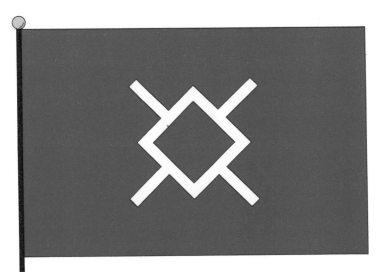

a.

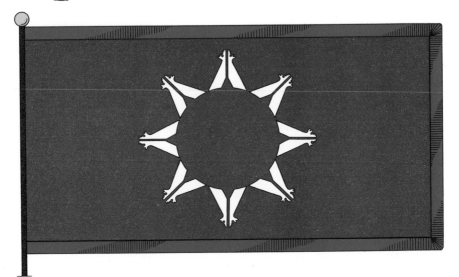

b.

c.

Medicine Root, Pass Creek, Eagle Nest, White Clay, and LaCreek Districts. The flag was first displayed during the Sun Dance ceremonies in 1961, following provisional Tribal Council approval. It became official on 9 March of the following year.

Originally part of the Creek confederacy living in Alabama and Georgia, the Seminoles moved into Florida during the 1700's. After the First Seminole War in 1818, the United States government began to encourage tribal resettlement in Oklahoma where the Seminole Nation was organized. Many Seminoles refused to leave, however, and antagonism between them and white settlers broke out in the Second Seminole War in 1835. A flag infamous in Seminole history is the flag of truce carried in this war by their leader Osceola, who was tricked into meeting General Thomas Jessup for peace talks. Jessup, disregarding the white flag, seized and imprisoned Osceola, although his people fought on for seven years. Formal peace was not finally concluded between the United States and the Seminoles until 1934.

SEMINOLE TRIBE (OKLAHOMA)
Seal
?–1907

The Seminole Tribe of Florida adopted a flag of its own in August 1966, when at the annual Powwow a flag-designing contest was held. The flag selected (LXIII-c) bears a general resemblance in design to the flag of Florida (XX-c) and includes the State motto, "In God We Trust." In the center is an emblem which combines the seals of the Tribe and of the Tribal Council with a palm tree for Florida. The dugout canoe, formerly the principal Seminole means of transportation, represents the business interests of the Tribe. The council fire and chickee (thatched-roof house) suggest the social affairs of the people. The chickee also appears in the Miccosukee seal (see p. 258), while the Indian paddling a canoe is the central feature of the seal of the Seminole Nation in Oklahoma.

The Oklahoma Seminoles are descendants of those who accepted the United States government offer of land in the West. They adopted the Indian and canoe emblem (opposite) because it recalled the happiness that they had had in the old days in Florida. The seal was used by the government of the Seminole Nation during the last years of its administration, which began in 1866 and ended in 1907 when Oklahoma became a State.

CONFEDERATE STATES OF AMERICA

Americans have hoisted flags to express their political sentiments since before the Revolution, and it is not surprising, therefore, to find a profusion of new banners accompanying the secessionist movement in the South. Hints of a desire for local sovereignty were given long before rebellion actually broke out, in such symbols as the 1845 flag of Florida (XIX-c). The real flowering of southern flags, however, began in November 1860 when the election of Lincoln to the Presidency caused widespread fear that the federal government would try to make changes in the institution of slavery. During the winter of 1860-1861 rallies and speeches were held throughout the South, and frequently the United States flag was replaced by a local banner. The familiar palmetto of South Carolina, the pelican of Louisiana, and the magnolia tree of Mississippi as well as other emblems and fiery mottoes appeared on these flags.

By far the most common device in the new Southern flags was the star, a symbol of independence and sovereignty. The development of the star as a special American symbol has already been cited (see p. 87), but special note should be given to its role in the South. As early as 1856 one South Carolina sea captain had hoisted a United States flag of only fifteen stars, to symbolize the regional unity of the South. By the spring of 1861 starry flags of rebellion had appeared in every southern State.

a.

b.

c.

Single-starred flags were flown to indicate that a particular State had severed its formal ties with the Union; see, for example, the North Carolina flag in XXXVII-b. The star was further popularized by the rousing song "The Bonnie Blue Flag," which was written and sung by Harry McCarthy, a comedian. The Bonnie Blue Flag itself (LXIV-a) was used, unofficially, throughout the South at this time. McCarthy composed the song after being inspired by the lone star banner raised when Mississippi seceded.

A bare three months after Lincoln's election, representatives of six of the seven seceding States gathered in Montgomery, Alabama, in February 1861 as a convention for the establishment of a new government. From all parts of the South designs were sent to the convention for adoption as a national flag to be displayed by the Confederate States of America. On 9 February William P. Miles was appointed chairman of a flag committee whose task was to sift through the proposed designs and select the one which should become official. The committee made its report the next month, recommending a flag of three horizontal red and white bars (so called to distinguish them from the stripes of the U. S. flag) with a blue canton bearing a white star for each southern State. This design (LXIV-b) met the requirements of the committee, which, obviously sensible to the essential elements of flag design, had insisted that "a flag should be simple, readily made, and, above all, capable of being made up in bunting; it should be different from the flag of any other country, place, or people; it should be significant; it should be

LXIV. EARLY FLAGS OF THE CONFEDERACY

a. **BONNIE BLUE FLAG** **Unofficial flag of the South, 1860–1861**

   WEST FLORIDA (REPUBLIC) **National flag 22 September–4 December 1810**

   TEXAS **Independence party flag 1835–1836**

   MISSISSIPPI **Unofficial national flag 9–26 January 1861**

b. **CONFEDERATE STATES OF AMERICA** **Unofficial national flag and ensign March 1861**

c. **CONFEDERATE STATES OF AMERICA** **Unofficial national flag and ensign September 1861–1 May 1863** readily distinguishable at a distance; the colors should be well contrasted and durable; and, lastly, and not the least important point, it should be effective and handsome."

It will be noted that the influence of the United States flag on the design of the first Confederate flag was very strong; this was intentional, as most Southerners in 1861 felt that they had as much claim to the glories of the Stars and Stripes as persons from any other part of the country. In fact the flag committee mentions in its report that there were two principal types of designs submitted to it: "those which copy and preserve the principal features of the United States flag . . . . [and] those which are very elaborate, complicated, or fantastical."

Although the flag committee made its report on 5 March, the convention voted to enter the record of its new flag in the *Journal* of the previous day, which had been Lincoln's inauguration. However, no formal action was taken to adopt this design then or later, and thus it remained, like the Continental Colors, a widely used but unofficial flag. Detailed specifications concerning the arrangement of the stars were never made, although the most common pattern was a ring of stars with or without one in the center. The number of stars varied from seven, at the time of the creation of the flag, to thirteen (LXIV-c) representing the States of Alabama, Arkansas, Florida, Georgia, Kentucky, Louisiana, Mississippi, Missouri, North Carolina, South Carolina, Tennessee, Texas, and Virginia. Both Kentucky and Missouri had two governments during the Civil War, one remaining loyal to the Union, the other participating in the Confederacy.

The first Stars and Bars, as the flag came to be called, rose over the State Capitol in Montgomery on 4 March. It was raised by the granddaughter of former United States President John Tyler, who himself was a member of the provisional Confederate Congress. While the honor of having made this flag is shared anonymously by several Montgomery women, there is a dispute over the name of the creator of the design. Major Orren Smith of North Carolina and Nicola Marschall, a Prussian living in Alabama at the time of the Convention, both claimed—long after the Civil War—to have submitted the winning design to the flag committee. The majority of those who have investigated the claims favor

Marschall, although it is not impossible that both men conceived of the same flag simultaneously.

A case of this kind of coincidence of ideas exists with regard to the best known Battle Flag of the Confederacy (LXV-a). At least five people independently arrived at the general concept embodied in the Battle Flag. First, a delegate from South Carolina presented to the Montgomery convention in February 1861 a design (like XLVI-b, but without the crescent or tree) for a Confederate national flag. The next month a pattern (LXV-b) even closer to the actual Battle Flag was proposed for a national flag by chariman Miles of the flag committee. At least two military men suggested almost the same design for army use that spring. Then in September 1861 the Battle Flag itself was established through the cooperation of Generals Joseph E. Johnston, G. T. Beauregard, and G. W. Smith, reputedly using a pattern suggested by Colonel J. B. Walton. (Other battle flags were also sometimes used.)

The need for a distinctive battle flag arose at the Battle of Bull Run (Manassas) in July 1861. In addition to their very important roles as symbols of national achievement and aspiration and as inspirational forces for the soldier on the field, flags have long served the practical purpose of rallying troops, indicating the flow of battle to commanders, signaling manoeuvers, and generally facilitating the course of battle. Unfortunately, the great similarity of the Stars and Bars to the Stars and Stripes made the former a poor battle flag for the South because troops could not easily distinguish friend from foe. After Bull Run, therefore, the three generals agreed upon the flag (LXV-a) which eventually came to be used by almost all the Southern armies. Many variations existed: the number of stars was reduced, or they were painted gold instead of white, or the border of the saltire was omitted.

The Battle Flag was made in three different sizes for the infantry, artillery, and cavalry, but normally the proportions were square. This made for a lighter flag that would fly in a light breeze and a shorter one than the usual military colors, so that it would be less likely to be torn by bayonets or tree branches. The brilliant colors and simple but bold arrangement guaranteed that the flag would be recognizable from a great distance. Many other flags were used by the Confederacy on the battlefield, especially State regimental colors, but the Battle Flag, although it was never officially recognized by the Confederate government, came to represent the Southern cause to most people.

In the twentieth century an erroneous idea about the design of the Battle Flag has become very common. The form now sold in stores and illustrated in many books (LXV-b) is rectangular rather than square and lacks the narrow white border around the outside. This was rarely used as a Battle Flag; in fact it was the jack of the Confederate Navy created on 26 May 1863 by Secretary of the Navy Stephen R. Mallory. In the same order Mallory had provided for a pennant and a naval ensign for Confederate warships. This ensign (LXV-c) bore the Battle Flag without its white border as a canton on a white field. (Previously, the Stars and Bars had served as a naval ensign as well as the flag for general use over public and private buildings, including forts and arsenals.) The new ensign lasted until the end of the war, and was struck for the last time on the *Shenandoah* in August 1865, four months after the capitulation at Appomattox.

The design of the naval ensign was apparently first suggested by the editor of the *Savannah Morning News* in April 1863. At that time the Confederate Congress, which had replaced the provisional government in 1862, was debating a report concerning an official national flag, which had been submitted to it by its flag committee. As a replacement for the Stars and Bars—a flag not only without official sanction and

LXV. FLAGS OF THE CONFEDERATE ARMED FORCES

a.   **CONFEDERATE STATES OF AMERICA   "Battle Flag"; "Southern Cross"; flag of the army (unofficial; variant) September 1861–April 1865**

b.   **CONFEDERATE STATES OF AMERICA   Navy jack   26 May 1863–August 1865   Proposed Confederate national flag, March 1861   Unofficial flag of the South, 1880?–present   Proportions 2 x 3**

c.   **CONFEDERATE STATES OF AMERICA   Ensign   26 May 1863–August 1865   Proportions 2 x 3**

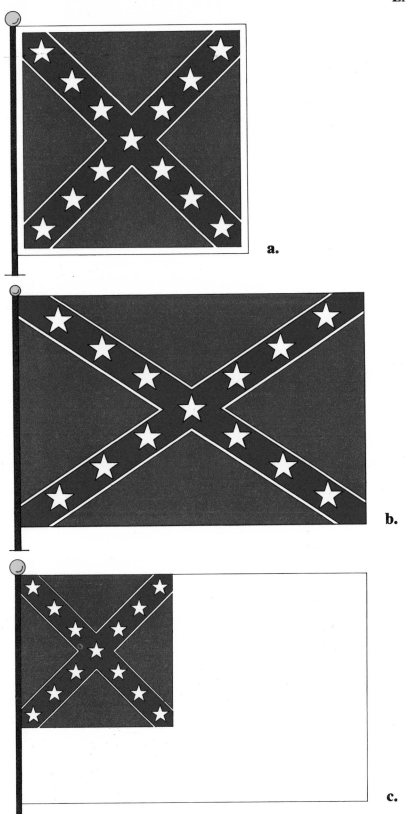

a.

b.

c.

distinctiveness in battle, but unfortunate in the eyes of many for being modeled after the United States flag—many designs were considered. One of these was white with a black horse, symbolizing the fact that Southerners were equestrians.* At last the Committee proposed a national flag vaguely similar to the Battle Flag. Its red field was divided by a white saltire and in the center appeared a rising yellow sun on a blue shield. The Senate rejected this flag and approved instead a flag with

**CONFEDERATE
STATES OF
AMERICA
Seal
30 April 1863–April 1865**

horizontal stripes of white, blue, and white and the Battle Flag as a canton. The version finally approved on 1 May 1863 as the first official national and state flag of the Confederacy (LXVI-a) was the same, omitting only the blue stripe in the middle.

This flag was known variously as the "Stainless Banner," the "White Man's Flag," or the "Jackson Flag" because it covered the coffin of General Stonewall Jackson soon after its adoption. Although the de-

---

* This concept was evident in the great seal of the Confederacy (see above) adopted on 30 April 1863, which showed George Washington, mounted and surrounded by a wreath of cotton, corn, and other southern agricultural products. The Confederate States never had a coat of arms and the seal appears never to have been used.

sign pleased those who had objected to the Stars and Bars, the new flag was not altogether a happy choice. The omission of the blue stripe left a wide white field which was easily soiled and might be mistaken for a flag of truce or, at sea, for the White Ensign of the British Navy.* To remedy its defects, Major Arthur L. Rogers of the Confederate Artillery proposed changing the proportions for the national flag from 1:2 to 2:3 and adding a red stripe at the fly. Such a flag (LXVI-b) was officially approved by the Confederate Congress on 4 March 1865, but only a few examples were actually made since the war was terminated little more than a month later. In this century this flag and its predecessors have been used by Southern patriotic and veterans' organizations. These Confederate flags also had a lasting influence in the design and meanings of the State flags of Alabama, Arkansas, Florida, Georgia, and Mississippi.

PRIVATE FLAGS

In any modern society men are divided into many interest groups based on occupation, language, religion, and other factors. To express their history and aspirations, many such groups create flags or other symbols. As a nation of joiners, the United States has thousands of these symbols, used especially in rallies, meetings, parades, and on organizational headquarters. Only a select few can be presented here from each of the principal categories—ethnic groups, associations and clubs, nonprofit corporations, and businesses. Lacking the heraldic tradition, the United States has never had more than one or two personal or family flags for every hundred thousand citizens.

The United States has long been justly proud of its ability to absorb large numbers of immigrants into a unified culture. Members of many of these nationalities, however, are equally proud of the heritage of their forefathers. Expressions of this are found in their formal and informal symbols and ceremonies. In club halls, shops, and on private homes the flag of "the old country" is often seen; the flags of Canada, China, Cuba,

---

* The Confederate Navy, in adopting this flag for use at sea, reduced the length in order to make it fly more readily and thus serve better as a distinguishing mark.

a.

b.

c.

LXVI

Greece, Ireland, and Italy are common. Especially in parades in big cities, one can see the flags of Hungary, Poland, Puerto Rico, and even countries like Armenia, Estonia, Serbia, and the Ukraine which are not independent.

In this general category is the green Irish flag (LXVI-c) which bears a harp and wreath of shamrock with the motto "Erin Go Bragh." (This is an erroneous version of the Gaelic motto "Éire Go Bráth," "Ireland Forever.") This flag is not used today in Ireland itself, although unofficially in the seventeenth and eighteenth centuries a somewhat similar flag was flown by Irish ships. Actually, the arms of Ireland are a gold harp on blue, the gold harp on green being only the coat of arms of the province of Leinster. The Fenian movement made the first use of the green flag in the United States. It was also seen in the Civil War when such colors were carried by Massachusetts and New York Irish regiments. Today the official green-white-orange tricolor of the Irish Republic is gradually replacing the old flag in the United States.

Another flag which has been transformed over time is the naval jack of the Confederate States of America (LXV-b). Originally flown only on the prow of ships, since the late nineteenth century it has been displayed extensively on land as an unofficial Southern banner—a kind of national flag of Dixieland, symbolizing adherence to the "Lost Cause" and the principles of racial segregation and "States' Rights." In the North it has also been widely used since World War II by some high school and college students on speedboats, hot rods, motorcycle helmets, in dormitories and similar situations. It is often mistakenly called the Battle Flag or the Stars and Bars. This is the only regional flag now used

LXVI. FLAGS OF THE CONFEDERACY; IRISH-AMERICAN FLAG

a.   **CONFEDERATE STATES OF AMERICA**   State and national flag
1 May 1863–4 March 1865   Proportions 1 x 2

b.   **CONFEDERATE STATES OF AMERICA**   State and national flag
4 March 1865–April 1865   Proportions 2 x 3

c.   **IRISH-AMERICAN FLAG**   Unofficial flag of the Fenian Movement
and other Irishmen in the United States   1860's–present

in the United States, although in the seventeenth and eighteenth centuries New England had its own flag.

Unlike other immigrant groups, the Africans whose descendants now constitute more than ten percent of the American population came to the New World involuntarily. As a minority constantly discriminated against in social, economic, and political life, black Americans long had no distinctive flags or other symbols, except for a few regimental colors like the Bucks of America flag (VII-c). Marcus Garvey, a leader of blacks in the 1920's, chose the colors red, black, and green to stand for the blood, the race, and the hopes of the Afro-American. A horizontal tricolor of those three colors known as the Black Liberation Flag is flown by many. Other actual or proposed flags representing black Americans were evolved in the 1960's, including those of the Republic of New Africa and the Nation of Islam ("Black Muslims"). Unlike other ethnic groups, blacks have not been able to trace symbols back directly to the lands of their ancestors, but their newly created flags reflect the ones used in modern African nations.

There are innumerable types of associations in the United States, some with flags and others without any. The major political parties have never used flags because neither the Democrats nor the Republicans have ever had the kind of ideological unity characteristic of many parties in Europe, Latin America, and elsewhere and hence have lacked any logical unifying symbols. Minor parties and movements of the extreme left and right occasionally fly flags, however. For example, the original Ku Klux Klan formed in 1867 had a triangular yellow flag with a red scalloped border; within was a motto and a black dragon.

The red flag of socialism and the black flag of anarchism known to Europeans are rare in American political life. In the 1960's, however, student groups protesting the war in Vietnam often flew the Viet Cong flag, which consists of a yellow star on a background of red over light-blue horizontal stripes. In the same era both leftists and rightists employed a form of the thirteen-star United States flag (IX-c) as a sign of their adherence to the revolutionary principles they felt should be essential in American life. Labor unions make little use of flags, although Mexican-Americans organized by the National Farm Workers Union carry a red flag bearing a black eagle on a white circle.

Veterans' organizations, fraternal associations, and clubs frequently have elaborate and widely used flags and other symbols. The American Legion and Veterans of Foreign Wars use dark-blue flags bearing their seals in the middle and inscriptions to indicate the number and location of the particular post. This pattern is obviously inspired by the blue regimental colors of the armed services. Similar flags are displayed by the Boy Scouts and Girl Scouts. The international Boy Scout flag is purple, a color rarely found in flags, with a white fleur-de-lys within a knotted cord. The Girl Scout world flag is somewhat similar; it bears a gold trefoil on blue. The troop flags used by United States Scout units are horizontally striped—red over white for the boys, blue over white for the girls, each bearing the national emblem in the center and encircling inscriptions. The Camp Fire Girls, YMCA, YWCA, 4-H Clubs, and similar youth organizations also have simple flags with the emblem of the association in the center. The Daughters of the American Revolution and the Sons of the American Revolution have vertically striped flags (blue-white-blue and yellow-blue-yellow respectively) with their emblems in the center.

Other flags are used, especially in parades, by groups such as the Eagles, Elks, Kiwanis, Knights of Columbus, Lions, Masons, and Shriners. The Rotary Clubs usually have small flags in pennant or gonfalon form, which are exchanged with members in other Rotary Clubs. Police and fire departments often have flags for parade use and sometimes plant special flags over the graves of dead comrades. The Mardi Gras festivities in New Orleans fly a green-, yellow-, and purple-striped flag; other traditional celebrations·also may have flags, including historical flags used in the area. High schools and especially their marching bands often have flags. In parts of the country, especially the Midwest, hundreds of precision color-guard groups are involved in competitions based on elaborate rules. This is roughly comparable to the folk-activity of "flag-tossing" which is found in Switzerland and the Netherlands.

Other flags associated with American sports are the skin-divers' flag (a white diagonal stripe on red) which warns of diving in the area where it is displayed, and the flags used at race tracks, including the well-known black-and-white-checkered starting flag. In professional sports, the major baseball teams compete annually for the famous pennant awarded the world champions. In other sports, such as skiing, signal flags or pennants may be used. Other signal flags include the red warning flag attached to trucks or flown over open manholes and the orange-and-white-checkered airport warning flag. The Weather Bureau has a number of flags and pennants which it displays along the coast to warn of impending gales and storms.

Perhaps the widest usage of associational flags and pennants exists in yachting and other forms of pleasure boating. The two most important flags in this category are the so-called yacht ensign (LXVII-b) and the flag of the United States Power Squadron. The former is like the national flag, except that in place of the stars it has a white fouled anchor surrounded by thirteen stars. This was originally not an ensign at all but a special signal, approved by the Government in 1848 for specially registered yachts so that they would not need to clear customs in every port. By common usage it quickly became an ensign in general usage among all pleasure craft, but in 1968 steps were taken to limit its use again to those entitled by law to hoist it. The U. S. Power Squadron flag has the same canton as the yacht ensign (except in red rather than blue), but the stripes are blue and white and are placed vertically.

All yacht clubs have pennants and most of them provide for flags or pennants of rank for use by their officers. Private distinguishing pennants are also seen on yachts. These two types frequently show great imagination in design, while retaining simplicity of form and color. In addition to these practical identifying signals, American boatmen often use racing flags, humorous flags (such as the Jolly Roger, the old pirate ensign with

LXVII. OTHER AMERICAN FLAGS

a.   **UNITED STATES ARMED FORCES**   **Service flag (flown by families and businesses to indicate a member is in military service) ?–present   Proportions 10 x 19**

b.   **UNITED STATES OF AMERICA   "Yacht ensign"   Yacht distinguishing flag   1848–present**

c.   **"CHRISTIAN FLAG"   Unofficial flag of several Protestant churches 1897–present**

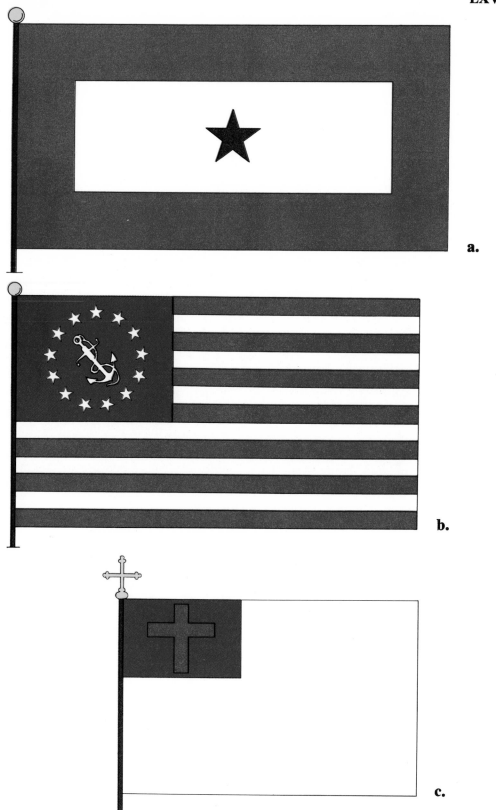

a.

b.

c.

skull and crossbones on black), and flags indicating the owner's absence, guests, etc. Also found at sea are the house flags of shipping companies, used on both freight and passenger ships. Indeed the whole subject of naval flags and pennants and the etiquette that is associated with them is very complex and will be given the separate, detailed treatment it deserves in another volume in this series.

Business firms in the United States do not tend to use flags to identify themselves, although pennants and banners are very frequently displayed for advertising purposes. Changes in corporate structure and in the "image" which the companies wish to convey to the public have probably prevented the development of general house flags. Heraldic flags bearing the arms of the firm, such as are found in Britain, are nonexistent in America. There are a few companies, however, such as the Sheraton Hotels, the Wabash Line, and Kemper Insurance, which regularly use flags.

Nonprofit corporations are in a similar position. Except for colleges and churches, few if any have flags of their own. At institutions of higher learning felt pennants may be used at sports events or in dormitories, and fraternities and sororities display their flags; but the colleges and universities themselves are less likely to have any flag. Two outstanding exceptions are Harvard and Yale Universities which have designed heraldic banners for each faculty or college for use at commencement and other ceremonies.

The flag of the Vatican is commonly displayed in Roman Catholic churches in the United States. The national flag of Israel is seen in many synagogues and is used by Zionist organizations. The so-called "Christian flag" (LXVII-c) found in some Protestant churches was conceived in 1897 by Charles Overton. A few Protestant sects have church flags of their own: the Protestant Episcopal or Anglican Church, for instance, has a white flag with an off-center St. George's cross of red. In the canton is a St. Andrew's saltire made up of nine small white crosses. Naval regulations prescribe the use of a special "church pennant" consisting of a blue Latin cross on a long white triangular field. It is flown above the national flag during religious services on warships. The practice dates back to at least 1826.

BIBLIOGRAPHY

There have been literally hundreds of books, booklets, articles, and other items written about the flags of the United States, but those who wish to pursue specific aspects of American vexillology may find the choice of good sources difficult. Much of what has been published is of little value since it consists largely of careless copying from those rare volumes which have, like this work, been thoroughly researched. Also a large number of items in the field are intended to be entertaining or patriotic rather than informative. The following books and articles are not all of equal worth and certain parts of each are better than other sections; but taken as a whole they represent the best available American flag literature. Each has been frequently consulted in the preparation of *The Flag Book of the United States.*

AIKMAN, Lonnelle. "New stars for Old Glory," *National geographic magazine,* Vol. 116, No. 1, (July 1959), pp. 86-121.

CHAPIN, Howard. *The artistic motives in the United States flag.* Providence: Pavillon Club, 1930. 19 p.

——. "Colonial military flags," *The New England quarterly,* Vol. IV, No. 3 (1931), pp. 448-459.

——. *The New England flag.* Providence: Pavillon Club, 1930. 15 p.

COOPER, Grace M. *Thirteen-star flags: keys to identification.* Washington: Smithsonian Institution, 1973. 62 p.

CUTLER, Alfred Morton. *The Continental "Great Union" flag.* Somerville (Mass.): School Committee, 1929. 48 p.

CUMBERLAND, Barlow. *History of the Union Jack.* Toronto: Briggs, 1911. 320 p.

DAVIS, Gherardi. *Regimental colors in the War of the Revolution.* New York: Gilliss, 1907. 50 p.

THE FLAG BULLETIN. This bimonthly journal has been published since 1961 by the Flag Research Center, Winchester, Mass. 01890. It contains articles on all kinds and aspects of flags, including flags of the United States.

MASTAI, Boleslaw, and Marie-Louise d'Otrange Mastai. *The stars and the stripes.* New York: Knopf, 1973. 248 p.

PERRIN, W. G. *British flags.* Cambridge: Cambridge University Press, 1922. 207 p.

PREBLE, George Henry. *History of the flag of the United States.* Boston: Houghton, Mifflin, 1894. 808 p.

QUAIFE, Milo M. *The flag of the United States.* New York: Grosset and Dunlap, 1942. 182 p.

—— *et al. The history of the United States flag.* New York: Harper, 1961. 210 p.

SMITH, Whitney. *Flags through the ages and across the world.* New York: McGraw-Hill, 1975. 360 p.

SPARGO, John. *The Stars and Stripes in 1777.* Bennington (Vt.): Bennington Battle Monument and Historical Association, 1928. 57 p.

Appendix I

THE FLAGS OF
THE UNITED STATES

As indicated in Chapters III and IV, the United States has had twenty-seven official flags and one unofficial one. (This does not include variations, official and unofficial, found in the arrangement of the stars.) The following table gives the dates for all twenty-eight flags and their designs and lists cumulatively the States they represented. Except for the third flag, which had fifteen stripes, all these flags had thirteen stripes. Flags 1, 2, 3, 4, 11, 24, 26 and 28 are shown in VIII-a, IX-a, X-a, X-b, XIX-c, XXIV-b, XXXVI-a, and the Frontispiece, respectively.

FLAG NUMBER	*DATES OF USE*	*NUMBER OF STARS*	*STATES REPRESENTED*
1	late 1775–13 June 1777 (unofficial)	(no stars; the first British Union Jack appeared in the canton)	Connecticut, Delaware, Georgia, Maryland, Massachusetts, New Hampshire, New Jersey, New York, North Carolina Pennsylvania, Rhode Island, South Carolina, Virginia

FLAG NUMBER	DATES OF USE	NUMBER OF STARS	STATES REPRESENTED
2	14 June 1777–30 April 1795	13	the same States as above
3	1 May 1795–3 July 1818	15	Kentucky, Vermont
4	4 July 1818–3 July 1819	20	Indiana, Louisiana, Mississippi, Ohio, Tennessee
5	4 July 1819–3 July 1820	21	Illinois
6	4 July 1820–3 July 1822	23	Alabama, Maine
7	4 July 1822–3 July 1836	24	Missouri
8	4 July 1836–3 July 1837	25	Arkansas
9	4 July 1837–3 July 1845	26	Michigan
10	4 July 1845–3 July 1846	27	Florida
11	4 July 1846–3 July 1847	28	Texas
12	4 July 1847–3 July 1848	29	Iowa
13	4 July 1848–3 July 1851	30	Wisconsin
14	4 July 1851–3 July 1858	31	California
15	4 July 1858–3 July 1859	32	Minnesota
16	4 July 1859–3 July 1861	33	Oregon

FLAG NUMBER	DATES OF USE	NUMBER OF STARS	STATES REPRESENTED
17	4 July 1861– 3 July 1863	34	Kansas
18	4 July 1863– 3 July 1865	35	West Virginia
19	4 July 1865– 3 July 1867	36	Nevada
20	4 July 1867– 3 July 1877	37	Nebraska
21	4 July 1877– 3 July 1890	38	Colorado
22	4 July 1890– 3 July 1891	43	Idaho, Montana, North Dakota, South Dakota, Washington
23	4 July 1891– 3 July 1896	44	Wyoming
24	4 July 1896– 3 July 1908	45	Utah
25	4 July 1908– 3 July 1912	46	Oklahoma
26	4 July 1912– 3 July 1959	48	Arizona, New Mexico
27	4 July 1959– 3 July 1960	49	Alaska
28	4 July 1960– present	50	Hawaii

THE FLAGS OF THE STATES AND TERRITORIES

In many States and communities in the United States it is the custom to give recognition to the various nations which have ruled the area. Although most States and Territories have existed under many different flags, exhibits and displays generally choose one flag for each country which has held sovereignty; thus, for example, in Texas there is a large amusement park called "Six Flags Over Texas" which hoists one flag each from Spain, France, Mexico, the Texas Republic, the Confederacy, and the United States.

This listing gives a complete résumé of the flags which have been official in each State and Territory, even if only for a part of its present area. Flags carried only by explorers or occupying armies have not been included. It should also be noted that in many cases a flag may have been official without ever actually having been flown; thus, except for scattered forts, the French flag would rarely have been flown in the Louisiana Territory. In the listing below, the numbers under each country and State refer to the illustrations in this book, except in the case of United States flags where the numbers refer to the flags listed in Appendix I.

State or Territory	United States	France II-a-b-c	France (see p. 18)	Britain IV-c, V-a-b-c	Spain I-a-b-c	Other
Alabama	1-16, 18-28	x		x	x	XI-b-c, Confederacy
Alaska	20-28					Russia, III-c
American Samoa	24-28					XIII-a
Arizona	11-28				x	Mexico
Arkansas	1-16, 18-28	x	x		x	Confederacy
California	11-28				x	Russia, Mexico
Canal Zone	24-28				x	XVI-b
Colorado	3-28	x	x		x	Mexico
Connecticut	1-28			x		Netherlands
Delaware	1-28			x		Netherlands, Sweden
District of Columbia	1-28			x		
Florida	3-28			x	x	Confederacy, XIX-c, L-c
Georgia	1-16, 18-28	x		x	x	Confederacy
Guam	24-28				x	
Hawaii	24-28					XXII-b-c
Idaho	10-28			x		
Illinois	1-28	x		x		
Indiana	1-28	x		x		
Iowa	3-28	x	x		x	
Kansas	3-28	x	x		x	

State or Territory	United States	France II-a-b-c	France (see p. 18)	Britain IV-c, V-a-b-c	Spain I-a-b-c	Other
Kentucky	1-28	x		x		Confederacy
Louisiana	3-28	x	x	x	x	Confederacy, XXVII-b, LXIV-a
Maine	1-28	x		x		
Maryland	1-28			x		
Massachusetts	1-28			x		
Michigan	1-28	x		x		
Minnesota	1-28	x	x	x	x	
Mississippi	1-16, 18-28	x		x	x	Confederacy, LXIV-a, XXXII-a
Missouri	3-28	x	x		x	Confederacy
Montana	3-28	x	x		x	
Nebraska	3-28	x	x		x	
Nevada	11-28				x	Mexico
New Hampshire	1-28			x		
New Jersey	1-28			x		Netherlands, Sweden
New Mexico	11-28				x	Mexico
New York	1-28	x		x		Netherlands
North Carolina	1-16, 18-28			x		Confederacy
North Dakota	3-28	x	x	x	x	
Ohio	1-28	x		x		
Oklahoma	3-28	x	x		x	Texas, Confederacy
Oregon	10-28			x		

State or Territory	United States	France II-a-b-c	France (see p. 18)	Britain IV-c, V-a-b-c	Spain I-a-b-c	Other
Pennsylvania	1-28	x		x		Sweden
Puerto Rico	24-28				x	
Rhode Island	1-28			x		
Ryukyus	26-28					Japan, XLIV-b
South Carolina	1-16, 18-28			x		Confederacy, XLVI-a-b-c, XLVII-a
South Dakota	3-28	x	x		x	
Tennessee	1-28	x		x		Confederacy
Texas	10-16, 18-28				x	Mexico, Confederacy, Texas
Trust Territory of the Pacific Islands	26-28				x	Japan, LII-c, LIII-a
Utah	11-28				x	Mexico
Vermont	1-28	x		x		
Virgin Islands	26-28	x		x	x	Denmark
Virginia	1-16, 18-28			x		Confederacy
Washington	10-28			x		
West Virginia	1-28			x		
Wisconsin	1-28	x		x		
Wyoming	3-28	x	x		x	Mexico

Appendix III

FLAG ETIQUETTE

Here is the complete text of the Flag Code adopted by Congress in 1942 and subsequently amended:

Resolved, . . .

That the following codification of existing rules and customs pertaining to the display and use of the flag of the United States of America be, and it is hereby, established for the use of such civilians or civilian groups or organizations as may not be required to conform with regulations promulgated by one or more executive departments of the Government of the United States.

SEC. 2. (a) It is the universal custom to display the flag only from sunrise to sunset on buildings and on stationary flagstaffs in the open. However, the flag may be displayed at night upon special occasions when it is desired to produce a patriotic effect.

(b) The flag should be hoisted briskly and lowered ceremoniously.

(c) The flag should not be displayed on days when the weather is inclement.

(d) The flag should be displayed on all days when the weather permits, especially on New Year's Day, January 1; Inauguration Day, January 20; Lincoln's Birthday, February 12; Washington's Birthday, February 22; Army Day, April 6; Easter Sunday (variable); Mother's Day, second Sunday in May; Memorial Day (half staff until noon), May 30; Flag Day, June 14; Independence Day, July 4; Labor Day, first

Monday in September; Constitution Day, September 17; Columbus Day, October 12; Navy Day, October 27; Veterans' Day, November 11; Thanksgiving Day, fourth Thursday in November; Christmas Day, December 25; such other days as may be proclaimed by the President of the United States; the birthdays of States (dates of admission); and on the State holidays.

(e) The flag should be displayed daily, weather permitting, on or near the main administration building of every public institution.

(f) The flag should be displayed in or near every polling place on election days.

(g) The flag should be displayed during school days in or near every schoolhouse.

Sec. 3. That the flag, when carried in a procession with another flag or flags, should be either on the marching right; that is, the flag's own right, or, if there is a line of other flags, in front of the center of that line.

(a) The flag should not be displayed on a float in a parade except from a staff, or as provided in subsection (i).

(b) The flag should not be draped over the hood, top, sides, or back of a vehicle or of a railroad train or a boat. When the flag is displayed on a motorcar, the staff shall be fixed firmly to the chassis or clamped to the radiator cap.

(c) No other flag or pennant should be placed above or, if on the same level, to the right of the flag of the United States of America, except during church services conducted by naval chaplains at sea, when ·the church pennant may be flown above the flag during church services for the personnel of the Navy.

No person shall display the flag of the United Nations or any other national or international flag equal, above, or in a position of superior prominence or honor to, or in place of, the flag of the United States at any place within the United States or any Territory or possession thereof: *Provided,* That nothing in this section shall make unlawful the continuance of the practice heretofore followed of displaying the flag of the United Nations in a position of superior prominence or honor, and other national flags in positions of equal prominence or honor, with that of the flag of the United States at the headquarters of the United Nations.

(d) The flag of the United States of America, when it is displayed with another flag against a wall from crossed staffs, should be on the right, the flag's own right, and its staff should be in front of the staff of the other flag.

(e) The flag of the United States of America should be at the center and at the highest point of the group when a number of flags of States or localities or pennants of societies are grouped and displayed from staffs.

(f) When flags of States, cities, or localities, or pennants of societies are flown on the same halyard with the flag of the United States, the latter should always be at the peak. When the flags are flown from adjacent staffs, the flag of the United States should be hoisted first and lowered last. No such flag or pennant may be placed above the flag of the United States or to the right of the flag of the United States.

(g) When flags of two or more nations are displayed, they are to be flown from separate staffs of the same height. The flags should be of approximately equal size. International usage forbids the display of the flag of one nation above that of another nation in time of peace.

(h) When the flag of the United States is displayed from a staff projecting horizontally or at an angle from the window sill, balcony, or front of a building, the union of the flag should be placed at the peak of the staff unless the flag is at half staff. When the flag is suspended over a sidewalk from a rope extending from a house to a pole at the edge of the sidewalk, the flag should be hoisted out, union first, from the building.

(i) When the flag is displayed otherwise than by being flown from a staff, it should be displayed flat, whether indoors or out, or so suspended that its folds fall as free as though the flag were staffed.

(j) When the flag is displayed over the middle of the street, it should be suspended vertically with the union to the north in an east and west street or to the east in a north and south street.

(k) When used on a speaker's platform, the flag, if displayed flat, should be displayed above and behind the speaker. When displayed from a staff in a church or public auditorium, if it is displayed in the chancel of a church, or on the speaker's platform in a public auditorium, the flag should occupy the position of honor and be placed at the clergyman's or speaker's right as he faces the congregation or audience. Any other flag so displayed in the chancel or on the platform should be placed at the clergyman's or speaker's left as he faces the congregation or audience. But when the flag is displayed from a staff in a church or public auditorium elsewhere than in the chancel or on the platform it shall be placed in the position of honor at the right of the congregation or audience as they face the chancel or platform. Any other flag so displayed should be placed on the left of the congregation or audience as they face the chancel or platform.

(1) The flag should form a distinctive feature of the ceremony of unveiling a statue or monument, but it should never be used as the covering for the statue or monument.

(m) The flag, when flown at half staff, should be first hoisted to the peak for an instant and then lowered to the half-staff position. The flag should be again raised to the peak before it is lowered for the day. By "half staff" is meant lowering the flag to one-half the distance between the top and bottom of the staff. Crepe streamers may be affixed to spear heads or flagstaffs in a parade only by order of the President of the United States.

(n) When the flag is used to cover a casket, it should be so placed that the union is at the head and over the left shoulder. The flag should not be lowered into the grave or allowed to touch the ground.

Sec. 4. That no disrespect should be shown to the flag of the United States of America; the flag should not be dipped to any person or thing. Regimental colors, State flags, and organization or institutional flags are to be dipped as a mark of honor.

(a) The flag should never be displayed with the union down save as a signal of dire distress.

(b) The flag should never touch anything beneath it, such as the ground, the floor, water, or merchandise.

(c) The flag should never be carried flat or horizontally, but always aloft and free.

(d) The flag should never be used as drapery of any sort whatsoever, never festooned, drawn back, nor up, in folds, but always allowed to fall free. Bunting of blue, white, and red, always arranged with the blue above, the white in the middle, and the red below, should be used for covering a speaker's desk, draping the front of a platform, and for decoration in general.

(e) The flag should never be fastened, displayed, used, or stored in such a manner as will permit it to be easily torn, soiled, or damaged in any way.

(f) The flag should never be used as a covering for a ceiling.

(g) The flag should never have placed upon it, nor on any part of it, nor attached to it any mark, insignia, letter, word, figure, design, picture, or drawing of any nature.

(h) The flag should never be used as a receptacle for receiving, holding, carrying, or delivering anything.

(i) The flag should never be used for advertising purposes in any manner whatsoever. It should not be embroidered on such articles as cushions or handkerchiefs and the like, printed or otherwise impressed on paper napkins or boxes or anything that is designed for temporary use and discard; or used as any portion of a costume or athletic uniform. Advertising signs should not be fastened to a staff or halyard from which the flag is flown.

(j) The flag, when it is in such condition that it is no longer a fitting emblem for display, should be destroyed in a dignified way, preferably by burning.

SEC. 5. That during the ceremony of hoisting or lowering the flag or when the flag is passing in a parade or in a review, all persons present should face the flag, stand at attention, and salute. Those present in uniform should render the military salute. When not in uniform, men should remove the headdress with the right hand holding it at the left shoulder, the hand being over the heart. Men without hats should salute in the same manner. Aliens should stand at attention. Women should salute by placing the right hand over the heart. The salute to the flag in the moving column should be rendered at the moment the flag passes.

SEC. 6. That when the national anthem is played and the flag is not displayed, all present should stand and face toward the music. Those in uniform should salute at the first note of the anthem, retaining this position until the last note. All others should stand at attention, men removing the headdress. When the flag is displayed, all present should face the flag and salute.

SEC. 7. That the following is designated as the pledge of allegiance to the flag: "I pledge allegiance to the flag of the United States of America and to the Republic for which it stands, one Nation under God, indivisible, with liberty and justice for all." Such pledge should be rendered by standing with the right hand over the heart. However, civilians will always show full respect to the flag when the pledge is given by merely standing at attention, men removing the headdress. Persons in uniform shall render the military salute.

SEC. 8. Any rule or custom pertaining to the display of the flag of the United States of America, set forth herein, may be altered, modified, or repealed, or additional rules with respect thereto may be prescribed, by the Commander in Chief of the Army and Navy of the United States, whenever he deems it to be appropriate or desirable; and any such alteration or additional rule shall be set forth in a proclamation.

GLOSSARY

The following terms are commonly used in vexillology (v) and heraldry (h). There are many other heraldic terms which are not listed here but can be found in any good book on the subject. Particular attention should be paid to the definitions of ENSIGN, GENERAL USAGE FLAG, GOVERNMENT FLAG, STATE FLAG, MERCHANT FLAG, and NATIONAL FLAG, since these terms are used in the captions of illustrations in this book.

ARMS (v, h) or COAT OF ARMS refers to the graphic emblem used by a person, corporation, or political entity to distinguish itself. The whole arms may consist of a shield, crest, motto, and supporters and is sometimes referred to as an ACHIEVEMENT or ARMORIAL BEARINGS. Arms also sometimes means the shield alone since in heraldry the shield is the essential part of a coat of arms. Example: the arms of Alabama (XI-a).

BADGE (v, h) is a graphic emblem other than a coat of arms used as a distinctive mark; it often is composed of part of a coat of arms or a coat of arms with an added background. Example: the Coast Guard badge appears on its ensign (LX-c).

BANNER (v, h) is a term which has changed its meaning several times. Today it generally means a flag suspended along its top edge or between two poles. To the heraldist it is a flag bearing the shield design from a coat of arms. Example: the banner of the Calvert family (XXIX-b).

CANTON (v, h) is the rectangular upper corner of a flag nearest the staff. In heraldry the upper corner is called a canton if it is less than one-fourth of a shield and a QUARTER if it is exactly one-fourth. In flags the word canton is used no matter how large or small the area involved. Example: the Confederate Battle Flag canton in the Mississippi flag (XXXII-b).

CHARGE (*v, h*) refers to a coat of arms or simpler emblem placed (or CHARGED) on a flag or shield. Example: the Arizona flag (XIII-c) is charged in the center with a star.

CHIEF (*h*) is the top third of a shield. Example: the shield of the United States has a blue chief (Frontispiece).

COAT OF ARMS—see ARMS.

COLORS (*v*) are flags carried by military units or used by a military officer. Formerly in the United States the term was limited to infantry and other dismounted units, STANDARD being the term for the flag of cavalry, mechanized, and motorized units. Now that the flags of both are the same size, the terms are used interchangeably. Centuries ago, colors were synonymous with ensign (*q. v.*). Example: the color of the Second Rhode Island Regiment (VII-b).

CREST (*h*) is the part of a coat of arms appearing above the shield, often on a helmet and torse (*q.v.*). The word is often falsely used in reference to a whole coat of arms. Example: the crest of the North Dakota coat of arms is a bow with three arrows (XXXVIII-b).

DEFACED (*v*) refers to a flag which has had a special emblem added. Example: the colonial jack (V-b) is the British Union Jack defaced with a white shield.

DEXTER (*h*) means right and SINISTER means left in heraldic terminology: this refers to the point of view of someone standing behind a flag (or shield), not the viewer. Example: the letter V appears on the dexter side of the Virgin Islands flag (LV-a).

DIMENSIONS (*v*) refer to the exact sizes in which a flag is made, as contrasted with its relative size (PROPORTIONS). Example: the dimensions of the Pennsylvania (XLI-c) flag are four feet six inches by six feet two inches; its proportions are twenty-seven by thirty-seven.

ENSIGN (*v*) was originally the distinguishing flag of nationality flown at the poop or stern of a ship; it continues to have this meaning, except that in certain countries there are now some ensigns used on land. Example: the ensign of Russia (see p. 23).

FIELD (*v*) is the background of a flag. Example: the flag of Arkansas has a red field (XIV-c).

FIMBRIATED (*v, h*) means framed by a color; a FIMBRIATION is the same as a BORDER, but narrower. Example: the blue circle of the Tennessee flag is fimbriated in white (XLVIII-b).

FLY (*v*) is the length of a flag, as contrasted to its hoist (*q.v.*). The fly or FLY END of a flag also refers to that part farthest from the pole. Example: the old New Mexico flag has a seal in the lower fly (XXXVI-a).

GOVERNMENT FLAG (*v*) is flown by the government of a political entity such as a nation or province; i.e., its use is restricted to official buildings and official persons. Since it represents the whole state, however, it is often called the STATE FLAG (as opposed to the national flag, *q.v.*), but this term cannot conveniently be used in the United States, Brazil, or Australia whose principal subdivisions are called States. Examples: North Dakota has a government or state flag (XXXVIII-b) as well as a State or general usage flag (XXXVIII-a).

GROUND (*v*)—the same as FIELD.

GUIDON (*v*) is a small flag, usually swallow-tailed (*q.v.*), which is carried by military units as a guide. Example: the old guidon of the United States (X-c).

HALYARDS (*v*) are the ropes by which a flag is hoisted. Other technical parts of the hoisting equipment may include GROMMETS, INGLEFIELD CLIPS, and RUNNING EYE OVER TOGGLE.

HOIST (*v*) is the width (British BREADTH) of a flag. The hoist is also that part of the flag nearest the pole. Example: the North Carolina flag has a red stripe along (or at) the hoist (XXXVII-b).

JACK (*v*) is a small flag, often square, flown from the jackstaff at the prow of a ship or, by extension, a flag of the same design—such as a union jack (*q.v.*)—flown elsewhere. Example: the jack of the Confederacy (LXV-b).

MERCHANT FLAG (*v*) is technically a flag reserved for use by privately owned vessels carrying cargo, but is often used by extension to mean "national flag at sea" (*q.v.*). Example: the merchant flag of France (II-b).

NATIONAL FLAG (*v*) is flown by the private citizens of a country. Where there is no special government flag (*q.v.*), the national flag is also flown by the government. Thus the flag of the United States (Frontispiece) is both a national flag and a government flag. In subnational political units like the individual States of the United States, instead of a national flag it is more proper to speak of a "CITIZENS'

FLAG" or "GENERAL USAGE FLAG." In some countries there are different designs for the NATIONAL FLAG ON LAND and the NATIONAL FLAG AT SEA. Examples: the national flag of England (IV-a); the flag of Maine for general usage at sea (XXVIII-c).

OBVERSE (*v*) is the front of a flag or seal; REVERSE is the other side. For a flag, obverse is that side of the flag seen when the hoist (*q.v.*) is on the observer's left—except for Arab flags where the reverse is true. Example: the flag of Massachusetts (XXX-b and XXX-c).

PENNANT (*v*) is a flag, often quite long, which tapers toward the fly. It is usually triangular or swallow-tailed and is often flown at sea. Example: the Ryukyu pennant (top of XLV-b).

POLE (*v*) is a long cylindrical piece of metal or wood from which a flag is flown. Generally, a pole is permanently fixed in the ground or on a building, while a STAFF is smaller and not fixed in place so that it can be carried.

PROPORTIONS—see DIMENSIONS.

PROTOVEXILLOID (*v*) is a primitive flaglike object, usually consisting of a staff with some object affixed to the top.

QUARTERED (*v, h*) refers to a flag or shield that is divided into four parts by perpendicular lines; a shield may, however, have more than four QUARTERINGS. Example: the flag of Panama (XVI-c).

SALTIRE (*v, h*) is a diagonal cross. Example: the flag of Spain (see p. 15).

SINISTER—see DEXTER.

STAFF—see POLE.

STANDARD (*v*) has had numerous meanings in the course of history. Originally, it meant a standing pole to which a flag might or might not be attached; most protovexilloids (*q.v.*) were standards in this sense. Later the term came to be applied successively to a long pennant containing heraldic emblems; to a rectangular flag bearing the arms or emblem of a head of state; and to the flag of a cavalry unit (see COLORS). It is frequently used by nonspecialists as a general word for a flag around which men rally, as in the Standard of the Coast Guard (LX-b).

STATE FLAG—see GOVERNMENT FLAG.

SUPPORTERS (*h*) are figures of men or animals on either side of a coat of arms. Example: the arms of Virginia (LV-c).

SWALLOW-TAILED (*v*) is a term applied to a flag with a V-shaped cut in the fly. Example: the flag of Sweden (III-b).

TORSE (*h*) or WREATH is a stylized picture of a bar of twisted silk, placed between the helmet and crest (*q.v.*) in a coat of arms. Example: the torse in the Tennessee National Guard badge (XLVIII-c).

UNION (*v*) or UNION DEVICE is a badge or flag symbolizing the union of political entities. In American and British practice, the union device has served as both a canton for the naval ensign and separately as a jack—hence UNION JACK. Examples: the union device in the Bucks of America flag (VII-c); the union jack of the United States (LVIII-c).

VEXILLOID (*v*) is an object which is used like a flag and usually looks something like a flag. Examples: the *puela* and *kahili* of Hawaii (see p. 133).

VEXILLOLOGIST (*v*) is one who studies VEXILLOLOGY, i.e., the history and symbolism of flags.

WREATH—see TORSE.

INDEX